GRAHAM WHITE

The Ontario Legislature:
A Political Analysis

UNIVERSITY OF TORONTO PRESS
Toronto Buffalo London

© University of Toronto Press 1989
Toronto Buffalo London
Printed in Canada

ISBN 0-8020-5817-5 (cloth)
ISBN 0-8020-6730-1 (paper)

Canadian Cataloguing in Publication Data

White, Graham, 1948–
  The Ontario legislature

  Includes index.
  ISBN 0-8020-5817-5 (bound). – ISBN 0-8020-6730-1 (pbk.)

  1. Ontario. Legislative Assembly.
  2. Ontario – Politics and government – 1943–1985.*
  I. Title.

JL273.W48 1989   328.713'07   C89-093685-4

Cover photo by Sandra Russell,
Legislative Assembly of Ontario

THE ONTARIO LEGISLATURE: A POLITICAL ANALYSIS

The biggest government in Canada outside Ottawa is at Queen's Park in Toronto. Graham White explores the structure, operations, and politics of this powerful body. His study deals with important developments through the 1970s, but concentrates on more recent history; his analysis extends through the time of the Liberal-NDP 'Accord' into the massive Liberal majority following the 1987 election.

White's underlying concern is the influence on political and policy decisions that can be exercised by members of a modern parliament of the Westminster model. Accordingly, he devotes considerable attention to exploring the sources and directions of reforms over the past two decades, the effectiveness of current ways of doing things, and the structural and attitudinal impediments to an enhanced role for the Legislature in forming policy.

The book presents a comprehensive picture of one of Canada's most active and progressive parliamentary bodies. It covers a wide range of topics including the organization of the parties within the Legislature, the non-partisan legislative bureaucracy, the Speakership, the operation and effectiveness of question period, committee activities, accountability mechanisms, and support services for members. White provides a wealth of data on the Legislature and its workings while avoiding needless technical detail. Emphasis is on the political rather than procedural.

Informed by a broadly comparative perspective, the book analyses the Ontario Legislature within the context of developments elsewhere in Canada, most notably in the House of Commons, as well as in parliamentary institutions abroad.

GRAHAM WHITE is Assistant Professor, Department of Political Science, University of Toronto. He was Assistant Clerk in the Ontario Legislature from 1978 to 1984 and is currently director of the Legislature Internships Programme. He is co-author, with Paul W. Fox, of *Politics: Canada*, 6th edition.

Contents

PREFACE ix

1 The setting 3
   The physical setting 3
   Historical overview 5
   The accord 10
   Parties 13
   Political culture 16

2 The participants 21
   The members 21
   Party organization in the legislature 36
   The Speaker 53
   Non-partisan staff 61
   The press gallery 65

3 The legislature at work 1: An overview 69
   Atmosphere and folkways 69
   Parliamentary practice in Ontario 73
   Party discipline 77
   Debate 80
   Time limits, closure, and time allocation 83
   The House routine 86
   How the legislature spends its time 89

vi Contents

4 The legislature at work II: Routine proceedings 92
   Members' statements 92
   Statements by the ministry 94
   Question period 96
   Adjournment debates 107
   Written questions 108
   Petitions 110
   Reports 112
   Motions 112
   Emergency debates 113

5 The legislature at work III: Legislation and finances 117
   Government legislation 117
   Private members' business 133
   Private legislation 140
   Financial procedures 142

6 Committees 154
   The setting and atmosphere of committee meetings 154
   History of the committee system 157
   Terms of reference and powers 160
   Select and standing committees 164
   Committee activities 166
   Special studies 169
   The committee chairman 173
   Resources 175
   Reports 179
   Conclusion 182

7 Services to members 184
   Physical facilities 185
   Members' indemnities and benefits 187
   Members' support services 188
   The member as constituency caseworker 192
   Television in the House 195
   Board of internal economy 199

8 The legislature and accountability 204
   The Public Accounts Committee 208
   The Government Agencies Committee 214

Contents

The Ombudsman Committee 216
Delegated legislation 220
Conclusion 222

9 The process of reform 225
  The Camp Commission 225
  Minority government and reform 1975–81 229
  Majority government and stagnation 1981–85 233
  The Liberal-NDP accord 236
  The phoenix of reform 1987–88 244
  Conclusion 246

10 The Ontario legislature: An assessment 251

NOTES 263

INDEX 297

Preface

The unspoken premise underlying this book is that parliaments matter. Without doubt they are overshadowed – in this country at least – by cabinets and by bureaucracies so far as the exercise of governmental power is concerned. Yet they remain our foremost representative institutions, the centre-piece of our claim to govern ourselves according to democratic precepts. Understanding how they function is thus an important political question in its own right as well as a necessary precursor to reform and improvement.

This book draws heavily on official legislative documents, Hansard, *Journals*, and committee reports, and on the surprisingly rich academic literature on the Ontario legislature, including a number of papers written by legislative interns. As well, it incorporates material gleaned from extensive interviews conducted between 1984 and 1988 with key members, staff, and observers of the legislature. Important as these sources of information were, however, the book is primarily a reflection of the seven years I spent working in the legislature – from 1976 to 1977 as a legislative intern and from 1978 to 1984 as an employee of the Clerk's Office. This experience afforded me a marvellous vantage-point on the political processes of the legislature and of the people behind them.

It also left with me an abiding partiality to the legislature and its members despite their manifold failings, many of which are commented upon in this book.

In a work of this nature it is folly to chase history by attempting to keep perfectly current. The book covers developments up to the fall of 1988, though it is mostly written in the context of the legislature as it operated prior to the Liberal landslide of September 1987. An underlying theme of the book is that the House as it functioned under the Tory majority of 1981–85 was remarkably similar to the House under the Liberal minority. The inference that basic principles would not change under a Liberal majority was borne out in the early days of the current parliament. The illustrative statistical material about legislative processes, taken from the 1986–87 session (which ran from April 1986 until February 1987), has not been relegated to the status of historical curiosity by the outcome of the 1987 election; an analysis of subsequent sessions would probably turn up similar results. This is not to suggest, however, that the 1986–87 session was a 'typical' one, for no such animal exists. Rather, the intent was to provide a detailed overview of one session as a means of fleshing out the more general observations pertaining to legislative activities in recent years.

Inevitably, change continues apace and instantly outdates any account of how the legislature operates. The most obvious loose end in the fall of 1988 was the future of the reform proposals thrashed out by a small ad hoc group of members in the winter of 1987–88. As is noted throughout the text and described briefly in Chapter 9, the recommendations of this group portended a fair number of important changes to procedure and to the committee system.

A great many people deserve thanks for assisting me with this book. Most didn't know that they were doing so, for I formed the intention of writing the book in the later stages of my time at Queen's Park. Accordingly, I have for the most part refrained from identifying in the notes persons who supplied information or opinion. Unquestionably, my most valuable sources were the members themselves, both in conversations about the legislature and its workings and in their behaviour, which I was able to observe at first hand. I hope that my affection for them and my empathy for their often trying lot shows through more clearly than the frustration I sometimes felt at their failure to grasp opportunities to improve the legislature or at their shortsightedness and their venality (particularly when they didn't do what I thought they should!). Thanks are also due to many of the legislature's staff, who provided information and documents to me. Their numbers are truly legion, and only a few can be singled out for special recognition. My friends and former colleagues in the Clerk's Office, particularly Ed Burke, Alex McFedries, and Ann Ford, cheerfully responded to endless requests; Mary Dickerson and her able staff in the Information and Reference Service of the Legislative Library assisted me in many ways; Barbara Hibbard, formerly of the Government House

Leader's Office, frequently shared with me her expertise and gave me access to valuable statistics she had collected. Over the years Thomas Stelling, the sergeant-at-arms, Douglas Arnott of the Clerk's Office, and Tom Mitchinson, the former director of the legislature's Information Services Branch, all contributed to my understanding of the legislature through their insights and advice. Professor Fred Fletcher of York University, with whom I have long worked on the internship program, helped in a number of ways, as did many of the interns. Ron Blair and John Holtby, who were my mentors when I was an intern, did not contribute directly to this book, but were responsible for first stimulating my interest in matters parliamentary. My former colleague at the legislature, John Eichmanis, now of the Information and Privacy Commission, read the entire manuscript and offered many perceptive suggestions. Donald MacDonald, the 'happy warrior' of Ontario politics, also read the manuscript and saved me from making a number of errors. The most important contribution of all came from my wife Cathy, who helped not only by assembling data and improving my prose, but simply by being there.

I also wish to express my appreciation to Virgil Duff of the University of Toronto Press for the support and enthusiasm shown for this book, and to Kathy Johnson for applying her formidable copy-editing skills so effectively. I gratefully acknowledge that this book has been published with the help of a grant from the Social Sciences Federation of Canada, using funds provided by the Social Sciences and Humanities Research Council of Canada.

In a book that sets considerable store by accountability, I can hardly do other than assume complete responsibility for errors and shortcomings.

THE ONTARIO LEGISLATURE: A POLITICAL ANALYSIS

1
The setting

THE PHYSICAL SETTING

The Ontario Legislative Building confirms that beauty is in the eye of the beholder. For some it is profoundly ugly, a stolid symbol of fusty Ontario; others find dignity and elegance in the massive form that offers reassurance of governmental respectability within.

The Legislative Building sits amid some fifteen acres of treed parkland in central Toronto. From this pleasant setting, which was owned until recently by the University of Toronto, the legislature takes its popular name, Queen's Park (a title also commonly applied to the entire Ontario government).[1] The present building, opened in 1893 after six years of construction, is the fourth in provincial history. Its predecessor, which served Upper Canada from 1832 to 1841, the United Province of Canada intermittently from 1841 to 1867, and Ontario from 1867 on, was located at Front and Simcoe streets, at the site of the CBC headquarters. The building that was torn down to make way for the new Legislative Building was a lunatic asylum, a fact that has generated all manner of unsubtle humour.

Italian Romanesque in style, the five-storey building is clad in pink sandstone from the Credit Valley northwest of the city, and sports a patinated copper roof.[2] It is laid out on an elongated H-pattern, with the bar of the H roughly three-quarters of the way to the bottom, which is to say the front of the building; in the courtyard at the rear is a four-storey annex. Facing south on University Avenue, the city's broadest thoroughfare, the principal axis is 490 feet long, and the east and west wings (the vertical bars of the H) are 230 feet in length. The building was originally symmetrical, but the entire west part of the structure was destroyed by fire in 1909, and the consequent restoration was executed in a fashion 'haphazard and flagrant in its disregard of all aesthetic criteria.'[3] Not only is the front façade now somewhat asymmetrical, but, more strikingly, the east and west parts of the main corridor are entirely out of harmony. Wood and bronze dominate the original eastern section; its western counterpart is finished in whitish-grey marble. Save for the Chamber itself, the most noteworthy feature of the interior is the large, red-carpeted main lobby, which gives onto the magnificent grand staircase where public ceremonies and celebrations are held. Externally, the building is remarkable for its stone carvings, by turns intricate, bizarre, and stately.[4]

Though it is a sizeable room (eighty feet by sixty-five feet, with a fifty-foot ceiling), the Chamber has a comfortable, inviting air created by the extensive woodwork in rich brown tones, principally of sycamore and mahogany. Set upon a dark red carpet, the members' desks are arrayed in the traditional opposing rows, though during the Liberal regime of Mitchell Hepburn in the 1930s and 1940s they were arranged in a continuous horseshoe. The huge Conservative majorities of the Frost and Robarts era required that large numbers of government supporters be seated to the left of the Speaker, all but surrounding the meagre band of opposition MPPs. Following the 1987 election, which returned ninety-five Liberals, the thirty-five opposition MPPs were again joined by a large cohort of government members on their side of the House. The traditional configuration of three rows of desks on banked risers was expanded in 1987 to include a fourth row to accommodate the five members added in the 1986 redistribution.[5] With four tiers of desks the Chamber is noticeably more crowded, and the atmosphere when the House is full seems correspondingly more tense. Government and opposition are separated by a gulf of thirteen feet, in which are located the long clerk's table, a small table for Hansard reporters, and the desk of the sergeant-at-arms.

Above and behind the Speaker is the press gallery, with writing tables for forty reporters; opposite it, above the main door, is the Speaker's gallery, where visiting dignitaries and special guests are seated. Two small recessed galleries underneath the Speaker's gallery are reserved for members' guests. Large public galleries accommodating 115 spectators apiece face both sides of the House from high above and behind the members. Something of an unusual feature is the row of chairs under the press gallery occupied by ministerial assistants and opposition party staff; they are literally seated on the floor of the Chamber, though they

5 The setting

are not permitted to venture beyond the back of the Speaker's dais. The unobtrusive television cameras detract only slightly from the nineteenth-century aura fostered by such appointments as a huge wooden clock facing the Speaker, ten large, ornate chandeliers, intricately detailed wood carvings, and the bulky, blue-upholstered furniture (some of which, like the clerk's table and chair, date from pre-Confederation times).[6]

HISTORICAL OVERVIEW

F.F. Schindeler's admirable *Responsible Government in Ontario*[7] covers many of the key points in the development of legislative procedures and rules; beyond this essential source, little historical research has been carried out on the Ontario legislature. Accordingly, I can offer here only the briefest gloss to set the historical context for an inquiry into the legislature of the 1980s.

As Schindeler wrote two decades ago, the foremost characteristic of the legislature through most of this century has been its debilitating subservience to the executive. In the twentieth century, government dominance over the legislature is hardly unique to Ontario; all Canadian provincial assemblies as well as the House of Commons share that characteristic, if not all parliaments of the Westminster model. The government dominance assumes many forms, but the more important include the legislature's minimal role in policy development and an inability to hold the government accountable for its actions. Perhaps of greatest moment is the inability of private members, government as well as opposition, to have their views and ideas taken into account in governmental decision-making over the entrenched power of the cabinet and the senior bureaucracy.

It is neither possible nor necessary for our purposes to examine historically the roots or the manifestations of the dominance of the Ontario executive over its legislature, but it is worth examining in passing the validity of the 'decline of parliament thesis' for the Ontario legislature. In Canada, at least, it has become commonplace to discount interpretations which presume that parliamentary effectiveness and independence have declined on the grounds that legislatures in this country have always been executive-dominated. Sir John A. Macdonald's preference that provincial assemblies resemble 'glorified county councils'[8] would seem to point to their lack of power. Yet, though county councils may be severely limited in jurisdiction, they are characteristically powerful within their own spheres of activity; individual councillors contribute significantly to policy development and decision-making. And indeed, the indications are that the Ontario legislature and its individual members were important forces to be reckoned with in the nineteenth century. Certainly, the newspapers of the day covered legislative proceedings extensively, and often printed only slightly condensed verbatim accounts of debates. More telling evidence is found in the *Journals* of the sessions of the 1870s and 1880s. Even a cursory study of those most enlightening documents reveals that many important public policy issues were raised, debated, and resolved as items of private members' business; that even after the first chaotic years of shifting voting coalitions,[9] the outcome of crucial divisions was often uncertain; and that opposition amendments enjoyed some prospect of success.

The extent to which Premier Oliver Mowat and his cabinet bowed to the wishes of the legislature should not be reified into some mythic golden age. The House met for only a few weeks a year, though in an era when the premier was given to embarking on European tours lasting several months this was less significant than it might seem today. The legislature was by no means omnipotent, but neither was it the impotent cipher it was to become. The factors contributing to the diminution of the legislature's powers are familiar to students of legislative institutions: the rise of disciplined political parties in the last quarter of the nineteenth century; the exponential growth in the scope of government and the attendant development of specialization and expertise in policy-making; and long periods of one-party dominance. The Liberal party governed Ontario from 1871 until 1905, whereupon the Conservatives took power and held it until 1985 with only two interruptions – by the Farmer-Labour coalition of 1919–23 and the Hepburn aberration (1934–43). The decades of Tory hegemony differed from the years when the Liberals held sway in that they were often characterized by a weak opposition, which inclined the government to take the legislature for granted (Ontario has experienced only six changes of government in over a century).

The history of the structural elements of the Ontario legislature can be sketched succinctly. Ontario was the only province of the original four not to begin life with an upper chamber (the creation of which lies within provincial competence). This was a subject of some controversy at the time of Confederation,[10] but the issue was effectively settled in 1867. Until the 1920s the province's largest cities – Toronto, Hamilton,

7 The setting

and Ottawa, for varying periods returned members in dual-member ridings, but this arrangement was of little consequence to the legislature; since then, all MPPS have represented single-member ridings. Of more importance was the often substantial rural overrepresentation in the House; particularly in the years before the Great War, residents of the larger cities, especially Toronto, did not enjoy anything like the representation in the legislature that their numbers warranted. The House has increased from 82 to 130 members, a modest increase compared with the roughly sixfold growth in the population over the same period. Whether the dynamics of a House of 130 are qualitatively different from those of a House of 82 is open to debate – though it is perhaps a moot point, since no single expansion of the House increased its membership by more than 10 per cent.

Far more important than marginal increases in the size of the House have been changes in the constellation of party forces represented in the House. Table 1.1 indicates the number of seats won by various parties at provincial elections (by-elections, defections, and the like never significantly altered the party composition of the House). It demonstrates that except for the transitory upsurge in 1894 of the Patrons of Industry (a farmers' movement), Ontario had only two parties of any consequence from Confederation until the end of the Great War. Since 1919 more than two important parties have had a presence in the House. To be sure, from time to time third-party representation in the legislature was slight (though electoral support for third parties was typically much more robust), but far more often they were numerically important. Third parties with respectable numbers of seats raise the prospect of minority government; indeed Ontario has experienced more periods of minority government than any other province. From 1919 to 1923 the province was ruled by a minority Farmer-Labour Coalition government, and the Conservatives found themselves with a minority government from 1943 to 1945.[11] Neither of these episodes seems to have left any notable legacies in the redressing of the balance between executive and legislature, or in any other aspect of legislative behaviour.

This brief gloss may seem an entirely inadequate treatment of the history of an institution as steeped in tradition as a Westminster-style parliament. Yet in many crucial respects the Ontario Legislative Assembly as it existed prior to the mid-1960s is more of a historical curiosity than a guide to the present-day institution. Certainly, the traditional tenets of responsible government, as well as such formal elements as the three readings of a bill, the requirement for the passage

8 The Ontario legislature

TABLE 1.1
Distribution of seats in the Ontario legislature, 1867–1987

Election	Liberal	Conservative	Farmer	CCF/NDP	Other
1867	39	43			
1871	43	39			
1875	49	36			3
1879	58	29			1
1883	49	38			1
1886	58	32			
1890	55	35			1
1894	46	30	17		1
1898	51	43			
1902	50	48			
1905	28	69			1
1908	19	86			1
1911	22	83			1
1914	25	84			2
1919	27	25	45	13	1
1923	14	75	17	4	1
1926	21	74	16		
1929	13	92	6		1
1934	70	17		1	2
1937	66	23			1
1943	16	38		34	2
1945	14	66		8	2
1948	14	53		21	2
1951	8	79		2	1
1955	11	84		3	
1959	22	71		5	
1963	24	77		7	
1967	28	69		20	
1971	20	78		19	
1975	36	51		38	
1977	34	58		33	
1981	70	34		21	
1985	48	52		25	
1987	95	16		19	

SOURCE: Graham White, 'Social Change and Political Stability in Ontario: Electoral Forces 1867–1977,' PHD thesis, McMaster University, 1979, Table III-1; reports of the chief election officer.
'Farmer' includes Patrons of Industry (1894), United Farmers of Ontario (1919–23), and Progressives (1926–29); 'CCF/NDP' includes Independent Labour Party (1919–23).

9 The setting

of supply, and parliamentary privilege, remain fundamentally unchanged, but these are features common to all parliaments based on the Westminster model.

The Ontario legislature of the 1980s is marked by long sessions of six or seven months a year, with extensive committee activity for the balance of the year; a broad range of services and facilities for individual MPPs, caucuses, and committees; an active, effective committee system; a substantial degree of independence from the executive; highly institutionalized party organizations within the House, linked by sophisticated channels of interparty consultation; powerful accountability mechanisms such as question period and the Public Accounts Committee; a large, vigorous opposition; and repeated bouts of minority government. None of these elements was present in the legislature until the twenty years ago.

Some of these changes had their genesis in developments sanctioned by Premier John Robarts, who according to one long-time opposition MPP 'brought the Ontario Legislature into the twentieth century.'[12] William Davis's creation of the Camp Commission in 1972 was a key event in the modernization of the legislature. Yet most of the fundamental changes either were a direct result of the influence of minority government or were powerfully affected by it. Indeed, the current Ontario legislature cannot be understood except in terms of the residue of the minority governments of 1975–81 and 1985–87.[13] Aside from the obvious yet important way in which a minority situation greatly enhances the power of the legislature with respect to both the government and the policy-making process, minority government has left a lasting legacy in members' attitudes towards the House, in a sense that the legislature has an important role to play in the governance of the province, and in reforms that easily withstood a return to majority government. Among the latter may be numbered not only changes to House rules but also such developments as the orchestration of House business through co-operation among the party House leaders and the greatly improved level of services available to members.

A further consequence of minority government and its legacies has been the revival of responsible government in Ontario. When Schindeler wrote in the mid-1960s, the domination of the cabinet over the legislature had become so overwhelming that the assembly's ability to scrutinize the government and to hold it accountable for its actions and policies was severely in doubt. If responsible government is to mean more than simply an expectation of the government's resignation or a request for a dissolution after the government loses a vote of confidence, it must entail the prospect of the legislature's possessing the procedural means, the information, and the determination to make individual ministers answer to it for their activities.[14] Whether, in this sense, responsible government in Ontario was ever on the critical list is open to debate, but there can be no doubt that in the Legislative Assembly of the 1980s responsible government is very much alive and well. Certainly, other factors beyond the procedural reforms and service improvements of the minority era underpin this noteworthy change. In particular, the formal establishment of a free-wheeling question period in 1970 was a major advance. Yet the generally high level of accountability required of government by the legislature (a topic examined in Chapter 8) owes much to the minority experience.

THE ACCORD

The minority-majority distinction is by no means the only one that may be fruitfully applied to the Ontario legislature. Of the many ways in which political scientists have categorized legislatures, one of the more useful for analysing the development of the assembly is Nelson Polsby's distinction between the arena legislature and the transformative legislature. Transformative legislatures, in Polsby's schema, are true law-making (as opposed to law-passing) bodies; they have the capacity to transform ideas and policy proposals independent of other institutions, notably executives. An arena legislature primarily serves as a forum for the clash of ideas and policy proposals and for the representation of the various interests and groups in society, but lacks an independent law-making ability.[15] Arena legislatures may have substantial significance as the locus for contending political points of view, particularly the platforms and ideologies of the principal political parties, but this significance rests upon the words exchanged within them; their capacity to take independent action is sharply limited.

Westminster-style parliaments are inherently much closer to the arena end of the spectrum, but many of the recent developments in the Ontario legislature could be interpreted as enhancing its transformative capacity: the growing professionalization of the members, measured in terms of both their salaries and their full-time status; the extensive use of committees, not only for refining legislation, but for stimulating interest in new policy proposals; and the improved resources available to members, caucuses, and committees. These changes should not be overestimated, for even in minority settings the cabinet clearly remains paramount over the legislature; yet the transformative elements of the legislature, which may be crudely equated with an ability to impinge on the policy-making process, have certainly increased. The much discussed Liberal-New Democratic Party 'Accord' of 1985–87 represented an important attempt to expand and to institutionalize the Ontario legislature's transformative capacity.

To almost everyone's surprise, the 1985 election returned virtually equal numbers of Liberals (forty-eight) and Conservatives (fifty-two). These numbers made it apparent that Ontario would experience another minority government and that the twenty-five NDP members would hold the balance of power. Almost immediately, the NDP began negotiations with both parties to determine which would receive its support. At the time the outcome seemed uncertain, though in retrospect the NDP's decision to cast its lot with the Liberals was predictable. Not least among the factors in the New Democrats' decision was their much greater sense of camaraderie with the Liberals, born of long years of shared frustration in opposition. In addition, senior Liberals had come to the conclusion that they had erred fundamentally in 1975 in failing to deliver a knock-out blow to the Conservative government when it was on the ropes, and that, should the occasion arise again, they would do whatever was necessary to dispatch the Tories. The possibility of a Liberal-NDP coalition (that is, with New Democrats holding cabinet seats) was mooted, and indeed was the preferred option for an important segment of the NDP caucus, but it was never discussed seriously by the negotiating teams.[16]

Recognizing the political perils inherent in their position, the New Democrats insisted on a public, written agreement, that would commit a Liberal government to a wide range of progressive reforms and that would rule out the possibility of a snap election. Thus was born the Liberal-NDP 'accord.'

The accord set out a long list of policy changes to be brought about by a Liberal government, some within the first session of the new parliament, others over a longer term. More controversial, and for present purposes more significant, was the mechanism adopted to ensure that no election would take place for at least two years. The Liberals promised that no dissolution would be sought by their leader within that period, save on defeat on a formal non-confidence motion; the New Democrats promised that they would neither move nor vote non-confidence. Individual bills, including budget bills, would not be construed as matters of confidence, but the basic budget motion (on the overall budgetary policy of the government) and 'votes on supply' would be.[17]

This agreement, claimed by many to be unique in British parliamentary practice, immediately drew howls of outrage (principally from Conservative partisans). It was protested that centuries of parliamentary tradition were being violated through an unconstitutional abrogation of the legislature's powers. The accord, of course, did no such thing, for it had no legal status and simply represented an agreement between party leaders, the import of which was political, not constitutional.[18]

Nevertheless, the accord did significantly affect the legislature. The first section of the accord outlined a series of legislative reforms to be given high priority; included among these were the introduction of full-scale television coverage of the proceedings of the House and several proposals for strengthening legislative committees. In addition, by making explicit the possibility of the government's losing votes on legislation without entailing confidence, the accord served to demythologize the confidence convention.[19] Most important, it effectively eliminated the destructive brinkmanship that had characterized the 1975–81 minority period. Minority government is often criticized for its preoccupation with short-term political factors, which reflects the constant threat of an election, brought about either by accident or by design. Certainly, the political calculus of the Davis minority was one of day-to-day political manoeuvring rather than of longer-term policy concerns. For almost this entire period one or both of the opposition parties was anxious to avoid an election; therefore, the government was significantly less constrained by the minority situation than might have appeared. With the spectre of an election exorcised by the accord, the opposition parties were able to focus on policy without being concerned that a too vigorous defence of a position (for example, by defeating a government bill) might precipitate an election.

Many of the most significant changes arising out of minority government in the legislature's corporate culture and institutional arrangements can be interpreted as ways of bringing order and stability to minority-government situations. The accord stands as the logical result of the search for mechanisms to promote and ensure stability in what would otherwise be an innately unstable condition. The accord was particularly in the interest of the NDP, traditionally the party most concerned with making the legislature more transformative, since, despite the NDP's third-party status, its legitimacy in the policy-making process was institutionalized.

13 The setting

Attempting to judge the long-term significance of the accord would be premature, though it seems fair to suggest that its political consequences were less far-reaching than its impact on members' perceptions of the role of the legislature. If its effects were not so revolutionary as many expected, it none the less represented a noteworthy advance in setting out explicitly how the assembly could exercise a substantial degree of influence over the government and its policies.

PARTIES

The number and nature of political parties are central to an understanding of any legislature, and certainly the Ontario legislature must be understood within the context of the Ontario party system. In turn, the party system reflects key elements of the province's economy and society. Ontario has a strong, diverse economy built on extensive resource and extractive industries, and the country's most well-developed secondary manufacturing base; as well, it enjoys the widespread growth of a service-based post-industrial economy. Rural-urban divisions continue to mark Ontario, though their significance has declined as communications advances have lessened the psychological and social distances between country and city. Regional loyalties remain strong, in part because of the antagonisms generated by the metropolis-hinterland relationship of Toronto to the rest of the province. Ontario is becoming increasingly diverse in its ethnic and cultural composition, though these factors are not always of political salience. Though organized labour is a powerful force in Ontario, and though its politics continue to reflect the antagonisms of capital and labour typical of an urban industrial society (principally through a strong NDP presence), Ontario's economy and society are too complex to permit a polarization into two clearly defined political camps, as has occurred in several western provinces.

As a result, Ontario possesses Canada's only stable three-party system; since 1943, the third party (usually the Co-operative Commonwealth Federation–NDP) has never attracted less than one sixth of the vote, and normally garners between one fifth and one quarter. This has made Queen's Park the only provincial legislature with three strong parties. Since 1967 the third party has always held at least sixteen seats.

Parliaments with three substantial parties are qualitatively different from those with only two. Aside from giving rise to the fundamentally important possibility of minority government, the presence of three parties greatly complicates the political calculus in the House, mainly through the competition between the two opposition parties to prove which is the 'real opposition.' The Liberal government quickly became adept at a strategy that had helped to keep the Conservatives in power for so many decades: it ensured that the opposition parties dissipated much of their energy in fighting one another rather than concentrating their attacks on the government. As well, an opposition party's planning must be framed so as to anticipate not only the government's likely responses, but also the tactics the other opposition party might employ.

The effects on the Ontario legislature of the three-party system stem not just from the fact of the three parties, but also from the specific presence of the New Democratic Party: 'the political wars waged by Grits and Tories in those legislatures with limited NDP representation tend to be different from those in which the NDP is a major force. Disputes of government incompetence and wrongheadedness characterize the former to a far greater extent than the latter where disagreements over the role of the state in the economy and the distribution of wealth in society surface more regularly.'[20]

Though disagreements are rife as to the degree of 'moderation' in NDP ideology,[21] it remains unquestionably true that the party's social democratic program places it distinctly to the left of both the Liberals and the Conservatives. An important question emerges: is the basic division within the legislature structural (government versus opposition) or ideological (the NDP versus the old-line parties)?

The Liberal and Conservative parties have, in recent decades, both aspired to a moderate, centrist position in the political spectrum, and each has often sought to portray the other as tied to a narrowly based right-wing position. Both have been essentially brokerage parties, alliances of broad coalitions of interests and viewpoints, lacking a clearly defined ideology or a commitment to membership determination of party policy. In contrast, the NDP has a fairly coherent ideology (though its distance from the mainstream of Ontario politics should not be overestimated), and it does attempt to take more seriously than the old-line parties the policy views of its membership as codified in policy resolutions passed at party conventions. Moreover, the party's social democratic ethos is firmly premised on a strong belief in collective action, which is evident in various aspects of the party's behaviour in the House. For example, the NDP tends to enjoy greater solidarity on policy matters than do the Liberals and the Conservatives. Conversely, the NDP leader is afforded less leeway than the other party leaders in determining party policy, and the NDP caucus is a more significant force in party decision-making vis-à-vis the party leadership than is the case in the other parties.

Not the least of the parties' influences on the legislature is their role in candidate recruitment. Nominations are seldom contested by more than four or five self-selected candidates; the choice is more often between two or three. Most of the serious candidates for the three main parties are selected not because of their merits as prospective legislators, or because of their long-standing service and dedication to the party, or because of their experience or understanding of policy issues; they are chosen because, within a very limited field, they stand the best chance of winning, perhaps because they are well-known from municipal politics (or, with increasing frequency, because they are the most adroit at signing up hordes of new party members and packing them into nomination meetings). This process contrasts markedly with candidate selection in Britain, which is characterized by large numbers of candidates, extensive winnowing of the field (primarily on the basis of ability) by local party organizers, prohibitions against the packing of nomination meetings, and careful vetting of potential candidates by the central party offices.[22] Partly because truly 'safe' seats are a much rarer commodity in Ontario than in Britain, no tradition has emerged of reserving safe seats for outstanding members; indeed, safer seats often tend to return the less impressive members, while the better MPPS represent the competitive ridings. The upshot is that the better members often have to direct more of their efforts than they might wish to keeping their local political fences mended, and they are subject to high rates of turnover. In short, candidate-recruitment processes adversely affect the quality of MPPS.

Once they are elected, Ontario MPPS are almost never denied the party nomination, or even seriously challenged for it, as occasionally occurs in federal politics. Whatever the circumstances of their initial nomination, members of the Ontario legislature come to dominate their constituency associations. The local riding organizations generally do not constrain members' behaviour, and certainly do not, as in Britain, serve as a powerful force for the promotion of party discipline.[23]

Just as the Ontario legislature must be understood in terms of its political parties, so too the parties must be seen in the context of the province's institutional framework. A key factor in shaping the number and nature of the parties, especially in their representation in the legislature, is the electoral system. The single-member plurality ('first-past-the-post') system may not have had the same pernicious balkanizing effects on Ontario politics that it has had nationally,[24] but it does shape representation in the legislature. Election results in which the leading party garners between 40 and 45 per cent of the vote are regularly transformed into comfortable majorities in the House, thereby reducing the prospects for minority or coalition government. Moreover, the electoral system encourages large 'catch-all' parties at the expense of smaller, more ideologically based parties. Electing the Ontario House through some form of proportional representation would by no means ensure that fringe parties or special interests would gain formal representation, but the probability of their doing so would be greatly enhanced. And a legislature marked by a smattering of Greens, Libertarians, or Family Coalitionists[25] might be a very different place indeed.

The electoral system is not the only impediment to the representation in the legislature of interests outside the mainstream parties. Ontario's election-financing legislation, with its panoply of subsidies, tax credits, and formal registration of parties and candidates, strongly reinforces the primacy of the three principal parties and discriminates against independent candidates and small, emerging parties. On a different level, the mechanics of the regulation of election finances have greatly strengthened the hand of the local riding organizations at the expense of the central party machine (though the constituency associations' greatly enhanced financial independence has yet to be transformed into more independent behaviour on the part of MPPS).

POLITICAL CULTURE

Analysts of Ontario's political culture tend to emphasize the importance of features such as continuity, social order, stability, élitism, and ascription – in short, conservatism.[26] Yet it is commonly acknowledged that this conservatism tends to be leavened with a persistent concern with progress and reform, so that the province is more aptly characterized as 'progressive conservative' or 'red tory.'[27] As Horowitz has pointed out, Canadian socialism and conservatism share an organic collectivist notion of society,[28] which finds expression in a positive if paternalistic state,[29] and these characteristics are nowhere more prominent than in Ontario. Nevertheless, liberal values of individualism, liberty, and a restricted role for the state remain of great importance in the province's political culture. For the purposes of locating the Ontario legislature within that culture, it is less important to delineate precisely the significance of liberal, conservative, and socialist values than to recognize that the overriding characteristic is one of moderation. Ontario's political culture is perhaps best understood as a blending of the more moderate elements of liberalism and conservatism, with a slight tinge of socialism.

Both in historical terms and in comparison with the rest of the country, Ontario remains prosperous and economically stable. This reinforces the essentially moderate nature of Ontario politics and helps explain why an image of managerial competence is so important to governing parties. The consequences for the legislature are twofold. First, the overall tone of Ontario political discourse is relatively moderate; in the nation-wide range of ideological stances of the provincial wings of the three main parties, Ontario's parties fall in the middle. The sharp ideological polarization that characterizes other provinces is by and large absent from Ontario. A second and related consequence involves the relations between members of opposing parties. Disorder, unruliness, and bitter partisan squabbling are commonplace in the Ontario legislature, but much of the barracking and verbal abuse is essentially theatrical, and disguises extensive cross-party friendships and a generally high level of respect and understanding among MPPS.

Another aspect of the Ontario political culture affects the legislature. Ontario is unique among the provinces in that the political orientation of its populace is primarily national rather than provincial, so that Ontarians are more attentive to federal politics than to provincial.[30] Ontario politicians must struggle to distinguish themselves and their concerns from the goings-on of their counterparts in Ottawa; more generally, since provincial politics often rank below national and municipal politics in public interest and in media attention, the Ontario legislature probably has the lowest public salience of any Canadian legislature.

Finally, Ontario's political culture is characterized by high levels of trust and efficacy (the sense that citizens can have an influence on politics).[31] This positive orientation towards government, which is doubtless tied in with the general level of prosperity, together with Ontario's status as a subnational government, means that the legislature is not called upon to foster political legitimacy, to engage in nation-building, or to contribute to the maintenance of the political system in any but essentially routine ways. This reduces the strain on the legislature and permits it to concentrate more directly on such tasks as surveillance, leadership recruitment, and conflict management.

Political culture can be something of a will-o'-the-wisp, so that treatments of political culture, especially those premised on historical analysis, run the risk of equating the élite political culture (which is more readily identified) with mass political culture. Certainly, it could be argued that Ontario's mass political culture is rather more liberal-radical than the conservative, managerial orientation of its political élites. Whether a significant gulf separates mass and élite political cultures in Ontario is a question far beyond the scope of this work, yet it is a matter of some importance for the legislature. To the extent that the membership and operation of the legislature, which are very much grounded in élite political culture, fail to reflect the concerns and attitudes of the populace, the legislature's crucial role as a representative institution is undermined. This suggests the need for more fundamental reform to the legislature than most members and observers are inclined to consider.

The arena-transformative distinction, discussed above in the context of the accord, has more general analytic utility in an examination of the Ontario legislature. Indeed, a principal thesis of this book is that the recent history of the Ontario legislature, its current operations, and the course of its future development are best understood in terms of an evolution from an almost entirely arena-type legislature into one that is more transformative. 'Evolution' is an especially apt word to describe this process, for it has been by and large unplanned and gradual, punctuated by occasional quantum leaps as the institution adapted quickly to major changes in its environment. Moreover, some lines of innovation died out while others flourished; and, generally speaking, most of the participants are unaware of the processes at work and have not attempted to influence them.

A second, and in some ways more important, thesis is that the experience of the Ontario legislature demonstrates that although parliaments of the British model are capable of becoming markedly more transformative, they will necessarily remain primarily arena-type legislatures. This is an issue of wide applicability because, within the institutional framework typical of British parliaments – strong parties, single-member plurality electoral systems, the conventions of responsible government, and so on – conditions at the Ontario legislature have been highly conducive to fundamental change. Extended yet stable minority governments, multifaceted reform campaigns in a generally

19 The setting

receptive environment, and a manifold expansion of the support services available to members have combined to make the prospects for change especially propitious. And yet, even with these favourable conditions, at root the Ontario legislature remains a transformative body only in very limited ways.

At once the most obvious and the most effective restriction on major growth in the legislature's transformative abilities is the cabinet's unwillingness to countenance any significant devolution of its tremendous power to the legislature. This is not merely a straightforward power struggle; basic constitutional principles are also involved. Ministerial responsibility and, indeed, the whole notion of responsible government as it has come to be understood in Canada reinforce the legislature's subservience to the executive. This need not be so, of course; constitutional principles and conventions are not immutable. More subtle constraints are also at work. Party discipline, for example, is premised much less on threats or coercion than on team-play and willing acquiescence. A major constraint is imposed by the members themselves, few of whom reflect seriously on the fundamental nature of their institution, its inadequacies, and its possibilities. The limits on how transformative the Ontario legislature can become are set not so much by the members' reluctance to do political battle with cabinet as by their unwillingness to challenge accepted ways of doing things, to question constitutional conventions, or to ask such basic questions as when party discipline is really necessary, or when confidence in the government is truly at issue. All of this is largely conditioned by the moderate, conservative traditionalism of Ontario's political culture.

Two main themes underlie the account of the Ontario legislature throughout this book: (1) the myriad changes of the past two decades, and their effects in rendering the legislature more transformative; and (2) the failure of these changes to alter fundamentally the fact that the legislature's transformative capacity remains sharply limited. These themes address the frequently posed question of just how much scope exists for significant increases in policy-making power in a modern legislature that adheres to the basic precepts of the British parliamentary system. Although the processes at work are subtle and complex, the principal indicator of the Ontario legislature's becoming substantially more transformative would be the exercise of significant power by the opposition and by the government back-benchers. After all, the notion of a transformative legislature is really just political science jargon for the kind of true decision-making body that many critics argue our representative institutions should be and that most citizens expect them to be.

None the less, if few besides those with vested interests in the status quo would disagree that our parliaments should become more transformative, the strengths of arena legislatures should not be overlooked. Since all legislatures combine both transformative and arena elements (Polsby writes of a continuum rather than a dichotomy), perhaps the normative question should be what the appropriate balance is between the two. This book attempts to provide the empirical basis for addressing this issue.

Political institutions can be be understood only within the context of their historical, social, and political environment. In this chapter I have described some key elements of the Ontario legislature's setting. But just as a legislature must be viewed as a reflection of the society and polity around it, so too its organization and operations – and ultimately its effectiveness – are in substantial measure determined from within, independent of the outside environment. Polsby makes this point in the arena-transformative context, suggesting that the analyst of transformative legislatures is primarily concerned with internal variables, such as committee structure and the division of labour within the legislature, whereas the student of arena legislatures focuses on such concerns as the social background of members, the organization of parliamentary parties, and the nature of debate.[32] Subsequent chapters will examine these and other features of the Ontario legislature.

How the Ontario legislature works, and how well it works, is a function both of its structure and environment and of the attitudes and behaviour of its members and those who guide and assist the members' work. It is to the characteristics of the participants in the Ontario legislative system that the following chapter turns.

2
The participants

Now that the stage is set, it is time to turn our attention to the dramatis personae of the legislature. This chapter examines the members of the House, the structure of party organization within the legislature – leaders, whips, House leaders, critics, and the like – the Speaker, the non-partisan staff of the House, and the reporters in the press gallery. These people constantly interact with one another, and no analysis of the procedures or workings of the Ontario legislature would make sense without an understanding of the roles played by the various participants. The social characteristics of the members, the role of the House leaders, the duties of the Speaker, and so on may seem essentially similar to those in other parliamentary settings, particularly in other Canadian legislatures; yet each institution is in important measure unique. The chapter attempts to pay particular attention to distinguishing the unusual features of the Ontario legislature from those it shares with other legislative bodies, such as the House of Commons in Ottawa.

THE MEMBERS

The 125 MPPs elected in 1985 were a diverse lot who brought with them a broad range of experience. They included a man who survived the fire-bombing of Dresden, a former stand-up comedian, a man who represented Canada in the 1936 Olympics, a former CBC reporter who once covered Queen's Park, three ordained ministers, and five sons, grandsons, or great-grandsons of MPPs. Diverse though they may have been, they were in many important respects not representative of the general populace. This section reviews the social characteristics of the members of the Ontario legislature as of 1986 and summarizes previous research on their attitudes and behaviour.[1]

Before examining members' social backgrounds, we will briefly look at their political experience. Forty of those elected in 1985 had not served before in the Ontario legislature. Although this represents just under one third of the House, it is not, by recent standards, an abnormally high proportion, as may be seen from Table 2.1.[2] Since 1951 at least one seventh and as many as two-fifths of MPPs have been new to the House at the start of each parliament. Although this is a high degree of turnover, its effects on the legislature tend to be tempered by two factors. First, the large majority of MPPs have significant experience in the legislature, and initiate the new members into the ways of the House. Although no norm of apprenticeship exists in the Ontario legislature in the fashion described by Matthews for the American Senate in the 1950s,[3] new members clearly take their cues about how to behave and how the legislature ought to operate from more senior members.[4] Table 2.2 demonstrates that if few MPPs can claim decades of service, one third had more than ten years' experience (though only five members' careers spanned more than twenty years). Of the differences evident in the experience profiles of the three parties, the most notable stem from the very large proportion of Liberal MPPs first elected in 1985. This may have had a direct bearing on the behaviour of the back-bench Liberals in the Thirty-third Parliament, for their principal role models for caucus and committee participation were the older contingent of Liberals, who were generally not talented enough to be appointed to the cabinet and who tended to be deferential to ministers and passive in their approach to the House.

The second factor to be taken into account in analysing members' experience is the extent to which they have previously held elected office. Although a certain exchange occurs between the House of Commons and the Ontario legislature (in 1986 four MPPs had served in Ottawa, and six MPs had once been MPPs), for the most part, previous elective experience was at the municipal level. The data set out in Table 2.3 show that about 50 per cent of the members of the Ontario legislature served on municipal councils or school boards prior to their election (the Legislative Assembly Act prohibits MPPs from retaining local office), and thus had some familiarity with legislative bodies. In other provincial assemblies far fewer members have had previous municipal experience.[5] The percentage of MPPs with local elective experience is virtually unchanged from the late 1970s, when the Ontario House also

TABLE 2.1
First-time MPPS 1951–85*

Election	Number	Percentage
1951	33	38
1955	21	21
1959	26	26
1963	41	42
1967	44	41
1971	36	31
1975	45	36
1977	18	14
1981	25	20
1985	40	32

*Excludes MPPS who had served in any previous House
Data for 1951–67 from A.K. McDougall, 'Some Tentative Hypotheses Leading to a Generational Analysis of Legislatures,' paper presented at the University of Waterloo, November 1980

TABLE 2.2
Experience of Ontario MPPS 1986 (percentages)

Party	0–2 years	3–6 years	7–10 years	11–15 years	16+ years	Mean (years)	N
Liberal							
Cabinet	43	13	9	30	4	6.4	23
back-benchers	67	0	7	11	15	5.9	27
All	56	6	8	20	10	6.1	50
Conservative	18	36	16	24	6	7.9	51
NDP	20	8	20	44	4	8.3	24
Total	34	18	13	26	7	7.3	125

(N's are the same for tables 2.3 to 2.8)

had a far higher proportion of former municipal politicians than other provincial legislatures.[6] Municipal politics in Ontario are almost entirely devoid of party labels and discipline (though the party affiliations of many municipal politicians are widely known). It might be expected that members' local experience with councils and school boards that were truly decision-making bodies unconstrained by party discipline would incline them to resist rigid party lines imposed by party

TABLE 2.3
MPPs who had previously held elected municipal office (percentages)

	Yes	No
Liberal		
Cabinet	43	57
back-benchers	59	41
All	52	48
Conservative	59	41
NDP	25	75
Total	50	50

leadership. Such is the power of the spoken and unspoken norms of party discipline, however, that very few MPPs attempt to extend the non-partisan approach of their municipal days into their activity in the legislature. More generally, the scale is so much larger and the processes so much more structured and formal at Queen's Park than in municipal councils that members find their experience at the local level of limited value in their new careers. The very high proportion of MPPs who come to the legislature from a background in local politics may account in part for the repeated findings in academic surveys that Ontario members are strongly drawn to constituency service (see below).

Comparing the municipal political experience of members of the three parties points up the extent to which both the Liberals and the Conservatives are parties of local notables with organizations (particularly outside the large urban centres) deeply rooted in municipal politics; compared with the NDP, both their caucuses have proportionately more than twice as many members with local experience.

Sex ratios
Of all the ways in which the membership of the Ontario legislature is unrepresentative of major population groups, perhaps the most notable is the underrepresentation of women. According to the 1981 census, 50.7 per cent of Ontario's population was female,[7] but women constituted only 8 per cent of the legislature in 1986. The ten women MPPs – four Liberals, three Conservatives, and three New Democrats – were the largest female contingent in the House since the first woman was elected in Ontario in 1943. Indeed, they represented just over one-half

the total number of women *ever* elected in Ontario. The legislature is certainly less a 'men's club' than it was in the recent past, though this change may be as much attributed to the increasing number of senior female legislative and party staff as to the glacially increasing number of women in the House. Unquestionably, the low proportion of women reflects the tendency of political parties in Ontario, as elsewhere, to relegate most of the small number of female candidates to ridings where their chances of success are slim. It is also an indication of the greater difficulties encountered by women in raising the money and developing the political contacts necessary to secure nominations in seats with good prospects.[8]

An examination of the ridings held by women reveals a clear pattern: seven of the ten women represented constituencies in greater Toronto; the others were from Ottawa, London, and Hamilton. In other words, all female MPPS came from large cities. It might be wrong to attribute this result to hesitance on the part of the electorate in the province's rural areas and small cities to vote for women, but the ratio probably does reflect the male domination of the local party organizations. As well, one of the impediments to women's holding public office has been their inability or unwillingness to devote large amounts of time to politics or to relocate, which would interfere with the family responsibilities that still fall mainly to women.[9] This interpretation may explain the high concentration of women in the Toronto area as well as the fact that only one woman in the legislature in 1986 had children of primary-school age.[10]

Religion
In a way that is scarcely credible today, religion was a dominant force in Ontario politics for generations. The religious affiliation of MPPS, particularly those chosen as cabinet ministers, was a matter of wide public interest. If religion generally has become less salient in the province's political life, the question of denominational preference is even less significant. The data in Table 2.4[11] confirm this: with minor deviations – a slight underrepresentation of Catholics and a slight overrepresentation of United Church members and Jews – the religious composition of the Ontario legislature in 1986 quite closely mirrored the larger society. If religious affiliation were an important factor, we could expect systematic and major discrepancies between the members and the general populace, on the presumption that the more powerful and significant groups would be disproportionately represented. In the 1940s

TABLE 2.4
Religious affiliations of MPPS (percentages)

	Roman Catholic	Anglican	United	Pres.	Other Prot.*	Jewish	Other
Liberal							
Cabinet	43	13	30	4	0	8	0
back-benchers	33	8	41	4	11	4	0
All	38	10	36	4	6	6	0
Conservative	22	22	36	8	8	4	0
NDP	42	21	21	4	13	0	0
Total	32	17	33	6	8	5	0
Population†	39	15	21	7	13	2	1

*Includes MPPS who described themselves as 'Protestant'
†SOURCE: Census of Canada, 1981, Catalogue 92-912, vol. 1, Table 1-1; percentages have been calculated with the 7.2 per cent of the population who professed to have no religious affiliation removed.

and 1960s, the religious composition of the House was significantly different and did involve substantial over- and under-representation of particular groups. The proportion of Catholics in the general populace grew from 23 per cent in 1941 to 33 per cent in 1971; none the less, Catholics constituted only 10 per cent of the House in 1943 and 1963 and 14 per cent in 1967 and 1970. Conversely, during the same period, adherents of the United Church were between 11 and 16 percentage points more numerous in the legislature than they were in the provincial population.[12] The shift away from this imbalance probably indicates that Catholics are now well represented among successful provincial politicians and that, even in comparison with the early 1960s, religious affiliation is a much less central factor in Ontario politics.

The denominational differences that are evident among parties, such as in the proportion of Catholics, probably reflect ethnic origin rather than an underlying religious factor, especially since it is no longer common for candidates to make their religious affiliations publicly known.

Origin
Because it is often easily ascertained through one's name, accent, and even physical characteristics, origin remains of substantial import in

modern-day Ontario politics. It is no longer the case, as it was in nineteenth-century Ontario, that deep ethnic divisions exist between Scots, Irish, English, and Welsh. Ontario society has become much more cosmopolitan, so that, to the extent that origin is a significant political factor, the cleavages are between those of Anglo-Celtic background and those from eastern or southern Europe, and those whose roots lie outside Europe. Table 2.5 presents data on the ethnic origin of Ontario MPPS and on the province's ethnic composition as of the 1981 census. The manner in which members were assigned to ethnic groupings tends to inflate the proportion of those from other than Anglo-Celtic backgrounds, since anyone with forebears from the British Isles and from Europe was classified as European. Even allowing for this, Anglo-Celts are still substantially overrepresented in the legislature; they constitute only 53 per cent of the population,[13] but 69 per cent of the MPPS. This is hardly a surprising finding, given the long-standing dominance of Ontario society, commerce, and politics by those of British background. The remaining columns in the table convey a most interesting observation: the proportions in the overall population and in the House of those of French (which is to say French-Canadian), western European, eastern European, and southern European descent are on balance quite similar,[14] but the non-Europeans (including native Canadians) were significantly underrepresented. Approximately 7 per cent of Ontarians trace their origin to Asia, the Indian subcontinent, the Caribbean, and elsewhere,[15] but in 1986 only one of the 125 MPPS was drawn from this segment of society.[16]

According to the 1981 census, 24 per cent of Ontario residents were born outside Canada, and another 10 per cent were born in other provinces.[17] Since a substantial proportion of those born in other countries are non-European in origin, it is to be expected that the percentage of MPPS who immigrated to Canada (12 per cent) should be low by comparison with the overall population level. Following the same logic, it is not surprising that the proportion of MPPS born elsewhere in Canada (11 per cent) almost precisely matches the proportion in the general populace. All three parties have roughly the same number of members in the two categories. Five MPPS were born in the British Isles, four in Italy, two in Poland, two in the United States, and one each in Jamaica and Brazil. Of the Canadian-born from outside Ontario, six were from western Canada, six from Quebec, and two from the Maritimes. Persons born outside Canada are still underrepresented in the ranks of Ontario MPPS, but to a lesser extent than even a few years

28 The Ontario legislature

TABLE 2.5
Origins of MPPS (percentages)

	Anglo-Celtic	French	Western Europe	Eastern Europe	Southern Europe	Other
Liberal						
Cabinet	57	9	9	13	9	4
back-benchers	59	8	12	8	15	0
All	58	8	10	10	12	2
Conservative	77	6	4	12	2	0
NDP	75	8	4	0	12	0
Total	69	7	7	8	8	1
Population*	53	10	12	7	9	7

*SOURCE: Census of Canada, 1981, Catalogue 92-911, Vol. 1, Table 1-1. For the population, 'French' includes those indicating combined British and French origin; those whose origins were partly British or French and partly Western, Eastern, or Southern European or Other were included among the latter groups; those reporting 'Jewish' origin were divided evenly between Northern and Eastern Europe.
Principal origins defining categories: *Western Europe*: Belgium, Netherlands, Germany, Scandinavia, Austria, Baltic States; *Eastern Europe*: Poland, Hungary, Czechoslovakia, Russia, Ukraine; *Southern Europe*: Italy, Portugal, Greece, Spain.

ago: in 1970 only 8 per cent of the members were not born in Canada, and more than half of those had emigrated from the British Isles.[18]

Occupation
Table 2.6 presents data on MPPS' occupations. Information was solicited on the member's principal occupation prior to election; in some instances the responses were vague or capable of being categorized in more than one way. The small-business category primarily includes independent merchants, but owners or operators of medium-sized construction, manufacturing, or service firms were also placed in this grouping on the premise that they were characterized by a fundamental similarity of entrepreneurial outlook. Since lawyers and teachers constituted such large and distinctive groups, they were separated from 'professionals.' The 'professional' category comprised for the most part managers and administrators in large organizations, as well as doctors, financial analysts, and the like; two members who had never had any real occupation prior to running for office were classified as 'professional' (including one minister who was elected before completing university).

29 The participants

TABLE 2.6
Occupations of MPPS (percentages)

	Farmer	Small business	Lawyer	Teacher	Professional	Worker
Liberal						
Cabinet	4	30	13	26	21	4
back-benchers	26	26	19	11	15	0
All	15	28	16	18	18	2
Conservative	14	34	20	8	20	4
NDP	0	4	4	33	37	21
Total	13	25	14	19	22	7

Those classified as 'workers' were for the most part clerical or skilled craftsmen, though two trade union organizers are included. Data are not presented on the distribution of the population according to these occupational categories, owing to the difficulty of matching them to the census categories.

Several noteworthy observations emerge from an inspection of Table 2.6. First, far more than in any other table, a clear distinction is evident between parties: more than one-half of the Liberal and Conservative members were farmers, lawyers, or small businessmen; fewer than one-tenth of the NDP members came from these callings. Moreover, though the NDP was hardly awash in members with genuinely working-class occupations, it did have a much higher proportion than either of the other parties. Nearly one-half of the NDP members were drawn from the traditional NDP occupations of teaching and social work (three of the nine NDP professionals were social workers; these were the only social workers in the House). Despite the lack of systematic data on earlier cabinets, it seems unlikely that any Ontario cabinet has ever had such a high proportion of teachers (30 per cent).

Even though complete and directly comparable data on the structure of the Ontario labour force are not available, it is clear that in their occupational backgrounds the members of the Thirty-third Parliament were highly unrepresentative of the electorate. Only about 5.3 per cent of the Ontario labour force are farmers,[19] though every eighth MPP was a farmer; roughly 3.9 per cent are teachers, though this occupation accounted for one in five MPPs. Lawyers are of course the single most overrepresented profession, since only about three-tenths of 1 per cent of the work force have legal training, but they are much less dominant in Canadian legislatures than was the case a few decades ago.[20] Possibly the most significant findings to emerge from this table are the relatively large number of MPPs from small-business backgrounds and the relatively small number who worked at manual or clerical jobs before their election. Neither of these observations is unexpected, mirroring as they do both the findings of earlier research on the occupational background of Canadian legislators.[21] Still, with the government and the legislature called upon constantly to develop redistributive economic policy and deal with matters of social welfare and labour relations, the work experiences and ideological predispositions these MPPs bring with them are potentially of great import. Although the categories they employed were somewhat different, Schindeler's and Morley's data on the composition of the 1943, 1963, and 1967 Houses suggest that members' occupational backgrounds have not changed greatly since the Second World War. Farmers constituted between 11 and 22 per cent of the membership of the House, lawyers accounted for another 10–23 per cent, and between 43 and 51 per cent were engaged in other managerial or professional occupations. The one major difference over the years is the difference in the proportion of members who were either craftsmen, production workers, or trade union organizers: 20 per cent in 1943 and 7 per cent in 1967. This was not so much a secular trend as a reflection of the highly unusual composition of the House in 1943, when nearly one-half of the large CCF caucus came from blue-collar or union occupations.[22] Perhaps the most telling comparison lies between the CCF group of 1943 and more recent NDP caucuses.[23]

Education and age
No surprises emerge from Table 2.7, which sets out data on members' educational attainment. Just over three-fifths of the MPPs had university degrees, and nearly one-third had post-graduate schooling (almost all of those who attended professional schools were lawyers and doctors). Members of the Ontario legislature are, as a group far better educated than the general population, whose educational achievements are shown in the last line of the table (the figures in the table overstate levels of education, for they pertain only to those in the labour force). Still, one-quarter of the members had no more than high school training (which does not necessarily imply graduation from high school). Members in 1986 were somewhat better educated than members in 1970, 38 per cent of whom had no more than a high school education.[24] The

31 The participants

TABLE 2.7
MPPS' education (percentages)

	High school	Some post-secondary	University degree	Prof. school	Graduate school
Liberal					
Cabinet	13	17	30	17	22
back-benchers	26	19	30	22	4
All	20	18	30	20	12
Conservative	31	12	28	24	6
NDP	21	8	45	4	21
Total	25	14	32	18	11
Population*	63	25	12		

*Labour force only. SOURCE: Census of Canada, 1981, Catalogue 93-966, Table 1

TABLE 2.8
MPPS' ages (percentages)

	Under 40	40–49	50–59	Over 59	Mean
Liberal					
Cabinet	13	35	44	9	49.2
back-benchers	33	22	22	22	49.0
All	26	28	32	16	49.1
Conservative	8	46	30	14	49.3
NDP	20	48	20	8	46.6
Total	18	39	29	14	49.0
Population*	48	16	16	20	

*Voting age population only. SOURCE: Census of Canada, 1981, Catalogue 92-901, Table 1

highest overall level of education is found, not unexpectedly, among cabinet ministers; some differences are apparent between the parties, with the Conservatives on balance having the lowest educational attainment, but these differences are not of sufficient magnitude to warrant a detailed analysis.[25]

The same might be said of the age distribution of members and the electorate, presented in Table 2.8; the New Democrats were marginally younger than their colleagues in the other parties, but in overall terms the three parties had roughly similar proportions of MPPS in the various age groupings. Taking the membership of the House as a whole, two-thirds of the MPPS in 1986 were between 40 and 60, and the mean age was 49.0 years. Clearly, the typical member was significantly older than most of his constituents (and indeed significantly older than most of his electors), yet, considering the experience and background expected of candidates for the legislature, they were by no means an 'old' group.[26] More members were in their twenties and thirties than in their sixties and seventies; for better or worse, many more MPPS are raising young families than experiencing their 'golden years.' Persons aged 60 or more are in fact somewhat underrepresented, though not nearly to the same extent as those in the 20–39 age group. The age profile of members in 1986 was similar to that of the 1970 MPPS.[27]

The composite picture of the 'typical' Ontario MPP that emerges from the preceding discussion is of a middle-aged, well-educated male of Anglo-Celtic or European descent who came to the legislature, after experience in municipal politics, from a middle-class job. With the exception of the unusually high degree of previous involvement in local government, this pattern is similar to that which generally characterizes Canadian legislatures.[28] Yet even though the members of the Ontario legislature are unrepresentative of the general population in these and other respects, it does not necessarily follow that their social characteristics are of great consequence. One need not belong to a particular economic or social group to understand or empathize with its problems and aspirations. Through their dealings with constituents, all MPPS come into contact with a broad spectrum of society on an almost daily basis. Moreover, both their sense of duty and their political self-interest dictate that they must strive to represent all their constituents.

None the less, the unrepresentativeness of the MPPS does matter, for several reasons. First, members' backgrounds are an important element in determining the issues to which they give priority in their legislative careers. Since many social groups are underrepresented among the MPPS, sometimes to the point of a total lack of representation, the special interests of these groups tend not to be actively promoted by members as much as they might be if some MPPS shared their characteristics. This argument is often made with respect to the small number of female MPPS available to direct attention to 'women's issues,' but it applies with greater force to native peoples, the physically handicapped, unemployed teenagers, and similar groups who are not represented at all in the legislature.

Second, though it is true that, for example, a member needn't be poor to understand poverty, it does take an uncommon determination to genuinely appreciate problems with which one has no first-hand experience; and while an unusual number of MPPs exhibit precisely this dedication to understanding the social and economic situations of others, it is too much to expect that they can do so over a broad range of problems. Put differently, their backgrounds render members less likely to appreciate the difficulties of, among others, single mothers, Asian immigrants, or injured workers. Of course, not all political issues can be understood in terms of social groups that may or may not be represented in the legislature. General issues such as the environment, which often are not closely tied to identifiable groups or classes, may also suffer from a lack of attention because members' backgrounds do not incline them to take an active interest in them.

Finally, even if these tendencies were entirely overcome, representation of social groups in political institutions has much to do with the legitimacy those institutions enjoy. To the extent that politically salient groups observe that their members are excluded from such a visible – and supposedly representative – governmental body as the Ontario legislature, the legitimacy of the legislature (and of the political system generally) will be lessened.

Studies of members' attitudes
Five major surveys of the members of the Ontario legislature were conducted in the early 1970s. Though the principal findings of these studies are certainly worth summarizing, we must be wary of applying them to the membership of the late 1980s. Membership in the Ontario legislature must be understood as a series of generations with differing experiences and outlooks;[29] only 15 per cent of the 1986 MPPs were serving in the House at the time the surveys were conducted. Moreover, as is documented throughout this book, the facilities and opportunities open to members have changed remarkably since the time the 1970s.

In the first paper published from these surveys, Walter White and Lawrence Leduc found that in explaining statistically several key attitudes among members, 'the major differences were less between government and opposition than between the members of the two opposition parties.'[30] From this they argued that because Ontario had been a one-party dominant system for so long, many of the Liberal members, who were not sustained by the distinctive ideology of their NDP colleagues, had come to concentrate their principal efforts not on policy questions, or even on criticism of the government, but on serving their ridings. Since the securing of favours for their ridings and for individual constituents was so dependent on the largesse of cabinet ministers, these Liberal MPPs had adopted a co-operative rather than a confrontational stance in dealing with the government. Frederick J. Fletcher and Arthur Goddard disputed the contention that 'opposition members had turned to constituency matters and away from policy in coping with their inability to influence government decisions.'[31] They found that the primal cleavage dividing members of the Ontario legislature lay, as would be expected in a parliamentary system, between government and opposition, not between parties. These contradictory interpretations may be accounted for in part by the fact that the White-Leduc survey was conducted in 1970, whereas the data used by Fletcher and Goddard were gathered in 1973 (just under one-quarter of the opposition was newly elected in the 1971 election).

In a paper based on 1973 data, Conrad Winn and James Twiss performed a factor analysis on a series of measures of MPPs' attitudes towards various social groups and policy issues. They uncovered significant interparty differences in members' attitudes, and presented evidence establishing that, within the legislature at least, the Conservatives were a right-wing party, the NDP left-wing, and the Liberals centrist.[32] This conclusion ran counter to the conventional wisdom which saw the Conservatives as a broad centrist party, with the Liberals as either slightly to the right of the Tories or essentially indistinguishable from them in ideology.[33] The explanation for this discrepancy probably lies in the substantial degree to which Premier William Davis and his top ministers were more leftist than the typical Tory back-bencher. The profound split in Conservative ranks over the sexual-orientation amendment to the Ontario Human Rights Code in the fall of 1986 adds plausibility to this interpretation: only four of the forty-five Conservative MPPs present for the vote supported the amendment, but they included Larry Grossman, the party leader, Dennis Timbrell, who was the runner-up at the leadership convention at Grossman was chosen, and two leading front-benchers.

Data supporting the Winn-Twiss interpretation can be found in the 1972 study of provincial back-benchers by Harold D. Clarke, Richard Price, and Robert Krause. Although most of the published papers from this project aggregated back-benchers across jurisdictions, a revealing provincial breakdown showed that although 93 per cent of Ontario Liberal MPPs described themselves as 'centre' or 'moderately left,' only 30 per cent of the Tory back-benchers did so (the balance labelled themselves either as 'moderately right' or 'right').[34] This study also determined that Ontario MPPS were among the most devoted to constituency service of any group of provincial members, with the NDP members spending somewhat less time on constituency matters than their Liberal or Conservative colleagues,[35] and tending to focus more on province-wide issues than on constituency problems.[36] Finally, in the standard trustee-politico-delegate categorization of legislative roles, roughly one quarter of Ontario MPPS were trustees, two-thirds were politicos, and only a small proportion were delegates; almost no variation could be detected across parties in the proportions of members assuming these roles.[37]

In two papers comparing Ontario and Nova Scotia back-benchers, Michael Atkinson explored members' policy orientations. He was able to discern a strong negative relationship between members' constituency interests and the breadth of their policy goals, and found he that the degree to which members' policy interests were broadly inclusive was clearly related to their level of ambition. In all parties, those with keener ambitions were less likely to focus their attention on particular decisions or on narrowly defined policy areas. In addition, he demonstrated that members with more electorally competitive ridings tended towards broad policy interests, which led him to conclude that 'provincial politicians do not feel compelled to cultivate narrow or local interests out of a fear of electoral retribution.'[38] Other of his findings are germane to the White-Leduc hypothesis discussed above: opposition MPPS tended to be 'policy critics,' whereas government back-benchers were more likely to see themselves as 'policy facilitators.'[39] Finally, the higher levels of services and professionalization in the Ontario House did not lead Ontario MPPS to a greater interest or involvement in policy than their Nova Scotia colleagues.[40]

Though it is unquestionably worthwhile and important to know about the social characteristics of MPPS, the extent to which those characteristics reflect the composition of the general populace, and the social and political bases of members' behaviour, one fact is perhaps more important for an understanding of the members of the Ontario legislature. Like all other human beings, they combine and display altruism and self-interest in varying proportions throughout their legislative careers. The self-interested side of the MPP's character, which subsumes ego gratification, personal ambition, and actions designed to further one's party, is clearly evident to the most casual observer. Yet it is all too easy to lose sight of members' altruism, for it takes more subtle

36 The Ontario legislature

forms and is unlikely to generate as much publicity as self-interested behaviour. I do not want to portray the members of the Ontario legislature as thoroughgoing humanitarians whose activities are misinterpreted as crassly political and self-interested by a cynical press and public; none the less, it would be wrong to discount their altruism. A great many MPPs first entered public life, and continue in it, at least in part out of a genuine desire to help others. Even more telling in this regard is the unusually high proportion of members of the Ontario legislature who have adopted children.[41] In short, the Ontario legislature cannot be fully understood without the recognition that the self-interested politicking of its members is significantly leavened with altruism.

One final aspect of members' attitudes concerns the legislature itself. Although the members certainly would not use the terminology, and few have a fully thought out concept of what the legislature should be, their views of it may be categorized in terms of 'arena' and 'transformative' models. Most lean implicitly towards an arena model, and see the legislature less as a place for doing – making policy – than for talking: fighting the 'continuous election campaign,' raising and debating the great issues of the day, and calling the government to account for its actions. Others (a minority to be sure), would prefer to see a legislature with a significant transformative capacity – that is, the power to determine policy. All members believe that they should have a certain degree of influence on policy, especially in local issues, but they are prepared to accept that the current system severely limits the power of individual members and of the institution as a whole.

An important qualification to this assessment is the substantial shift that has occurred over the past two decades in members' views about the proper balance between arena and transformative elements in the legislature. Ontario MPPs have come to accept and expect that they will exercise policy influence to a markedly greater extent than their recent predecessors. Moreover, although disagreement is rife about how much reform is called for, most members would probably be in favour of at least some enhancement of the legislature's transformative capabilities.

PARTY ORGANIZATION IN THE LEGISLATURE

Paul Thomas, writing of the Canadian House of Commons, has said that 'most legislatureislative behaviour by individuals must be understood as, in fact, being party behaviour.'[42] Parties are certainly no less omnipresent in the Ontario legislature. No independent has been elected in Ontario for decades, though one member left the Liberal party to sit as an independent in the 1940s. With rare exceptions, such as the flamboyant maverick MPP Morton Shulman,[43] the mathematics of the Ontario House are based on a denominator not of 130 members, but of three parties.

Important as they are for the conduct of elections and for their influence on the activities of MPPS, the extra-parliamentary aspects of Ontario's mainstream parties – organization, ideology, membership, electoral support, and the like – cannot be considered here.[44] The discussion will be confined to the party apparatus within the legislature, principally the party leaders and their offices, the whips and House leaders, and the party caucuses.

Party leaders
Whether in this age of electronic media and 'image politics' party leaders dominate their caucuses significantly more than in earlier times is an uncertain proposition. What is not open to question is the fact of that dominance. The leaders attract many times the press attention of the most well-publicized private member; both the cause and the effect of this attention is the much greater public recognition enjoyed by leaders. In turn, the elected members know that their prospects for re-election and the success of the party are heavily dependent on the leader. Thus, within broad limits, the leader's role as principal party spokesman, chief strategist, and policy-maker is accepted with little question by most MPPS. Moreover, particularly on the opposition side, the leaders have a hugely disproportionate share of party resources: whereas party members are entitled to three full-time staff, one or two of whom are completely occupied with constituency business, leaders have personal staffs of more than a dozen, including press aides and expert policy advisers, and have first call on such nominally common resources as caucus research groups. The favoured position of the leaders is symbolized in the standing orders governing the most important part of the legislative day, question period. The first four questions are reserved for the opposition leaders, and they are permitted two supplementaries; private members are allowed only one.

One might expect that the premier would dominate his caucus more thoroughly than the opposition leaders, since he has the power to appoint and dismiss cabinet ministers, to offer patronage within the legislature (parliamentary assistantships, committee chairs, and so on), and to grant or withhold major political favours for members' ridings. By contrast, the opposition leaders have very limited opportunities for patronage;[45] partly for this reason they can and do experience serious problems keeping their caucuses united and responsive to their wishes. Yet in some respects the premier may be a less dominant figure, for cabinet ministers are well-known across the province, have substantial personal staff and enormous bureaucratic resources at their command, and often have their own political power-bases. A more accurate assessment would show that the dominance of the government party's back-bench MPPs by the party leadership (headed by the premier) is far more pronounced than is the case on the opposition side.

On a day-to-day basis, party leaders, especially the premier, are too busy to take an active role personally in the management and direction of the parliamentary party. These tasks are delegated to the House leaders and to the whips. The increasing press of business outside the House has meant that the custom of all party leaders being present for most proceedings in the House, which was the norm as recently as the Robarts era, has given way to a presumption that neither the premier nor the opposition leaders will be in their seats except during question period. Indeed, it is something of an occasion when any party leader speaks in debate (other than in question period) or takes part in a committee meeting.

Whips and House leaders
The House leaders are of far greater importance in the Ontario legislature than the whips, despite the office's being much more recent origin.[46] The position of whip was recognized as early as the nineteenth century,[47] but it was only in the mid-1960s that Premier John Robarts formally turned the leadership of the House over to specific ministers. Opposition House leaders were appointed a few years later. A 1974 amendment to the Legislative Assembly Act established House leaders in law, but only for the purpose of paying them extra emoluments; whips had enjoyed similar status for some years. Currently, the chief government whip is paid an extra $10,516 annually, the same amount received by the House leader of the official opposition; the third party's House leader gets $7,916. Assistant government whips and the chief and deputy whips of the opposition parties receive between $4,726 and $7,207.

Conservative and Liberal whips and House leaders are appointed by the leader; in the NDP these offices are filled by caucus elections, though

39 The participants

the leader tends to get the whip and House leader of his choice. Those appointed or elected to these positions tend to be among the more experienced and capable members, and they usually serve for several years (from 1975 until 1984, the Conservatives and the Liberals had only two House leaders, and the NDP three). The Executive Council Act does not require the government House leader to be a member of cabinet, but the standing orders provide that only a minister can 'call' the business of the House (that is, stipulate what matters the House is to debate) should the government House leader be absent. All government House leaders have been very senior ministers; some have held key portfolios such as Treasury or Intergovernmental Affairs, but others have been assigned relatively undemanding portfolios such as Mines or Culture and Recreation. Ontario has yet to follow the lead of Ottawa in freeing the government House leader of all portfolio responsibilities. From 1976 on, the Conservative chief government whip sat in cabinet as a minister without portfolio. In the Liberal regime this position was first given to a neophyte MPP who was not included in the cabinet; even after the 1987 election, the new chief government whip was not given cabinet rank.[48]

Each party's whip and House leader work closely together, but the division of labour is clear. House leaders are responsible for the development and implementation of House strategy, for most interparty negotiation and consultation, and for orchestrating the operation of the House. The whips' prime duty is to ensure that every possible member is available for votes, either in the House or in committee, that party discipline is enforced, and that morale is maintained.

Until the advent of minority government in 1975, consultations among parties about House business were rudimentary and tentative. The opposition often had no notice of the items of business called for debate by the government House leader, a situation that frequently gave rise to needless wrangling over the arbitrary way in which the government conducted House business. The uncertainties of minority government demanded more structured channels of communication among parties, and the House leaders quickly developed sophisticated and effective mechanisms for consultation; these have remained essentially unchanged for over a decade.

When the House is in session the House leaders, usually accompanied by the whips, meet every Thursday morning in the office of the government House leader. At these meetings the business of the House for the following week is agreed upon; the agenda is announced in the House at the end of the day by the government House leader. Deals are struck on amendments to bills, on the amount of time to be allocated to particular debates, and on other matters; and information about party positions and preferences is exchanged. An atmosphere of give and take prevails, and is fostered by a high degree of trust. A House leader will not give away his strategy or plans, but outright falsehoods are avoided; this sometimes means that certain questions about a party's intentions are not asked. Much of the time is taken up by routine scheduling, on which all recent governments have been quite accommodating; by way of illustration, estimates or debates on legislation will usually be postponed if a party critic is unavailable. The government retains the undoubted authority to schedule the business of the House, and this type of accommodation represents a significant curtailment of government prerogative. If there is a significant element of altruism in the government's stance – a recognition that the opposition has a legitimate right to be involved in scheduling House time – that altruism is none the less tempered by a strong dose of self-interest, for the government has come to appreciate that a well-orchestrated House, with few surprises, is a more efficient mechanism for the passage of its program. An opposition outraged over arbitrary 'steamroller' tactics is an obstructionist, uncooperative opposition. The measure of the amicable and professional relationship that prevails among the House leaders is that even during the most bitter, protracted partisan clashes, such as occurred in the fall of 1982 when House business came to a standstill for weeks owing to the opposition's stalling of the government's inflation restraint bill, the House leaders continued to consult and negotiate with one another.

In addition to their regular weekly meetings, the House leaders confer frequently by telephone and in person in the Chamber. Any number of circumstances arise that may require consultation among the House leaders in order to clarify or amend previous agreements. Many of the details, the routine negotiations or consultations, and the implementation of agreements and plans are delegated to the executive assistants of the House leaders, who are among the most indispensable and influential staff in the legislature. When the House is recessed, the House leaders meet only occasionally.

The government's willingness to take into account the needs and preferences of the opposition, and the success of the House leaders in smoothly orchestrating the conduct of House business, are measures of the Ontario legislature's maturity. Compare these procedures with, for example, the British Columbia legislature, where until very recently

41 The participants

the notion of party House leaders' consulting or attempting to reach agreement on anything would have been an anathema, and where the government revelled in taking advantage of an opposition critic's absence to debate bills and estimates in his field.

It would be difficult to overestimate the influence of the House leaders in the operation of the Ontario legislature. They are responsible not only for the short-term planning of House business, but also for a good deal of the (necessarily limited) longer-term planning. The government House leader is primarily responsible for working out the government's long-range plans for the legislature, but the opposition House leaders also play a central role in establishing, inter alia, the session-long schedule for estimates and the distribution of committee workloads. Any serious efforts at reform, even those originating with legislative committees, must meet with the approval of the House leaders, and are likely to be modified during negotiations. In addition, the House leaders are usually members of the Board of Internal Economy, and thus play key roles in decisions relating to members' services and in the administration of the legislature. Not surprisingly, many MPPs tend to defer to the collective will of the House leaders on almost any matter of consequence. This fosters a tendency for members to dump their problems into the laps of the House leaders rather than attempting to solve them themselves. For example, the House leaders usually prefer not to resolve impasses reached in committees, but this does not prevent committees whose members are unwilling to make hard decisions from turning to the House leaders for a solution.

In that he represents not just a caucus of several dozen MPPs but also the cabinet and the entire executive arm of government, the government House leader's responsibilities are far more extensive and complex than those of his opposition counterparts. As is the case in Ottawa, 'his duties fall into three related areas: the development and coordination of the government's legislative programme before and during the session, the management of the session itself, and the oversight of representation and procedural matters and reforms.'[49] Ontario has no equivalent to the federal Cabinet Committee on Legislation and House Planning, but the government House leader does meet regularly (usually on Thursday, prior to the House leaders' meeting) with the chief government whip and staff from the Premier's Office and the Cabinet Office. This small group meets to exchange information and avoid misunderstandings rather than to develop tactics and strategy,[50] which usually emerge from higher political levels. The government

House leader is also responsible for carrying legislation affecting the legislature, the cabinet or electoral processes, such as the Legislative Assembly Act, the Executive Council Act, the Representation Act, the Election Act and the Election Finances Act. After the Liberal landslide in the 1987 election, Sean Conway was appointed government House leader, with special responsibility for managing and motivating the huge government caucus.

For all three parties the House leaders' offices are important centres for the dissemination of advice and information. The Government House Leader's Office is particularly significant, since it is the main operational link between the government and the legislature. Through it flows most of the official paper that passes between the House and the government – answers to written questions, documents for tabling, estimates briefing books, government notices, and the like. The scheduling of House and committee appearances by ministers and civil servants for estimates and legislation is co-ordinated by the Government House Leader's Office. The task of communicating to all those in government who need to be informed of the agreements reached by the House leaders and the plans developed by the government's legislative strategists also falls to that office. Conveying the information is much easier than ensuring that it is understood and acted upon.

Ministry staff, both 'exempt' political staff and civil servants, are encouraged to tap the expertise of the office and to keep the House leader's staff informed of any problems they encounter relating to the House or committees. The government House leader and his staff spend a good deal of time explaining the operation of the House to members and to ministry staff. Ministry staff typically have only a rudimentary understanding of the political intricacies of the House, and must be made aware that inadvertent oversights or unthinking actions can lead to major rows with the opposition. Even more difficult to resolve may be the problems arising from what has been termed in the Ottawa setting 'the carelessness and inconstancy of his ministerial colleagues.'[51]

It has been said of the British House of Commons that 'the duties of the whips have been much misunderstood and maligned.'[52] The same can accurately be said of whips in the Ontario legislature. The whips of all three parties carry out the principal functions of enforcing party discipline, maintaining party cohesion and morale, and implementing legislative tactics. For the government party, it is particularly important that they be performed well.

Most of the whips' time is devoted to ensuring that all members are aware of impending votes in the House and in committee, that all available members do vote, that a respectable number of MPPs are present in the House at all times, and that substitutes are arranged for members absent from committee meetings. Constant cajoling, pleading, and reminding are required not because members are inclined to defy the party, but because they can easily find more interesting and productive uses for their time than 'House duty' or waiting around for votes. In consequence, the whips, and particularly those on the government side, have developed extensive scheduling and monitoring systems to keep track of MPPs and to ensure that they know where they are supposed to be.[53]

The primary responsibility for lining up speakers for debates falls to the whips, as does the allocation of MPPs to committees. The whips work closely with the House leaders and attend their weekly meetings. In the opposition the communication and implementation of party tactics tends to be shared by the whip and the House leader; for the government, these tasks are left largely to the whip. To the surprisingly limited extent that strategy sessions are convened for government back-benchers on legislative committees, they are organized through the whip rather than through the House leader's office (although individual ministers may also organize such sessions). The Government House Leader's Office advises members on procedural questions but usually refers queries on tactics or policy stances to the whip, the minister, or the Premier's Office.[54] The Government Whip's Office is also responsible for coordinating government members' contributions to 'members' statements.' As well, any government member who proposes to ask a question during question period must inform the whip's office in advance; virtually all do so.

The enforcement of party discipline is the whips' province, but only rarely do they use of threaten to use sanctions against rebellious behaviour. Ultimately, whether a member's transgression is a spotty attendance record or open defiance of party policy, the whips have few weapons at their disposal, and a determined MPP can ignore them. Members can be assigned prime or undesirable offices; they can be put on or kept off their preferred committees; interparliamentary or committee junkets can be granted or withheld; and MPPs can be appointed or removed from paid positions such as committee chairmanships and parliamentary assistantships. Should such carrots and sticks fail to have an effect, the party leader may be asked to speak to the recalcitrant member, but even the leader must rely more on suasion than on threats; no sitting member in Ontario has been denied renomination or refused electoral help by party headquarters for breaking party discipline. In an ultimate test of wills, then, neither the whips nor the party leadership can force an MPP to toe the party line. (In fact, as is discussed in Chapter 3, members of the Ontario legislature tend to accept party discipline, so there is little need for it to be imposed upon them.)

To a limited degree in the opposition parties, and to a sometimes significant extent in the government party, whips promote party morale and serve as a conduit for back-bench opinion to the party leadership. The chief government whip owed his place in the Conservative cabinet to his claim to speak for the private members and to his ability to transmit the views of cabinet to the Tory back-benches. In the Liberal government, the chief whip does not sit in cabinet and thus figures less prominently in linking the cabinet to the back-bench, though his role in transmitting information and discontent from the private members to the cabinet remains important. The chief Liberal whip devotes less attention to morale-building within the caucus, which was a high priority for the chief whip when the Conservatives were in power. Nevertheless, the techniques used by Tory whips for this purpose – parties, softball games, and an open bar in the whips' office opposite the main entrance to the Chamber – are still employed by the Liberals.

The chief government whip assigns one member to serve as whip on each legislative committee. These committee whips are primarily responsible for ensuring adequate Liberal attendance, but they are also expected to provide political intelligence concerning committee activities and to ensure that government committee members know what is expected of them. As was the case under the Conservatives, who used a similar system, the committee whips' record of success in their tasks is mixed.

As is discussed in Chapter 9, in the interparty negotiations and the detailed implementation of the 1986 revision of the standing orders the whips rather than the House leaders took the lead. The whips had been involved in previous consultations on reform proposals, but had been clearly secondary to the House leaders. Although this reflected a peculiar set of circumstances (the government House leader was too busy attending to his duties as treasurer, and the Conservative House leadership was in a state of flux owing to changes in the party leadership), this episode may augur a lasting enhancement of the whips' role. Indeed, during late 1987 and early 1988 the key player on the government side in the work of the ad hoc committee to revise the standing orders was the chief government whip.

45 The participants

Parliamentary assistants
Parliamentary assistants are neither fish nor fowl. They are more than ordinary back-benchers but far less than ministers, and their duties vary widely. Some do little more than fill in for their ministers at ceremonial events; others are in effect junior ministers with important administrative and political responsibilities. Although such considerations as ability and ministry workloads come into play in determining the scope of their activities, the most significant factor is the attitude of the ministers to whom they are assigned. If the minister cares to share the workload, and if he likes and trusts his 'PA,' then the parliamentary assistant will be given interesting and important things to do; otherwise, he will merely cut the occasional ribbon and meet the occasional class of school children.

Parliamentary assistants came into being in the early 1970s following the recommendation of the Committee on Government Productivity, which envisioned them as junior ministers who would lighten the burden on hard-pressed ministers.[55] It soon became evident, however, that parliamentary assistantships were more useful as patronage, as consolation prizes for those left out of cabinet (PAs are currently paid an extra $8,506 per year). Few assistantships were given out as ways of testing promising back-benchers. When the Conservatives were in office, some assistantships regularly carried substantial responsibility: the parliamentary assistant to the minister of intergovernmental affairs (and later to the minister of municipal affairs and housing) dealt with much of the routine liaison with municipalities and was the government spokesman on private bills; the parliamentary assistant to the provincial secretary for social development ran the Youth Secretariat, a major component of the provincial secretary's portfolio. It is too early to discern a pattern in the present government, though it is clear that some parliamentary assistants have been put to good use by their ministers. Several have acted as leaders of the government forces on committees dealing with key bills. The parliamentary assistant to the minister of consumer and commercial relations was assigned to head a major task force examining the province's liquor legislation, and when the minister of education became acting minister of government services owing to a resignation, he delegated most of that ministry's business to his parliamentary assistant. In the later stages of the Tory regime, the cabinet committee on regulations was chaired by a minister without portfolio but otherwise was entirely composed of parliamentary assistants. When they came to power the Liberals revamped the committee so that it became a true cabinet committee, with only ministers as members; but after the 1987 election only two ministers were retained (as chairman and vice-chairman). Significantly, only back-benchers who were not parliamentary assistants were appointed to it.

Like the ministers they serve, parliamentary assistants are appointed, transferred, and dismissed by the premier. Parliamentary assistantships are distributed almost as an afterthought in the wake of cabinet shuffles; until recently, there has been no expectation (as there had been in Ottawa during the Trudeau administration), of regular rotation of parliamentary assistantships.[56] A parliamentary assistantship tends to be a stepping-stone to cabinet: under the Conservatives, very few members were brought into cabinet who had never been parliamentary assistants, though a handful of parliamentary assistants were repeatedly passed over for cabinet. Certain parliamentary assistantships have been perceived as more prestigious than others; the members holding them have been virtually certain of promotion to cabinet (most notably, during the Tory regime, the parliamentary assistants to the treasurer and to the attorney-general).[57] In 1986 fifteen of twenty-seven Liberal back-benchers held appointments as parliamentary assistants; the numbers were somewhat higher under the Conservatives. An unspoken rule has prevailed for some years, doubtless attributable to the need to share the spoils: no MPP can serve as both a committee chairman and as a parliamentary assistant. Committee chairmanships are generally viewed as less prestigious and less desirable than parliamentary assistantships.

Parliamentary assistants are not considered part of the ministry; they do not attend cabinet meetings or cabinet committee meetings. In the House some parliamentary assistants carry routine legislation for their ministers, or represent them in committee meetings (though not for estimates). The standing orders permit parliamentary assistants to answer on their ministers' behalf during question period if they are so authorized by the premier; in contrast to Ottawa, where parliamentary secretaries field occasional questions, no Ontario premier has ever allowed a parliamentary assistant to answer a question.

Caucuses
The word 'caucus' has two separate though related meanings in the Ontario legislature. First, it refers to the private meetings, held every Tuesday morning when the House is in session, of each party's MPPS. Although the party leaders (and, on the government side, the cabinet)

are members of caucus, the term in this sense is often synonymous with 'the private members.' In a second and much larger sense, the term includes not only the MPPs, but also their staff and ancillary services such as research bureaus. As is true of so many other spheres, the influence and operation of caucus (used here in the first sense) is fundamentally different in government and in opposition. The government caucus may have some limited influence on the development of government policy, but its prime functions are the transmission of information and the maintenance of morale. In opposition, the views of caucus tend to have a significantly greater impact on party leadership and policy, though caucus is most important as a means of developing and co-ordinating political attacks on the government.

The regular weekly caucus sessions last about two hours. During the summer recess and in the winter interval between sessions, one or two-day long caucuses are held, often outside Toronto. Each party has a chairman of caucus who chairs the formal meetings of caucus and may have other administrative duties relating to the operation of caucus in the larger sense. These chairmen tend to be veteran members, and it is generally true, as is the case in Ottawa, that 'the position of caucus chairman is an honour and carries some influence, but it is not a highly prized position.'[58] Because of the political importance of maintaining good relations with its large caucus, the Liberal majority government has significantly upgraded the position of caucus chairman. Although the person selected for the post, Barbara Sullivan, was a first-time member, she was hardly a political neophyte, having had long experience in the higher echelons of the Ontario Liberal party.[59] Together with the whip, the caucus chairman is responsible for the well-being and effectiveness of the caucus. As part of this mandate, she oversees the administrative arm of caucus, including the caucus research unit and a series of 'regional desks.' The size and sophistication of the government caucus operation has grown significantly since the Conservatives were in power.

Caucus has been a source of great frustration for government back-benchers under both the Conservatives and the Liberals. The private members would like to see caucus exercise influence over the policy-making process and serve as a forum for keeping ministers accountable to them, but by and large this does not happen. The back-benchers do have the opportunity of making their views known to ministers, but often the ministers are more interested in using caucus as a means of informing their members about decisions already taken than

48 The Ontario legislature

in consulting them in advance. Moreover, the attendance of ministers is spotty unless they have a specific matter to bring forward, and is clearly related to the presence or absence of the premier. The potential influence of caucus is not realized, because members typically have little advance notice of business to be discussed and thus have little opportunity for research or for organizing among themselves to promote a particular approach. The Liberal government caucus has a formal agenda compiled by the chairman of caucus, but it is not circulated in advance; back-benchers' requests for specific matters to be placed on the agenda are scheduled at her discretion. On occasion the chairman will circulate briefing material prior to caucus meetings.

Each government caucus begins with brief remarks from the premier, followed by reports from the House leader and the whip and by brief reports from the caucus committees. These formalities generally take little time, so that the bulk of the meeting is given over to discussing policy matters. No formal rules regulate speeches, but the chairman restrains talkative MPPs and attempts to ensure that anyone who wishes to speak has the opportunity. Votes are not taken and no 'summing up' is done by the premier. (When the Liberals were in opposition, the leader would regularly sum up the discussion, and occasional non-binding votes were held.) Legislation is not routinely brought before caucus prior to first reading; however, there is an expectation that major policies will be discussed. Caucus has on occasion modified or even blocked proposed policy initiatives, but as a group its influence is limited; it is by no means a decision-making body. Within a very few months of the Liberal government's coming to power, the 'we-versus-them' mentality that characterized the Conservative caucus's attitude towards cabinet had become evident, and attempts were underway by government back-benchers to make the government more responsive to caucus. Special efforts have been directed to ensuring that the extraordinarily large government caucus created by the 1987 Liberal landslide feels itself a valued and active participant in the political process. Primarily, this has taken the form of an extensive caucus committee system, described below, but it also involves encouraging ministers to take caucus seriously.

Members on the government side recognize that caucus represents a unique opportunity to make their views known directly to ministers and to the premier without the usual phalanx of protective staff. Caucus meetings are viewed as 'members-only' time; the only non-members permitted to attend are one or two staff from the whip's and caucus offices and one or two representatives from the premier's office, and even they are sometimes asked to leave. On occasion the president of the party attends.

An important organizing device within opposition caucuses is the assignment of MPPS as 'critics.' Individual members are designated by the party leaders as official caucus spokesmen on various fields. For the most part, the critics' responsibilities parallel the structure of government. A critic is appointed for each ministry; in addition, a few MPPS will be assigned to cover policy fields that overlap more than one ministry, such as native affairs or Metropolitan Toronto issues. This division of labour is important, for critics take the lead in formulating and co-ordinating caucus response to government legislation and other policy initiatives, are responsible for the principal work on estimates reviews, tend to ask most of the (non-leaders') questions of 'their' ministers in question period, and often are called upon to put forward the party's position on particular issues in public meetings and in the media. Although the broad outlines of party policy normally will be set down by the leader and the caucus (and, in the NDP, by party policy resolutions), critics frequently have substantial leeway in establishing the details of party positions. The distribution of critics' responsibilities can be a severe test of a leader's diplomatic skills, for certain high-profile 'portfolios' may be much in demand, and every member expects to be appointed to some official role. An example of the extremes to which leaders may be forced, particularly with a large caucus, was the Conservatives' designation during the 1986–87 session of a chief critic for the Ministry of Agriculture and Food, along with four deputy critics for agriculture and rural affairs in eastern, western, central, and northern Ontario. This practice differs somewhat from that in other commonwealth parliaments; even in the small state legislatures of Australia, for example, not all opposition members will be included in the shadow cabinet.

Since the government has changed hands only once in the last forty-five years, no generalizations can be made about the extent to which critics are appointed to the portfolios they shadowed in opposition. Of the dozen experienced Liberal MPPS appointed to the cabinet in 1985, roughly half were assigned to portfolios for which they had served as critics prior to the election. Critics are periodically shuffled by their leaders for many of the same reasons the premier shuffles ministers: to reward ability, to downgrade mediocrity, to breathe new life into the organization, and to replace those who retire or resign.

The fundamental reliance of both opposition caucuses on their critics is quite similar, but in other important respects the caucuses differ substantially from one another. This has been due in part to a significant size differential; from 1985 to 1987 the Tory caucus was almost precisely twice the size of the NDP caucus. More fundamental, however, are the different natures of the parties. As a programmatic party with a strong belief in collective action, the NDP caucus is limited by formal party policy, but it exercises greater influence over the leader than is the case in the old-line parties. Both in tactics and in policy, the NDP caucus is a genuine decision-making body; the Conservative caucus, in contrast, is essentially a sounding-board for the leader.

Meetings of the Conservative caucus are roughly evenly divided between routine business, which includes the leader's report, comments from the House leader on upcoming business, and a report from the whip. In addition, at each meeting a few minutes are set aside for discussion of the private members' business scheduled for that week; if possible, a common stance is agreed upon, and speakers are lined up for the debates. The balance of the caucus meeting is given over to a wide-ranging discussion of current policy issues and party strategy, with the critic for the area often taking the lead. As was the case when the Conservatives formed the government, votes are virtually unknown, and the leader sometimes, but not always, sums up the meeting. A small number of caucus staff regularly attend caucus meetings, and though high-ranking party executives have a standing invitation to attend, they rarely do.

NDP caucus meetings follow a roughly similar format, though they differ in that the party's provincial secretary regularly attends in order to monitor caucus for adherence to party policy. In addition, nominated candidates are permitted to attend caucus, though few do. So long as the CCF/NDP caucus remained small, it was unquestionably subservient to party apparatus outside the legislature; but because of the tremendous growth in its size and sophistication in the late 1960s and early 1970s, the caucus now dominates the party.[60] The party in convention and the quarterly provincial council meetings between conventions still exercise far more influence over the caucus than do the extra-parliamentary wings of the older parties, but fundamentally the leadership of the party lies with the caucus.

In all parties caucus committees generally have been of little consequence, particularly in comparison with the regional caucuses in Ottawa[61] and the subject-matter committees of the Conservative caucus in Alberta.[62] Before the 1987 election, the government caucus had only two formally constituted committees: the Metropolitan Toronto caucus and the rural caucus. A small, informal francophone caucus also existed. After the election, when the government was blessed with an unprecedented number of back-benchers, an elaborate caucus committee system was established. In addition to six regional caucuses (Southwestern Ontario, Hamilton-Niagara, Central Ontario, Eastern Ontario, Northern Ontario and Metropolitan Toronto), four subject-matter committees were struck: Economic, Social, Justice, and Rural Affairs. The informal grouping of francophone MPPs, under the leadership of the minister for francophone affairs, continues to exist outside the regular caucus committee structure. Members were permitted to join one or more of the subject-matter committees, whose membership ranges from twenty-six to thirty-four members. A few subcommittees have been hived off from the committees to deal with specific policy areas, such as housing and waste management. All but one of the committee chairmen, who are appointed by the premier, are first-time members. The caucus committee chairmen, together with the chairman of caucus and the whip, comprise the caucus executive, which meets weekly. Several of the caucus staff members spend substantial amounts of their time working on research and organization for the committees.

The caucus committees meet roughly twice a month while the House is in session. Turnout, though not as high as for full caucus, is good: twenty to twenty-five members are usually present. In addition to meeting with delegations from interest groups, the committees hear presentations from ministers on current policy issues, serve as vehicles for members to pursue their pet projects, and generally offer greater opportunity than full caucus for back-benchers to become involved in specific issues and to keep in touch with their colleagues' views and problems. All the same, the committees' scope for influence is limited; ministers attend less frequently than they do meetings of the full caucus, and they involve the caucus committees in policy concerns only so far as suits their purposes. At least one caucus committee has experimented with making formal reports, complete with recommendations, to cabinet. In sum, the formidable array of caucus committees represents a genuine attempt by the government to harness the energies and abilities of its great horde of back-benchers without granting them any real power. The success of this endeavour remains uncertain.

The previous Conservative government had a less extensive network of caucus committees. Two regional committees (Toronto and Northern Ontario) and several subject-matter committees (usually the government members on the legislative policy-field committees) met irregularly and exercised little influence. (An attempt by eastern Ontario members to form their own caucus was scuppered by a powerful minister from the region.) Once in opposition, the Conservatives established an elaborate caucus committee system, which was far more active than the committees that had existed when the party governed. In addition to the rural caucus, a comprehensive set of regional caucuses was complemented by four permanent policy committees: Justice, Resources, Social Policy, and Economics and Finance. In addition, the Tories frequently formed ad hoc caucus committees on specific bills. The chairmen of the committees were appointed by the leader. The major critics, along with a few other interested MPPS, usually formed the policy committees, with regular staff assistance from the caucus research office; members' assistants were permitted to attend committee meetings.

The Conservative caucus committees met with interest groups and played an advisory role in developing party policy and in devising responses to government legislation, though the decisions on such matters remained very much the prerogative of the leader. The committees also enjoyed some success in promoting a broader understanding of unfamiliar problems among the Tory MPPS, and an empathy for the political situations of their colleagues. Most of this came to an end in the aftermath of the 1987 election, which diminished the Conservative caucus by two-thirds, thereby reducing both the need for and the possibility of an extensive committee structure. In 1988 committees of the Tory caucus were either informal and ad hoc, or were devoted to internal party matters rather than legislative concerns.

Similarly, the relatively small NDP caucus sees no need for policy or regional committees (an informal northern Ontario caucus does exist), though it has three functional committees. An administrative committee deals with labour relations within the caucus and other administrative matters. The executive committee, made up of the leader, the deputy leader, the whip, the House leader, the chairman of the caucus Planning and Priorities Committee, and a few additional members, develops House tactics and takes decisions on behalf of the caucus between formal caucus meetings. The third committee, on planning and priorities, is made up of senior members and senior caucus staff. It develops long-term strategy and policy, and works closely with the party's election-planning committee to meld the party's work in the legislature with its activities on the hustings. For example, at a major

53 The participants

caucus meeting in the fall of 1986 held just prior to the resumption of the House, the 'P and P' committee proposed that the caucus concentrate during the upcoming sittings on seven high-priority issues which the party would carry into the election (which was expected to be called by mid-1987).

Opposition parties at Queen's Park have in recent years made frequent use of a form of caucus committee, the travelling task force. Composed of two or three MPPS, task forces are dispatched across the province to hold public hearings on issues of importance to the party. Such task forces have several purposes: they help the party develop new policies; they educate MPPS; they project an image of an innovative, consultative party open to new ideas and responsive to public opinion; they provide opportunities for parties to proselytize on behalf of cherished causes; they promote new contacts and solidify existing relations with interest groups; and they give opposition members a platform from which to criticize the government. Launching a task force entails substantial commitments of members' time and energy, and of caucus resources, and it is by no means certain that the political benefits will outweigh these costs. Most party task forces produce reports, but these tend to disappear quickly from sight. The product is usually less important than the process, especially the sometimes impressive media attention task forces can generate outside the Toronto area, which tends to be a great sink-hole for opposition policy initiatives.[63] In recent years the NDP has established task forces on occupational health and safety, agriculture, energy, forestry, technological change, poverty, and the insurance industry; when they were in opposition the Liberals mounted task forces to examine tax assessment, health care, youth unemployment, penal policy, and skills training. That task forces are indeed useful tools for the opposition is suggested by the fact that within months of losing office, the Conservative opposition had established task forces on Sunday shopping and the sale of beer and wine in corner grocery stores.

THE SPEAKER

The Speaker is, in parliamentary terms, the most important member of the legislature. Historically and constitutionally, he is the guardian of the members' rights and privileges and as Parliament's spokesman.[64] On a more prosaic and more realistic level, the Speaker's abilities and approach are crucial in setting the tenor of the conduct of House business. He presides over the political jousting matches of the province's leading politicos, who are at once his colleagues, his bosses, and his subordinates; his task is demanding in the extreme and calls for a rare blending of skills. When he is appointed Speaker, the practising party politician must instantaneously renounce his partisanship, sever his ties to his party caucus, and be fair and even-handed to political friend and foe alike.

Certainly the Ontario Speaker has all the trappings of authority and respect. Afforded the title 'Honourable,' he is fourth in official precedence (behind the lieutenant-governor, the premier and the chief justice of the Supreme Court); his pay is close to that of cabinet ministers; he presides over the deliberations of the assembly in formal dress; he is the administrative head of the Office of the Assembly and chairs the powerful Board of Internal Economy; and, as the only resident of the Legislative Building, he occupies a small suite on the third floor of the west wing. And yet the Speaker of the Ontario legislature is often not accorded great respect by its members, his rulings may be scrutinized suspiciously for partisan bias, and in many respects he lacks the wide-ranging and undoubted authority exercised by the Speaker at Westminster.

This unflattering comparison with the British Speaker must be placed in a Canadian context. With the possible exceptions of the Speaker of the House of Commons and the president of the Quebec National Assembly, the Ontario Speakership carries with it at least as much respect and authority, as well as independence from government, as any in Canada and more than most. Moreover, the importance of the Speaker has grown signally as the legislature has matured. Still, the fact that the call for a permanent Speaker has scarcely ever surfaced in Ontario reflects the MPPS' fundamental lack of a sense of the Speaker's importance.

Changes in the office of Speaker reflect the larger developments in the Ontario legislature over the past few decades. There is virtually no evidence by which to judge the independence or the significance of the Speakership in the early years, but certainly throughout most of the twentieth century the office was of no great consequence and the members who held it were generally not parliamentarians of the first rank. The Speakership was widely viewed as a consolation prize for long-time government back-benchers who never made it into cabinet, and considerations of patronage rather than merit loomed large in the premier's selection of the Speaker. Not surprisingly, some Speakers continued to view themselves as members of the government party, a perception bolstered by the fact that the typical Speaker would return to the government back-benches when his term expired. Accordingly, the Speakers' decisions tended, consciously or not, to favour the government, though certainly some Speakers took very seriously the neutrality of the office (most notably Speaker William Stewart, who unexpectedly resigned one day in the middle of the 1947 session, apparently in protest over government pressure).[65] The Camp Commission stated forthrightly that many of the legislature's problems could be traced to a weak Speakership lacking in independence from the government.[66] Since the late 1960s, however, successive Speakers have worked hard at being scrupulously neutral and non-partisan, although some have found that being fair and being seen as fair are two very different things.

In the nineteenth century the pattern became established that the premier would appoint a new Speaker for each parliament. Only three Speakers have served more than one such 'term': Charles Clarke (who later became clerk of the House) in 1880–86, Cooke Davies in 1949–55, and Hugh Edighoffer, the current Speaker. Save for the improbably named Speaker Nelson Parliament, who served during the United Farmers government, all Speakers prior to 1977 were from the government side; the opposition had little if any say in the choice of the Speaker, which was viewed as the premier's personal prerogative.

Jack Stokes's appointment as Speaker in 1977 marked a quantum leap for the Ontario Speakership. Stokes was the first Speaker drawn from the opposition ranks in modern times, and he brought to the Speakership a tough-minded impartiality, and a sense of the dignity of the office and the House far beyond that of his predecessors. A telling indication of his approach was the complaint of his former NDP caucus-mates that he was not favouring them as earlier Speakers had favoured the Tories. Some members saw Stokes's no-nonsense style as imperious and affected. If his brusqueness was at times excessive ('Sit down, there's nothing out of order' was a characteristic dismissal of members' attempts to raise points of order), he undoubtedly set new standards for the Speakership and raised expectations of the Speaker's impartiality. Yet the limit of Stokes's influence and the Conservative government's view of the Speakership was made evident when he was not even considered for reappointment when the 1981 election returned a Tory majority, and eliminated the need for government concessions to the opposition. Philip Laundy, who has written extensively about Commonwealth Speakers, observed that Stokes appointment was 'simply a matter of political convenience' for a hard-pressed minority government, and that his fate demonstrates that 'the politicians of Ontario have no interest in promoting the continuity and political independence of the Speaker.'[67] This assessment seems somewhat harsh, and overlooks the substantial strides made by the Ontario Speakership since the mid-1970s.

In 1980 the House passed a private members' resolution requiring the government to consult with the opposition leaders before nominating a member for the Speakership.[68] Following the March 1981 election, the government failed to consult the opposition about its nominee for Speaker, John M. Turner (who was asked to take on the post only two days before the House was to open). This caused the NDP leader, Michael Cassidy, to disrupt the normally placid opening-day ceremonies with bitter objections to the lack of consultation, although he emphasized that his complaint was with the process rather than with the nominee, and he did not offer an alternative nomination.[69]

This episode helped prompt the decision of the Procedural Affairs Committee to follow the lead of the McGrath Committee in Ottawa, which had recommended that the Speaker be nominated by private members rather than by the premier and, if more than one nomination was put forward, be elected by secret ballot.[70] This recommendation was one of those not acted upon in the rules revision of April 1986; however, as is described in Chapter 9, the idea was revived in 1988 by an informal reform committee. Even if such a change were formally instituted, though, it is likely that the Speaker would still be appointed by the premier. In Westminster, which inspired the committee's recommendation, the choice of the Speaker is truly made by the House, and the prime minister's choice may be rejected.[71] The key to this process, however, lies in the extraordinary respect accorded the Speakership in the British House of Commons and the independent-mindedness of British MPs. Without similar attitudes in the Ontario legislature, no amendments to the standing orders will change the way in which Speakers are chosen, although the government will no doubt engage in more extensive consultation with the opposition.[72]

The Speaker's lack of authority is both the cause and the effect of persistent appeals to rulings from the chair. Most provinces have done away with such appeals during the past decade, but Ontario has not progressed beyond the abolition, in 1970, of appeals to Speaker's rulings during question period. The 1985 Procedural Affairs Committee report recommended that all appeals be stopped, but no such change was included in the package of rule changes adopted in April 1986.[73] Challenges are not common (in 1985 only one division was held on an appeal from a Speaker's ruling, and there were none in 1986–87, though one ruling was appealed), and the reduction of the Speaker's role in sanctioning emergency debates has eliminated a significant source of appeals. None the less, appeals are not quests for procedural purity but stratagems to gain party advantage. More important, a challenge to a ruling from the chair also represents a challenge to the Speaker's authority and impartiality, and ultimately demonstrates the House's lack of confidence in him. The untoward effects of this practice, which never gained currency in Britain and was abandoned in Ottawa in the 1960s, are exacerbated in that challenges are almost invariably launched by the opposition, which forces the government to support the Speaker, thereby giving the impression of collusion between the Speaker and the government.

Such an impression is more than a theoretical possibility, as was demonstrated by the motion of censure against Speaker John Turner. Turner, having had no experience in the chair (or even as a committee chairman), was called upon to preside over a particularly fractious House. The government, returned to majority status after six frustrating minority years, was determined to exert its authority, and the opposition was bitter and angry about the election outcome. The New Democrats were particularly hostile, in part because of the Conservatives' refusal to reappoint Jack Stokes as Speaker and in part because they had hoped to recapture Turner's seat, which they had won several times in the past. Not surprisingly, he had trouble controlling the House, and he also made a number of questionable rulings. Moreover, his natural deference, which inclined him away from clamping down on the premier and cabinet ministers in question period, was interpreted by the opposition as partisanship. Finally, Turner raised opposition hackles by his ill-advised public presentation, on behalf of the government, of cheques to organizations in a Liberal riding adjacent to his own. The New Democrats brought forward a motion calling for his resignation, which occasioned a highly emotional debate in November 1981. The Liberals declined to support the motion, and blamed the situation on the government's lack of respect for the House. Former Speaker Stokes spoke, in effect, against the motion, but was absent for the vote in which the motion lost 86 to 17.[74] Many felt that the motion was aimed less at the Speaker than at the government's attitude towards the legislature and at the influence of the clerk. At any rate, the debate proved something of a catharsis. As he gained experience and confidence, Turner's control over the House improved, as did his rulings. Still, though he was liked personally by the members, he never gained the full respect of opposition members, many of whom continued to view him as biased and incompetent. The episode of the censure motion must be understood in its politically supercharged context; nevertheless, it illustrates the fundamental lack of respect for and confidence in the office of the Speaker.

The powers of the Ontario Speaker are essentially similar to those exercised by his counterparts in other Commonwealth jurisdictions. The Speaker has a casting vote, though its only recorded use occurred in 1904[75] and 1985. The Speaker's authority to recognize members rarely comes into play since the rotation among parties is firmly established and in most cases the parties orchestrate their own line-ups of speakers. During one memorable period, however, Speaker Stokes would not recognize a particular MPP who refused to apologize for charges he had made against other members.[76] This drastic action was Stokes's response to the Speaker's inability to discipline MPPs beyond expelling them from the House for one day (after which the member can return to his place without apologizing), and his realization that naming a member for unparliamentary language or behaviour is often not a punishment but a boon for publicity-hungry MPPs. Since 1970 Ontario Speakers have been able to name a member without requiring passage of a motion moved by the government House leader as was the Ottawa practice until recently. A typical session will see two or three members ejected, almost invariably opposition members; two members were named in 1986–87.

The standing orders provide another means for the Speaker to enforce discipline: they permit an indefinite suspension 'for grave disorder.' Recent Speakers have had increasing recourse to this technique, on occasion because of disruptions in the public galleries, but more frequently as a way of cooling the House down. During the 1986–87 session, for example, Speaker Hugh Edighoffer suspended proceedings three times. Of course, the Speaker's most potent weapon is his personal authority, which derives from a variety of sources: the legislature's inherent respect for the office (limited, if growing, in Ontario); his ability to read the moods of the House and react appropriately; his reputation for fairness and impartiality; and the force of his personality.

Most members are probably aware that the Speaker has no authority to intervene in committee activities, to force ministers to answer questions, or to provide information to the satisfaction of the opposition, but they persist in asking the Speaker to order chairmen or ministers to do their bidding. Nor does the Speaker have the authority to

59 The participants

choose among or to combine amendments, as is the case in the United Kingdom; but, given the relative insignificance of the report stage of legislation in Ontario, this is not of great consequence. The traditions of the House and the standing orders often limit the Speaker's discretion; for example, the new standing orders direct the way in which the Speaker is to exercise his 'discretion' in permitting supplementary questions during question period. Yet leeway exists for the Speaker's personal predilections to affect substantially the procedures of the House. Several examples may be drawn from question period: Speaker Stokes's institutionalization of the larger number of supplementaries to leader's questions; Speaker Turner's ruling that ministers but not questioners may redirect questions to other ministers; and the attempts on the part of several recent Speakers to maximize the number of back-benchers participating in question period.

The Speaker is assisted in his travails by a deputy Speaker, who is also chairman of the Committees of the Whole House, and a deputy chairman of the Committees of the Whole House.[77] The deputy Speaker and the deputy chairman are appointed on the motion of the government House leader. During recent times of minority government, it has come to be expected that the presiding officers will be drawn, to an extent, from the opposition parties. During the period from 1975 to 1981 Jack Stokes (NDP) and Hugh Edighoffer (Liberal) were the deputy speakers, and Richard Treleaven, a Conservative, served as deputy Speaker in the Thirty-third Parliament. Several recent Speakers had previously served as deputy Speakers, but no expectation exists that the deputy will necessarily succeed to the Speakership.

If the Speaker is not out of town, he invariably presides over routine proceedings, following which the three presiding officers take turns in the chair. The Speaker never takes charge of the Committee of the Whole or the Committee of Supply, which are presided over from the clerk's chair by one of the deputies. Occasionally, other private members are asked to relieve one of the presiding officers, particularly when the House is in committee, but they are expected to turn any difficult situations or tricky rulings over to one of the regular occupants of the chair. Nevertheless, the Speaker has no authority to reconsider decisions made by the deputy Speaker – or, for that matter, any other member occupying the chair.[78]

The deputy Speaker ranks far below the Speaker in importance, although he is substantially more important than the deputy chairman, as is symbolized by the inclusion of the deputy Speaker's office within the Speaker's suite of offices. He has relatively little involvement in administration, and though he is expected to remain neutral while in the chair, he is not subject to the same rigid norms of non-partisanship as the Speaker. Recent deputy Speakers have regularly attended their party caucuses, voted in the House,[79] and taken part in debate from their places. Deputy Speaker Richard Treleaven raised some eyebrows – and triggered speculation that he would be removed by the House leaders – when he engaged in a vocal campaign to improve health facilities in his riding using such tactics as 'mini-filibusters' (including a memorable six-hour speech during an all-night sitting). On the whole, however, deputies have tended to be restrained in their political uses of the House. For example, the deputy Speaker asked no questions in question period during 1986–87, and the deputy chairman asked only one. The extent to which the Speaker consults with and takes advice from his deputies varies widely, and is to a large extent a function of personality. Some Speakers have held regular meetings of presiding officers to discuss problems and to anticipate difficult situations. Terry Jones, who was deputy Speaker in the early 1980s, was the first to don formal apparel to perform his duties in the House. Now, the deputy chairman also dresses in formal attire.

Under the Legislative Assembly Act, the Speaker and the deputy Speaker continue in office after dissolution until a new Speaker and deputy Speaker are elected, even if they do not stand for re-election or are defeated.[80] Since the first item of business to be dealt with in a new parliament, even before the Speech from the Throne is read, is the election of the Speaker, this provision is primarily administrative, and is aimed at ensuring that the assembly always has an administrative head, just as defeated or retiring ministers remain in office until their successors are sworn in.

A significant change in the Speakership, dating from the early 1970s and the establishment of the Office of the Assembly and the Board of Internal Economy, has been the exponential growth of the administrative responsibilities of the Speaker. Two decades ago, almost all the legislature's administrative work was handled by the government. The Speaker's duties did not go far beyond his procedural role in the Chamber. Today, the Speaker is the head of an enterprise employing several hundred, with an annual budget of more than $70 million; his administrative work is virtually a full-time calling, and in some ways is more demanding and onerous than his responsibility for presiding over the House.[81] Included among these administrative duties are the chairmanship of the Board of Internal Economy, the ultimate authority to hire and fire assembly staff, and the direction of the Ontario branch of the Commonwealth Parliamentary Association. The last position primarily entails serving as the legislature's official host at innumerable receptions for visiting parliamentarians, and leading delegations to vast numbers of interparliamentary gatherings in Canada and abroad. In a sense the Speaker can call on the expertise and advice of all assembly personnel; yet his personal office is small – typically only one or two medium rank special assistants in addition to his constituency assistants – and the threat of co-option or subversion by the legislature's permanent bureaucracy is ever present.

NON-PARTISAN STAFF

A small army of non-partisan staff supports the activities of the Ontario legislature. For the purposes of understanding its operation, the most important are the clerk of the House, the controller, the director of legislative services, the director of the Legislative Library and the sergeant-at-arms. Though they are not legislative staff in the conventional sense, the ombudsman and the provincial auditor are also servants of the House and are discussed briefly in this section. The chief election officer and the chairman of the Commission on Election Finances are also responsible to the House, but since their functions are electoral rather than legislative they are not considered here. The work of the information and privacy commissioner and the commissioner appointed to administer the Members' Conflict of Interest Act is of more immediate concern to the House, but assessments of these recently established offices would be premature. Neither, however, appears likely to develop the direct, intense relationship with legislative committees that characterize the offices of the ombudsman and the provincial auditor.

The clerk of the House is the chief procedural adviser to the House and to the Speaker. He is also responsible for compiling the official documents of the House – the order paper, *Votes and Proceedings*, and the *Journals* (but not Hansard) – and for maintaining House records and papers, such as the sessional papers, the documents tabled in the House. Assisted by two or three 'table clerks,' the clerk sits directly in front of the Speaker at the traditional clerk's table, from which he dispenses advice and maintains an unobtrusive watch over the procedural purity of House business. He and his staff are the central repositories of the accumulated precedents and traditions of the House. The Speaker relies heavily on them for research and advice when he is faced with ruling on a disputed point. The table officers are responsible for timekeeping during debates, and for keeping track of details such as the status of amendments when legislation is being reviewed in the Committee of the Whole. In addition, the staff of the clerk of the House includes some half-dozen committee clerks who provide procedural advice and administrative support for the various committees.

The clerk of the House is appointed by order in council (that is, by cabinet decree), and holds office for life; he may be removed from office only for cause on address of the House.[82] When a new clerk was to be appointed in 1986, the government, recognizing that the clerk is the central officer of the House, turned its authority over to the Legislative Assembly Committee, which screened and interviewed applicants and, in concert with the Speaker, effectively made the appointment. Although the Legislative Assembly Act provides for a first clerk assistant, a clear second in command, for a variety of reasons none has been appointed since 1981, when the government dismissed the first clerk amid substantial controversy.[83]

Until his retirement in the fall of 1986, Roderick Lewis had served as clerk of the House since 1955, when he succeeded his father, who had been appointed clerk in 1926. Lewis was very much a traditionalist with little enthusiasm for reform or innovation;[84] many Liberal and NDP members suspected him of favouring the Conservative government at their expense. This, together with his lack of interest in the House's burgeoning administrative apparatus, meant that the clerk's office, especially in Lewis's final years, did not provide an impetus to change (as has been the case in other Canadian legislatures).

The vacuum left by the clerk was largely filled by the director of administration. In line with the recommendations of the Camp Commission, this office was responsible for finance, personnel, Hansard, television and public relations, food services, and the like. The director of administration also filled the key position of secretary to the Board of Internal Economy. The first director of administration was Robert Fleming, who had served as executive secretary to the Camp Commission. Fleming spearheaded a number of important projects, such as the development of the House's computer system and an extensive legislative *Manual of Administration*, and brought an uncommon passion to the arcane field of legislative administration, not least through publication of an annual reference book, *Canadian Legislatures*. Fleming was

63 The participants

not universally popular among the members, however, and in the summer of 1987 his appointment was not renewed by the Liberal government.

With a new activist clerk, Claude DesRosiers, in place, the Board of Internal Economy moved to avoid a bifurcation of responsibilities, with the attendant possibility of endless bureaucratic rivalry. Fleming's position was not filled, and the Office of the Assembly was reorganized by creating two lesser positions, a controller and a director of assembly services. At the same time, the clerk was clearly designated as the principal legislative bureaucrat by virtue of his chairmanship of the important Management Advisory Committee and through an organizational restructuring under which the other senior Office of the Assembly officials report to him.[85]

The director of the Legislative Library is responsible for ensuring that members' insatiable needs for timely, accurate, and often obscure information are met. He is supported by a staff of nearly one hundred, including not only professional librarians, but a range of specialist researchers who prepare background papers for individual members and for committees.

The position of sergeant-at-arms is one of the most ancient of parliamentary offices; it hearkens back to an era when the Speaker and the members of the Commons were in genuine need of armed protection against violence from the king or from other enemies of Parliament. The sergeant, who holds appointment at pleasure, carries the mace in the Speaker's parade, escorts from the Chamber MPPS who have been named by the Speaker, and directs the staff of attendants and pages who see to the members' needs in the House. He is responsible for the service of Speaker's warrants compelling the attendance of witnesses before legislative committees. In some Canadian legislatures, notably the House of Commons and the Quebec National Assembly, the sergeant-at-arms has extensive administrative duties. In Ontario his responsibilities are more limited; he maintains security in the Chamber and in committee rooms, oversees House furnishings, and directs the legislative page program. The first Ontario sergeant-at-arms served an astonishing sixty-six years; after his death, the position devolved into an honorary one occupied by former military men who had been decorated for wartime service. In 1976 a full-time sergeant, Thomas Stelling, was appointed; he has moved the office away from purely ceremonial functions into substantive policy areas, particularly security.

A report from the Legislative Assembly Committee in 1986 proposed that appointments to senior legislative positions no longer be the gift of the government; the clerk, the first clerk, sergeant-at-arms, and the director of the library would be selected by a legislative committee, subject to House approval, and the director of administration would be selected by the Board of Internal Economy.[86] Although this report had not been debated by the time the new clerk was appointed in 1986, the government followed the committee's recommendation, and, according to its official response to the report, considered that the recommendation was 'in force.'[87] Late in 1987 the Board of Internal Economy adopted a procedure whereby all five senior assembly staff would be selected by a committee composed of the Speaker, the clerk, and three members (representing the three parties) of the Legislative Assembly Committee.[88]

Ontario has had a separate provincial auditor since 1886, but only in the last two or three decades has the office achieved genuine independence from government and developed the resources and techniques to act as an effective critic of and adviser on government expenditure processes.[89] Until the early 1970s the Auditor was primarily engaged in 'pre-audit' (the authorizing of cheques and payments against legislative appropriations before the money is spent). This concentration on narrow legality sharply limited the auditor's usefulness to the legislature. The auditor's current 'post-audit' mandate, with its key 'value for money' provision, now focuses on evaluating the efficiency, effectiveness, and economy of government spending. His annual reports to the legislature are vital to the work of the Public Accounts Committee and in generally fostering legislative accountability in the expenditure of public moneys.[90] The auditor is appointed by the government, on address of the assembly after 'consultation with the Chairman of the standing Public Accounts Committee.'[91] The appointment has no specific term, but ends with the auditor's sixty-fifth birthday. The auditor has a staff of approximately 110, most of whom are professional accountants or accounting students.

After several years of discussion, occasioned in part by repeated private members' bills, an Ombudsman was appointed in 1975 to investigate and report upon citizens' complaints against unfair or arbitrary treatment by bureaucrats. The ombudsman is an officer of the legislature, to which he reports through the Speaker; like the auditor, he is appointed by address of the assembly, though his is a ten-year renewable term. His function is clearly one that MPPS can and do perform, but the ombudsman has a number of advantages over the members in performing this task on their behalf: a large staff (of roughly 120 in 1986), the authority to compel the production of papers and the taking of evidence under oath, and the respect and trust accorded by the bureaucrats to a high-profile, non-partisan official of the legislature.[92]

The ombudsman and the auditor share certain obvious similarities, such as their formal positions as servants of the legislature and their limited powers – both may investigate, report, and recommend, but neither can compel the acceptance or implementation of their recommendations. None the less, important differences are evident, particularly in the way the offices are perceived by members. The provincial auditor is viewed as an expert adviser to the House and to the Public Accounts Committee; he is a trusted colleague in the fight against government waste and mismanagement, and his impartiality and findings are almost never called into question by MPPs. This is symbolized by the auditor's being seated beside the chairman of the Public Accounts Committee, and by his presence at the committee even when it meets in camera. In contrast, the ombudsman is viewed with suspicion (and jealousy) by not a few members, and antagonistic relations between the ombudsman and the members, if not common, are not unknown. In the Ombudsman Committee, the ombudsman is seated apart from the MPPs, and he is routinely excluded when the committee holds sessions in camera. One of the committee's principal purposes is to review and to support or reject the methods and the findings of the ombudsman in a way scarcely imaginable to the Public Accounts Committee. Members' divergent views of the two offices largely stem from fact that the ombudsman is doing work that many MPPs believe they could do better at a fraction of the cost; no member could hope to perform the specialized audits carried out by the provincial auditor and his staff.

THE PRESS GALLERY

Members of the press gallery are key players in the legislative process, and their perceptions and actions are of fundamental importance to all MPPs. As Frederick J. Fletcher has put it, 'the parliamentary ritual acquires its significance in large part from the public attention it gets, and this attention is conveyed almost entirely through the mass media, since few Ontarians attend sessions or read Hansard.'[93]

For special or particularly newsworthy events, non-gallery members will augment the usual Queen's Park complement, but most of the media coverage of the legislature is generated by the roughly three dozen permanent members of the Queen's Park press gallery. No formal studies have compared the social characteristics, the backgrounds, and the outlooks of the press gallery with other groups of reporters, but it is reasonable to assume is that they do not differ significantly from similar Canadian media groupings.

For many Queen's Park reporters, the legislature is their first major posting; they can expect to stay for a year or two before being reassigned. The Ontario beat (for reporters cover Ontario politics and government generally, not just the legislature) is typically viewed as of intermediate importance (particularly in comparison with a posting to Ottawa), and is seen as a stepping-stone in one's career. Accordingly, the turnover in the gallery is high. As of the fall of 1986, two gallery members had been covering Queen's Park more or less continuously since the 1960s, and three had been there since the late 1970s; most of the rest had less than three years' experience. This high rate of turnover is of some consequence, since it takes even experienced reporters considerable time to become familiar with the complexities of the Ontario government, the arcane ways of the House, the issues of Ontario politics, and the politicians themselves. Without such knowledge it is difficult to cover Queen's Park thoroughly; as one analyst has remarked, 'Because policies often develop over long periods, new reporters lack the background to understand events.'[94]

The *Toronto Star* and the *Globe and Mail* maintain bureaus of four or five reporters and one columnist while the Toronto *Sun*, the Canadian Press wire service, Thomson newspapers, and CBC radio normally assign two or three reporters to Queen's Park. Most other Queen's Park 'bureaus' consist of a single reporter (plus a cameraman, in the case of television reporters). In other words, many members of the press gallery must cover virtually all aspects of Ontario politics and government; this allows little time for specialization, detailed research, or thoughtful analysis, let alone investigative journalism. One implication of this pressure to cover everything is that few reporters pay much attention to the legislature, save for the burlesque of question period and the occasional committee meeting where pyrotechnics are expected.

The press gallery is more than a collection of individual reporters; it has a collective identity of sorts. A formal organization exists, but it tends to be mainly concerned with social events, though the gallery has adopted official positions on matters such as television coverage of the House, office space and service for gallery members, and access to events

67 The participants

and persons. Far more important is the fact of the gallery's physical presence in the Legislative Building. Office space is provided for all permanent gallery members, though some of it is of such poor quality that no one would want to use the space for anything other than storage. In addition, the gallery has a sizeable lounge, with bar service, on the third floor, adjacent to the Chamber. At any time during working hours several reporters may be found around the large table in the lounge, trading political gossip and putting forward their interpretations of political events. Whether this constitutes 'pack journalism' is open to debate, but it certainly provides the opportunity for reporters to shape one another's ideas and approaches, and for a conventional wisdom to emerge. One point about which there is all but universal agreement among reporters is the essential irrelevance and ineffectiveness of the House. Naturally, this view inclines reporters away from in-depth coverage of the legislature. Ironically, a good deal of legislature's ineffectiveness can be attributed to a lack of media coverage.

Much of the material in this chapter is either ambivalent on or unrelated to the issue of the Ontario legislature's becoming a more transformative body. It would be reasonable to hypothesize that the highly educated, professionally specialized MPPs of the 1980s would be more likely than their predecessors to demand a meaningful role in policy-making and to turn their expertise to particular policy areas; but without extensive data we can only speculate. However, the implication of the fact that half of the members were former municipal politicians is clear. Municipal councils and school boards are highly transformative, and members with municipal experience, accustomed to making policy and wielding power, might well be expected to bring about significant increases in the legislature's transformative capacity. Clearly, though, this has not occurred.

The heightened specialization, professionalization, and formality of organization within the party caucuses hold the potential for enhanced transformative activity in the legislature, and to a certain extent this has occurred. None the less, it is evident that these changes denote no major alteration in the distribution of power within the legislature. Changes in the ways in which the opposition parties organize themselves have been effective only in improving their ability to attack and discredit the government, something that is typical of arena rather than transformative legislatures. On the government side, regardless of the extensive new committee systems and other changes, the caucus plays only a very minor role in decision-making, and even that limited role tends to be one of blocking rather than formulating policy.

One set of changes that has been unequivocally transformative in nature is the expansion and professionalization of the assembly's non-partisan staff. Competent, specialized staff assistance to members and committees is a sine qua non of a transformative legislature in the modern world. The ramifications of the increase in staff and services are discussed more fully in Chapter 7.

The legislative activities of Ontario MPPs are not determined only by their social characteristics, their formal position within the legislature, the influence of the parties, and the nature and abilities of the non-partisan staff who serve them. In addition, the formal rules, as well as the political conventions of the House and its informal rules of conduct and procedure, channel and limit members' behaviour. The following three chapters set out the principles under which the Ontario legislature operates, and examine some of its more important processes.

3

The legislature at work 1: An overview

As a guide to how the Ontario legislature really works, a reading of its rules, the *Standing Orders*, would prove almost as incomplete and misleading as the Constitution Act does as a guide to the operation of the government of Canada. This chapter analyses the legislature's atmosphere and folkways, the bases of its procedure, the nature of debate, the reach of party discipline, and the operation of time limits and closure mechanisms. The routine of the House is briefly sketched; the amounts of House time devoted to various functions and procedures are analysed.

ATMOSPHERE AND FOLKWAYS

Some years ago the American political scientist David Truman pointed out that 'a legislative body has its own group life. Like others, it has its standards and conventions, its largely unwritten system of obligations and privileges.' These unwritten norms, he added, 'do much to moderate the conflicts inherent in the legislative process and to facilitate the adjustments without which the process could not go on.'[1] More recently, Edward Crowe succinctly summarized the significance of these conventions: 'The set of norms found in a particular legislature defines its character as an institution, serves to distinguish it from the outside world and from other elective assemblies, and also helps it to function effectively.'[2] What are the norms and conventions of the Ontario legislature?

The Ontario legislature is sometimes described as the 'rowdiest House in Canada.' The accuracy of this assessment is not germane here, but it is certainly true that visitors from other Canadian legislatures are frequently taken aback by the members' indecorous behaviour. By the same token, though, Ontario MPPs are very much surprised by the pandemonium of the British House of Commons during question time (in this, as in so many other ways, Ontario members tend to harbour idealized notions of the Mother of Parliaments). The two principal manifestations of this raucous atmosphere are the continual heckling (which is encouraged by the good quality of the floor-level acoustics) and the blatant disregard for the Speaker's calls to order. The insults, catcalls, and barracking, however, are generally boisterous rather than venomous, though they often have sharp political barbs imbedded in them. This reflects the nature of partisanship in the Ontario legislature: omnipresent and unmistakable, but not usually vicious or remorseless.

Much of the burlesque of the House, particularly during question period, is exactly that: theatre, in which members perform according to their roles. More often than not the apparent partisan rancour dissipates outside the Chamber. Deep enmity does exist between various individuals on opposite sides, but so too does genuine cross-party friendship. Most members get along with their fellows across the way; they recognize that each has a role to play and that criticism is not to be taken personally.

A recent study of the culture at Queen's Park asked current and former MPPS what qualities made for good members. One finding stood out:

almost every person included some finding on the following:
> those who can stick to their principles and fight hard for what they believe in, but who can also rise above partisan politics.

Rising above is interpreted in the political sense – putting aside party differences to come to creative compromise; and in the personal sense – respecting other members for their beliefs and maintaining friendly relations.[3]

A telling symbol of the nature of partisanship in the legislature lies in one of its more unusual folkways. Members wander freely about the Chamber and will not infrequently pull up a chair among opposing MPPs to talk with one of them.

Several factors contribute to the tolerance that leavens partisanship legislature. The first is the essential moderation of the province's political culture; unlike, say, British Columbia or Saskatchewan, Ontario is not politically polarized. Accordingly, although members do express significant policy disagreements stemming from differing outlooks on the role of the state in the economy, limits to individual freedoms, and the like, Liberals and Conservatives do not regard New Democrats as godless socialists who would nationalize the province if given half a chance, nor do NDP members look on MPPS from the older parties as soulless capitalists devoid of social conscience. Second, as full-time professionals, MPPS accept that their opponents have jobs to perform and roles to play. Indeed, all MPPS appear to share strong bonds and empathize with one another's lot. This is no mythic devotion to some noble parliamentary ideal, but the natural by-product of their unique common experiences – the rigours and uncertainties of getting elected and re-elected, the pressures on family life, the relentless demands of constituents and of party, the intrigues and trials of caucus life, and so on. Members may not agree with other members, but they understand them. They understand one another's motivations, their outlooks, and their foibles in a way, for example, that they do not understand (and therefore come to distrust) civil servants. Finally, animosity is muted by personal contact, principally through committee work and travel. Members get to know one another during prolonged service on committees, and the experience of committee travel, or travel with a parliamentary delegation, is particularly important in breaking down barriers. Ontario MPPS frequently travel in mixed-party groups ranging in size from three or four to a dozen or more; thrown together in unfamiliar locales, the members naturally spend a good deal of time socializing and getting to know one another as people.

These humanizing and moderating tendencies should not be misinterpreted: partisanship suffuses the MPP's every activity, and can, particularly just before or just after an election, become bitter and ruthless. Some individuals never develop personal ties with their political opponents. Moreover, MPPS from different parties seldom eat together in the legislative dining-room; most gravitate to one of the three large caucus tables. And to the extent that an MPP's friends are drawn from Queen's Park, they tend to come from within his own party. The tendency to concentrate one's personal life within the party is more pronounced among NDP members than among Liberals and Conservatives:

They have closer personal contacts and socialize more within the caucus. This may be because the New Democratic Party is the political reflection of a broader social and ideological movement, so party members have a deeper sense of group identity. It may also be a defense mechanism of the perennial runners-up, or banding together in an environment where often mindless 'red-baiting' is considered acceptable. The NDP is also a smaller caucus, physically grouped together more closely than the other two parties. The staff union offers further cause for group contact and identification.[4]

A final word on partisanship at Queen's Park: members are, as a rule, significantly less partisan than their staff. Political staff have little contact with their opposite numbers in the other parties, and thus, unlike the MPPs, don't see the human side of their opponents. Moreover, staff are less likely than members to appreciate the theatrical elements of the legislature, and they take partisan clashes more seriously.

The legislature has been styled 'the most exclusive club in Ontario.' Though the club metaphor retains a strong element of truth, it is substantially less accurate than it was even a few years ago. For one thing, although women remain outsiders in many ways, their presence, even in limited numbers, has undercut the essential maleness of the club. The most significant changes, however, arise from the growing professionalization of the members and the expansion in the scale of the legislature. Full-time professional MPPs with heavy constituency loads no longer have time for fraternization with their colleagues, opponents, and staff; the once ubiquitous card-games in the opposition lobby are now just memories. Attendance in the House, other than for question period, is low; instead of exchanging ideas and information formally through debate and informally though conversation in the lobbies, members work in their offices. Personal staff, who are increasingly ambitious and who take their jobs very seriously, encourage MPPs to do more 'productive' work than listening to debates and discussing all manner of things with colleagues or opponents. As the legislature has grown in scale, particularly the numbers of members' staff, caucus staff, and assembly staff, it has become decidedly more impersonal. In addition, the MPPs' offices are scattered throughout the legislative building, the Whitney Block, and (for ministers and parliamentary assistants) elsewhere in downtown Toronto; this has reduced members' proximity to one another, and thus their contact. The abolition of evening sittings in 1986 also sharply curtailed casual interaction. Evening sittings were far more relaxed than daytime sittings; relatively few staff were around, and the members were generally not inclined to work in their offices, so that they spent a good deal of time in relaxed conversation with their fellow MPPs. (The two-hour dinner break that accompanied the evening sittings also encouraged members to go out together in groups.) Finally, the advent of television has meant that members now spend less time in and around the Chamber, since they can monitor House business via their TV sets while working in their offices.

Just as the House is less important than in days past as an object of members' attentions, so too the value placed on seniority has declined substantially. The once-common expectation that newly elected members would bide their time, observe and learn from the veterans, and only slowly become actively involved in the legislature is essentially a thing of the past,[5] though inexperienced members still recognize that they can learn a good deal from the old-timers. Perhaps related to this change in attitude is the fact that the opposition parties cannot really be said to have back-benchers. To be sure, some members are obviously more effective than their colleagues and enjoy higher status within the caucus and in the estimation of the leader; yet there is nothing like a clear division between front-benchers and back-benchers in the opposition parties. In part, this reflects the relatively small size of opposition caucuses, which are typically in the range of twenty to forty members, and which thus require substantial contributions from all members. Conversely, the cult of professionalism (and the strong ambitions that often underlie it), together with the staggering growth in cabinet ministers' workloads, has broadened the gulf between cabinet and government back-bencher.

Still and all, the legislature is very much a club in which the informal rules and understandings are as important as the formal procedures. Among the unwritten rules and norms are those prohibiting public discussion of opponents' personal foibles; tolerating 'tap-dancing with the truth,' but not outright lies; placing a premium on maintaining confidences; prizing highly a sense of humour, conviviality, and lack of pretension; presuming a privileged status for members to which no non-member can really aspire; and frowning on taking advantage of procedural technicalities to thwart opponents.[6]

PARLIAMENTARY PRACTICE IN ONTARIO

Parliamentary practice in the Ontario legislature is a blend of written rules, British parliamentary conventions, and customs representing Canadian or Ontarian adaptations of the British model.

The fundamental principles underlying the Ontario legislature are those of the Westminster model of parliamentary government. These are in the nature of zero-order beliefs – so primal as to be accepted without

74 The Ontario legislature

justification and scarcely susceptible to rational challenge. They include the concept of responsible government, the notion of a loyal opposition, party discipline, and ministerial responsibility. A discussion of those principles need not detain us here. What is important is that Ontario MPPS tend to share an unspoken presumption that these constitutional cornerstones of the British parliamentary system are at once immutable and unambiguous. They are, of course, neither.

The written framework can be subdivided into provisions which in their permanence are analogous to a constitution, and into provisions which are more changeable and can be analogized to statute law. Among the first may be counted the Constitution Act, 1867. Section 69 of the act establishes a unicameral legislature; section 87 determines a number of features of the legislature, including its quorum; and section 90 retains for the government the prerogative of money bills, taxation, and appropriation. Similarly, sections 4 and 5 of the Constitution Act, 1982 limit the life of a legislature to five years (except in time of emergency), and require at least an annual sitting of the legislature. In addition, the amending procedure, set out in section 38 of the 'new' constitution, requires that amendments must be acceptable to not only the governments involved but to Parliament and the provincial legislatures.

Rather more significant is the provincial Legislative Assembly Act.[7] This act sets out such fundamentally important features of the legislature as the qualifications for membership, the power of the House and its committees to compel the attendance of witnesses and the production of papers, the immunity of members from civil actions arising from their work, the grounds on which persons may be found in contempt of the legislature, the power of the House to deal with contempt and breaches of privilege, and the penalties the House may impose for such offences. Apart from those relating to members' qualifications, these provisions have remained essentially unchanged since the act was first passed in 1876.[8] Some of these important principles were placed upon uncertain ground after the coming into force of The Charter of Rights and Freedoms, particularly those relating to the ability of the House to declare grounds of contempt and to punish offenders. So far, little attention has been devoted to potential problems. Other parts of the act concern themselves with less fundamental principles; they describe the indemnities and allowances of members and prescribe the legal framework for the Board of Internal Economy. In the day-to-day proceedings in the House and in other aspects of legislative routine, the Legislative

75 The legislature at work: An overview

Assembly Act is of little consequence. Similarly, the Members' Conflict of Interest Act is important in that it constrains and directs members' actions, but has little direct effect on the routine operation of the House.

Other statutes, including the Audit Act, the Ombudsman Act, the Freedom of Information and Personal Privacy Act, the Election Act, the Management Board of Cabinet Act, and the Workers' Compensation Act, contain provisions relating to the legislature, but these come into play only in special circumstances. All of the statutes, including the Legislative Assembly Act, are subject to amendment in the usual fashion.

Of the greatest practical importance for most House activities are the standing orders – the 'statute law' of the legislature. These are the House rules that set out, often in some detail, the basic procedures which govern consideration of bills, rules of debate, times of sitting, order of business, question period, and a host of other matters. The standing orders can be amended by simple majority on a motion or a committee report, but it is generally accepted that their organic nature renders them immune to cavalier change, and indeed they are amended only after extensive consultation between parties. Aside from minor adjustments, they have been revised only six times: in 1875, 1929, 1939, 1970, 1976, and 1986. Schindeler has identified a basic difference between Ontario and Westminster in the relationship between the written rules and established practice, a difference that stems from the origin of Ontario's rules as a codification of what was accepted by convention in Britain: 'In Ontario custom modifies the written rules whereas in Britain the standing orders modify ancient practice.'[9]

Ontario's standing orders are notable for the primacy they grant parties over private members and for their premise that the legislature is in effect composed of three parties. Many of the formal rules apportion opportunities for members to speak or to engage in various activites (such as moving non-confidence motions or chairing committees) according to their party affiliation. Party domination is a basic reality of the Ontario legislature, but its formalization in the standing orders seriously undercuts the options available to independent-minded MPPs. Moreover, should a member be elected independent of the three main parties (or should he defect from one of them once elected),[10] he would find himself at a serious disadvantage under the existing rules.

The standing orders cannot cover all contingencies, and their interpretation is not always clear. Speakers' rulings, the legislative analogue of judicial decisions, resolve issues not covered in the rules and disputes over interpretation; they are thus of considerable import, not only in settling the immediate point at issue but in building up a body of precedents and in codifying practice. Although the Speaker is continually called upon to make minor off-the-cuff decisions on routine matters, he delivers major, written rulings only a few times a session. These rulings are recorded in the *Journals* and are collected in precedent books maintained by the Clerk's Office. In 1986-87 major Speaker's rulings were delivered on, inter alia, the propriety of ministers' redirecting questions to other ministers, the limitations on opposition responses to ministerial statements, and the allegation that disclosure by government officials to the press of details of pending legislation prior to its introduction in the House constituted a breach of parliamentary privilege.[11] Like judicial precedents, Speakers' rulings are not cast in stone, but may be overturned by subsequent rulings (though this is not common).

The evolution of the current standing order 1(b) demonstrates the growing maturity of the Ontario legislature. At confederation, any contingencies not covered by the rules were to be decided by the 'rules, usages and forms' currently in force in the British House of Commons. In 1929 'the usages and precedents of this legislature' were explicitly ranked ahead of British practice as a source of guidance, and in 1970 the formula was changed to its current wording: 'In all contingencies not provided for in the Standing Orders the question shall be decided by the Speaker or Chairman, and in making his ruling the Speaker or Chairman shall base his decision on the usages and precedents of the Legislature and Parliamentary tradition.' 'Parliamentary tradition' is a vague notion, encompassing precedents from all over the globe. In practice, though, despite the occasional citation of rulings or conventions from Australian and other Commonwealth jurisdictions, if guidance beyond the Ontario precedents is sought, Speakers (and members) turn first to Ottawa, whose principal modern authority, *Beauchesne*,[12] is often cited, and then to Britain. *Erskine May*,[13] the classic volume on British practice, is used to formulate basic principles; but since British procedure is now so very different from Canadian, its value in matters of detail is slight. Sometimes reference is made to the practices of other provincial legislatures, but their value is limited by a lack of readily available, codified precedents and by the fact that the standing orders in several Canadian provinces specify reliance on the rules of the federal House of Commons in unprovided-for contingencies.

'Parliamentary tradition' weighs most heavily in quasi-constitutional matters such as privilege, committee powers, the sub judice convention, and the like.[14] In more routine matters, Ontario experience combined with a commonsense interpretation of the standing orders usually provides sufficient guidance for a ruling. Although Ontario lacks a *May* or a *Beauchesne*, its precedents as recorded in the *Journals* have been collected and codified by the Clerk's Office and are available to the Speaker and members. Only a few Ontario usages and practices are truly unwritten. Parties speak in rotation; divisions do not take place without the consent of all three whips; committees conduct business without a quorum but not without a representative of each party; and formal rules are not amended unless all parties agree to the change. Similarly, certain standing orders are entirely disregarded, such as the rule directing the Speaker, during question period, to disallow any question not of 'urgent public importance'; the rule proscribing remarks referring to matters on the order paper for future debate or to matters already dealt with by the House; and the rule requiring amendments to bills in committee to be filed with the clerk two hours before the bill is considered, 'when time permits.'

These examples point up what is perhaps the most important convention underlying parliamentary practice in Ontario: pragmatism. This pragmatism is evidenced by the frequency with which things are accomplished by suspending the standing orders with the explicit or implicit unanimous consent of the House; the presumption is that if the three House leaders or their surrogates agree on a course of action, then no harm is done in waiving the rules. Similarly, some dubious practices are followed because they are convenient and because no one objects. The acceptance of committees sitting between sessions is an illustration, as is the practice, standard until a very few years ago, of putting major procedural questions to the House without notice (for example, the amendment of committees' terms of reference or the deeming of legislation uncompleted at the end of a session to have had first and second reading in the next session). It is not that Ontario MPPs have no respect for the rules and break them willy-nilly, but rather that, given their essentially pragmatic outlook, they are untroubled about bending or ignoring them if it makes sense to do so and no one objects. If someone does object, or if someone insists on a literal application of the standing orders, then the proprieties are followed (though the objector risks being labelled 'difficult' or 'finicky').

PARTY DISCIPLINE

Party cohesion in the Ontario legislature is, as Samuel Beer remarked in describing the British House of Commons in the 1960s, 'so close to 100 per cent that there was no longer any point in measuring it.'[15] A study of voting records of the Thirty-second Parliament (1981–84) showed that, except for a handful of items of private members' business, all recorded votes were party votes, defined as votes wherein at least 90 per cent of each party's MPPS voted together.[16] The results would not have been much different had the criterion been 100 per cent, for many sessions pass without a single member's voting against his party in the House on a matter of any import.

This remarkable cohesion is a result of stringent party discipline; but party discipline involves far more than the punishments and rewards doled out by the whips and the leaders.[17] The discipline must be accepted by the members: indeed, the most effective aspect of party discipline is the self-discipline members impose on themselves. To be sure, it is widely understood, particularly on the government side, that life is much easier for those who conform, and that MPPS' self-censoring behaviour stems not so much from explicit direction as from anticipated consequences, which often render actual threats unnecessary.[18] Yet MPPS are more than timorous voting machines; they believe in their parties and they believe that a British-style parliament requires strong, cohesive parties lest it descend into the chaos of the congressional system. In other words, they vote the party line not only because they fear the consequences of not doing so, but also because they want to and because they believe it is their duty. The member who opposes the party incurs the wrath of the party leadership, but he also isolates himself from his colleagues, and deprives himself of crucial social and psychological support as well as essential sources of information.[19] Outspoken MPPS are shunned because other MPPS recognize the dangers in becoming too closely identified with those out of favour with the party leadership, but also because their fellows look with disfavour on those who don't play by the accepted rules.

The force of party discipline waxes and wanes with the circumstances. It is understood, for example, that, especially when they represent government policy, party positions that directly and adversely affect an MPP's riding may be cause for him to disagree publicly with the party. Bona fide constituency concerns of such seriousness are infrequent, however, and if they come to a vote, the party leadership prefers dissident members to stay away rather than vote against the party. Similarly, on those rare issues that give rise to profound moral qualms, such as abortion or gay rights, MPPS' consciences are respected; in return, members are expected to refrain from embarrassing the party.[20] Depending on how central an issue is to a party's program, members' expression of outspoken individual viewpoints may be tolerated, though members explore this nebulous area at their peril. If they pick their issues carefully, astute and aggressive members may even find dissension a useful means of bringing themselves to the attention of party notables and of securing promotion. What is certain, is the fate awaiting those who criticize basic party policy, as evidenced by the unfortunate Tory MPP who found himself ostracized for publicly questioning his government's purchase of a major oil company in 1981. His crime lay not in his opinion, which was shared by a large part of the caucus and by senior ministers, but in voicing it publicly.

The leeway accorded members is significantly wider in committee than it is in the House. Committees tend to deal not with principles but with matters of detail, on which parties may not have clearly defined positions. There may not be a specific party line to toe, and even if there is, the parties can be surprisingly lax in communicating it to their MPPS. Moreover, most committees toil in relative obscurity, so that deviation from the party position is much less likely to come to public attention. To equate this greater latitude in committee with the absence of party discipline, however, is a fundamental misinterpretation.

Party discipline assumes a different cast in each party, but within the New Democratic Party a unique form of discipline prevails: 'To a much greater degree than with either of the other caucuses, the greatest single motivator for cohesion within the New Democratic caucus is the explicit connection between the parliamentary wing of the party and party policy ... [all New Democrats asked to define discipline] mentioned the ideological and organizational bond between the caucus and party policy and platform.'[21] Party resolutions and policy decisions taken at party conferences are of far greater consequence in the NDP than in the other parties, and NDP members feel a correspondingly stronger commitment to support party policy. This cohesion among NDP members owes little to threats or inducements from the party leadership but instead reflects shared values, not the least of which is a strong belief in collective action. Because of the NDP's frequent third-party status, elements of a siege mentality – some would say paranoia – also contribute to party cohesion.

Discipline in the NDP has a programmatic basis, and the government party, be it Liberal or Conservative, can rely on what has been styled 'the discipline of power,' but the remaining opposition party can rely on neither. Not surprisingly, then, as brokerage parties without distinct ideologies, whose principal objective is tied not to policy goals but to regaining power, both the Liberals and Conservatives have had to work much harder at maintaining a rather shakier degree of discipline while in opposition.

DEBATE

In common with many other parliaments, the term 'debate' as used in the Ontario legislature is almost entirely a misnomer. Genuine debate entails an exchange of ideas and positions, a refutation of opposing viewpoints, and a reply and rebuttal. Only rarely the discussions in the Ontario legislature resemble this model. In the first place, the standing orders permit members to speak only once in most debates, and Ontario, unlike Westminster, has no tradition of members' 'giving way' during their speeches for questions and comments from other members. Ontario now has an analogue of Ottawa's recently established procedure which permits up to ten minutes of comments and questions about a member's speech and the member's response to them during debates on second and third reading of government bills, the throne and budget debates, and debates on interim supply. This has had a salutary effect on the quality of 'debate,' though it remains a good distance from the conventional cut-and-thrust of a genuine debate. Perhaps the most significant effect of the comment and question procedure has been that members take more pains to ensure that they understand the speeches their staffs have prepared for them. None the less, it remains essentially true that debate in the Ontario House consists in the main of a rotation of set-piece speeches given in isolation from one another. The rule requiring that remarks be relevant to the question before the House is laxly enforced, as is the prohibition against repetition, and this too the quality of debate.

Long-time observers routinely decry the decline of oratory in the Ontario House. Such laments betray a certain nostalgia, but there is little doubt that the overall quality of debate has declined in recent years, as has the number of skilled orators capable of delivering powerful extemporaneous speeches. The chief cause of this decline is the greatly reduced salience of what goes on in the House and the similarly diminished audiences for the debates. With the press of committee, constituency, and ministerial business, few members attend the House unless they have to, either because they are involved in the matter

81 The legislature at work: An overview

under discussion or because it is their assigned time for House duty. Attendance is of such low priority that party leaders are rarely in the House (except for question period) and probably make no more than half a dozen speeches during a session; in contrast, as late as the Robarts era (1961–71), the premier was present in the House as often as not, and served as his own House leader. Most speeches are delivered to small numbers of mainly inattentive members, and there is little incentive to develop oratorical skills. Moreover, with extensive staff resources at their beck and call, members now regularly rely on assistants to write their speeches for them; naturally, this practice does little to improve the quality of debate. The televising of House proceedings has reinforced members' tendency to rely on prepared texts so that they appear to be in control of their material and so that they do not reveal their weakness in speaking off-the-cuff. (Most members even have their questions written out for them in question period; such a practice was uncommon just a few years ago.)

The Speaker is nominally responsible for deciding who is to speak, but in practice he is rarely called upon to make a decision. By long-established tradition, MPPS speak in fixed rotation – government, official opposition, and third party – and each party normally has a speaking list so that it is almost always clear who is to speak next. The standing orders provide for motions to be offered that a particular MPP 'do now speak,' but recourse to this rule is almost unknown. Even in the less structured atmosphere typical of the Committee of the Whole, disputes about whose turn it is to speak are unusual.

Since 1970 French has been an official language of debate in the Ontario legislature, but only since the mid-1980s has it been taken seriously. Although only about 1 per cent of what is said in the House is said in French,[22] remarks in French have come to be accepted as unexceptional; only a few years ago 'to speak French in the legislature and to ask a question in French was regarded as almost a challenge to the political order.'[23] In recent years perhaps as many as two dozen MPPS have been able to speak in French without a text, and substantially more have had some passive understanding (though no Speaker since 1970 has had better than a rudimentary facility). Until 1986, debate in French was severely hampered by the lack of simultaneous translation facilities. Hansard prints remarks in the language in which they were made, but provides no translation; the order paper and *Votes and Proceedings* will provide a translation of symbolically important events or motions, and will publish in French any material submitted by members. A few bills are available in French, and a handful of major reports from committees have been published in both French and English, but English remains overwhelmingly dominant in House documents and in debate. Still, in the legislature as in the government, the use of French can be expected to increase exponentially in the future.[24] On special occasions MPPs deliver speeches with brief passages in other languages, such as Italian, Polish, Ukrainian, and Cree, but these are not recorded in Hansard.[25]

The usual proscriptions against unparliamentary language apply in the Ontario House. Members are not to accuse other members of lying, to impute to them 'false or unavowed motives,' to make allegations, or to use insulting or abusive language.[26] Ontario MPPs have generally not distinguished themselves by the inventiveness of their epithets, so that their contribution to the repertoire of acceptable and unacceptable parliamentary language is meagre; nevertheless, it has been judged that it is permissible to refer to members as 'grimy,' 'yappy,' and 'boring,' and as 'stooges'; but it is not permissible to call a member a 'hypocrite,' a 'trained seal,' a 'guttersnipe,' a 'complete ass,' a 'nitwit,' or a 'raving maniac.'[27] A member is addressed by the name of his riding or by his position in the ministry or in the House. In 1981 Speaker John Turner attempted to adopt the British practice of calling upon members by name, which he contended was the proper procedure, but was forced to abandon the change in the face of vociferous opposition from members unwilling to abandon a cherished custom.[28]

Debates are interrupted by aggrieved members rising on 'points of order' and 'points of privilege,' terms they tend to use interchangeably. It is not so much that they fail to understand the difference, as that they understand all too well their functional equivalence: they both provide a guaranteed method of gaining the floor, often illegitimately; of grabbing attention before question period; of asking, in effect, an extra supplementary question; or of otherwise scoring political points.[29] While he was still the leader of the opposition, David Peterson, upon rising to begin question period and finding few ministers in their places to be questioned, once inquired of the Speaker, 'Could we engage in some spurious points of order and privilege to delay and give them time to come in?'[30] Legitimate points of order do arise frequently, and on occasion generate substantial debate. Genuine points of privilege are rare, and the bogus nature of most so-called points of privilege is widely understood. The institution, in 1986, of an opportunity for members to make short speeches prior to ministerial statements has, as planned,

83 The legislature at work: An overview

drastically cut down on spurious points of privilege at the beginning of the legislative day.

TIME LIMITS, CLOSURE, AND TIME ALLOCATION

Few time limits constrain the length of debates; the standing orders restrict only the time that may be spent on emergency debates, on private members' business, on non-confidence motions, and on estimates (both initial consideration and concurrence). Fewer still are the limits on the length of speeches. Members may speak for only ten minutes in emergency debates, during private members' time, and on the extremely infrequent motions to recommit bills to committees. Otherwise, they are permitted to speak for as long as they wish; the extensive restrictions on the length of speeches found in several Canadian jurisdictions, such as British Columbia, Quebec, Saskatchewan, and the House of Commons, have not found favour in Ontario. In March 1984 the Procedural Affairs Committee proposed a forty-five-minute limit on speeches,[31] but by November 1985 the idea had been abandoned.[32] Certain informal or ad hoc limits occasionally come into play. The House leaders may agree, for example, that a particular committee report will be given only one afternoon's debate, and that speaking time will be apportioned equally among the parties; from time to time formal motions are passed to divide speaking time on specific items, but more often this is done through unofficial agreement.

The laissez-faire outlook on the length of speeches and debates makes it difficult to predict the length of various proceedings, especially on legislation. Rather more significant is the potential for opposition delay and obstruction offered by the absence of time limits and by the lack of any procedure for time allocation.

Despite substantial talk over the years, no action has been taken towards implementing a time-allocation rule. Although the Camp Commission found that opposition obstruction was not a serious problem in Ontario,[33] it did recommend a procedure for time allocation, which it styled 'closure by agreement.'[34]

In the fall of 1981 the Liberal opposition gave vent to its frustration at the government's refusal to table documents relating to the purchase of a major oil company by staging a filibuster and holding up interim supply for several days. The government was able to bring the debate to a conclusion by moving 'the previous question,' a mechanism requiring that a vote be held immediately on whether the matter before the House (that is, the previous question) should be put to an immediate vote. This seems to have been the first use of 'the previous question' since the 1930s, and its deployment drew a rancorous response from the opposition. It soon became apparent that this simple device for ending debate on a specific question before the House did not lend itself to neutralizing all forms of opposition obstruction.

In the fall of 1982 Bill 179, an inflation-restraint measure that the government had hoped to pass quickly, took nearly three months to become law, primarily because of the relentless stalling tactics of the NDP.[35] The bill was finally pushed through by the use of government motions to limit the time for public hearings in standing committee and to limit House debate on the committee report and at third reading, together with the odd application of 'the previous question.' In the wake of the delays caused by the opposition and the government's resort to time allocation, both of which were quite unprecedented in the Ontario legislature, interest was generated anew in institutionalizing a means of overcoming intransigent opposition obstruction.

Although time allocation has been used only a handful of times, it has become accepted as part of the government's procedural repertoire (as has 'the previous question,' which has been officially renamed 'closure'). Less draconian than closure, time allocation takes the form of a government motion, which requires notice and is itself debatable. It sets out a timetable for debate of the remaining stages of a bill by specifying when votes are to take place and limiting the length of time that the bells may ring for those divisions. Governments of both Liberal and Conservative stripe have moved to impose time allocation only on major pieces of legislation that have been subject to prolonged debate and on which the opposition is employing clearly obstructionist tactics. More than the convenience of the government must be at stake before the government will resort either to closure or to time allocation and thereby risk triggering the inevitable opposition jeremiads about the demise of parliamentary democracy.

Some argued that the Bill 179 episode demonstrated the need for more effective procedures by which the Government could end filibustering; others, myself included, contended that the episode showed that only minor modifications are necessary. The opposition went to extraordinary lengths to delay the bill, partly in the hope that, given additional time, a great groundswell of public opinion would force the government to abandon the bill or to modify it substantially, as had happened in 1974 with a controversial bill on teachers' right to strike. The means by which the government finally ended the impasse had been available to it from the outset. The issue whether or when to impose closure was essentially political, not procedural. So long as it was willing to accept the political consequences, the government could have used its majority to get its way whenever it wanted. It may be objected that minority governments lack the ability to enforce their will in this fashion, but if neither of the opposition parties can be persuaded to support the government's attempts to expedite its business, then perhaps that business ought not to be expedited. In short, the decision to obstruct or to impose closure is at root a question of political will and political calculation.

A potentially more serious dilemma, which does not admit of either the closure or the time-allocation solution, involves obstruction by prolonged bell-ringing. The House of Commons in 1982 and the Manitoba legislature in 1983 were brought to a standstill for weeks when the opposition refused to take part in votes, thus causing the division bells to ring until a political solution was reached. Ontario experienced a minor 'bells crisis' during a weekend in 1982, and on several occasions the opposition, piqued at some government action or inaction, has wasted a day's sitting by the simple expedient of not turning up for a vote. The Ontario legislature is particularly vulnerable to disruption by marathon bell-ringing: it has few rules governing the length of time the bells are to ring, and by convention the Speaker will not proceed with a vote unless all three party whips signal their readiness.

After the various bell-ringing episodes, the Procedural Affairs Committee grappled with the question. According to its 1984 report 'Some mechanism must be established to preclude the possibility of an opposition party hijacking Parliament for extended periods by refusing to participate in a vote. At the same time, the Committee recognizes that, under exceptional circumstances, it is legitimate for the opposition to signal extreme displeasure with proposed Government measures by forcing the division bells to ring for unusual lengths of time.'[36] In an attempt to reconcile these fundamentally divergent principles, the committee recommended a cumbersome procedure for enabling the opposition to delay a particular vote for up to three weeks while permitting the government to continue with other business. Not surprisingly, this proposal attracted little support. Nor did the party representatives negotiating the 1986 rule changes accept the committee's subsequent proposal that division bells be limited to fifteen minutes unless the whips advised the Speaker that more time was required to round up absent members, in which case the bells might ring for up to twenty-four hours.[37]

So far, the 'give-no-quarter' attitude that leads to prolonged bell-ringing episodes has, by and large, not been a feature of the Ontario legislature. Occasional bouts of obstruction occur, such as the filibuster that kept the House sitting between Christmas and New Year's Eve in 1987, and the continuous reading of petitions opposing Sunday shopping that consumed more than a week of House time in the spring of 1988. Still, the moderation that characterizes relations between government and opposition stands as the most effective means of preventing a serious bell-ringing crisis in Ontario, just as it inhibits abuse of the closure and time-allocation procedures. None the less, it is significant that the opposition has been unwilling to give up its potentially lethal weapon.

THE HOUSE ROUTINE

Until the 1960s, the sessions of the Ontario legislature were geared to the rhythms of rural life. The House sat for perhaps two or three months prior to spring planting, and if necessary, it sat again after the crops had been harvested in the fall. Although the legislature's work has expanded substantially over the past two decades, a fairly predictable cycle of activity still exists; that predictability arises not from formal requirements but from custom.

In a typical (which is primarily to say a non-election) year, the session begins in mid- to late March. The House takes a week off for the spring school break in late March, and then works until roughly the third week in June. On occasion, depending on the workload and the mood of the opposition, the House may sit into July before adjourning for the summer. Normally, the session does not resume until after Thanksgiving, in mid-October. In 1978 and 1984 the House was recalled briefly in August to end or prevent strikes by Toronto Transit Commission workers. When the government called the legislature back into session in mid-September 1982 to deal with its inflation restraint program, its expectation that after a few days the 'summer break' might be resumed proved hopelessly optimistic. Indeed, not only did the House sit straight through until the middle of December, it was unable to complete its work by Christmas and required four more weeks in January and February 1983. Following the cataclysm of the 1985 election, the House did not meet until June, and the flood of major legislation arising from the Liberal-NDP accord resulted in spill-overs of the sessions of 1985 and 1986 into the first few weeks of the following years. Normally, however, the House is prorogued by about the end of the third week in December.[38] The standing orders require the government House leader to announce at the end of the spring sitting the date for resumption in the fall; no similar provision exists at prorogation for setting a date for the new session.[39]

Schindeler reports that from 1867 to 1964, the average session lasted only 44.3 days.[40] In the period 1969-86, the House sat for an average of just over 100 days a year.[41] Not only is the House sitting much more often, but, even when it is not in session, committees tend to be very busy. Ontario is certainly not unique among British-style parliaments in having committees meet while the House is adjourned or prorogued,[42] but the extent of activity is unusual; during February and September four or five committees are often meeting at the same time. Usually the only times of the year when committees do not meet are early January and August. The level of 'off-season' committee activity is far higher than that characteristic of the British or Canadian parliaments, which of course have substantially longer sessions.

In its 1985 report, the Procedural Affairs Committee recommended a parliamentary calendar similar to the Ottawa model, which would have seen the House in session from the beginning of March to the end of June and from mid-September to mid-December; on the basis of 4 sitting days a week, this system would have provided for roughly 120 sitting days a year.[43] Despite general agreement on the merits of the idea, it was vetoed by the Liberal government when the rules were changed in the spring of 1986. The premier had already scheduled a well-publicized trip to Asia for the fall, and was uncomfortable with the prospect of travelling while the House was in session. The idea remains alive, however; the most recent proposal calls for a calendar similar to that suggested by Procedural Affairs, but with 'constituency weeks' added in the spring and fall sittings during which neither the House nor committees would meet; this system would provide just over 100 sessional days.[44]

From the late 1960s until 1986, the House sat on Monday, Tuesday, Thursday, and Friday mornings.[45] The Conservative government steadfastly refused to permit the House to meet on Wednesdays, which it reserved for cabinet meetings, except in the last week or two prior to the summer adjournment or the Christmas prorogation. Several committees usually met on Wednesday. This schedule was unpopular with out-of-town MPPs who were jealous of the opportunity it gave to Toronto members or members within easy commuting distance of Toronto (for example, MPPs from Ottawa) to spend a day working in their ridings. Moreover, the natural let-down and fatigue that accompanied at the end of the week meant that Fridays tended to be unproductive, with low attendance and a high propensity to silliness. As part of the 1986 reforms the example of the Quebec National Assembly was followed and Monday to Thursday sittings were instituted.

The same set of reforms saw the abolition of evening sittings, which had run from 8:00 PM to 10:30 PM every Tuesday and Thursday, and on occasional Mondays. Currently, the House meets every weekday except Friday from 1:30 pm until 6:00 pm.[46] A Thursday morning sitting (from 10:00 AM until noon) is earmarked for private members' business. All told, the House sits for twenty hours a week, just as it did prior to 1986.

One of the enduring legacies of minority government has been the infrequency of late-night (or, more accurately, early morning) sittings. Prior to 1975 it was not unknown for the House to sit past midnight. The standing orders now require a government motion to authorize sitting past the normal adjournment time, and in effect permit either opposition party to prevent a late sitting.[47] Thus, even before evening sittings were done away with, the House would continue to sit past 10:30 PM only two or three times a year and virtually never past midnight. Under the new timetable, sittings lasting past 6:00 pm are equally infrequent, though there are occasional 'late shows,' and the odd division may still be underway at the official adjournment time.

Similarly, the minority era of the 1970s signalled the end of the 'legislation by last-minute-rush' strategy, in which the government would wait until the last few days of the session to introduce important measures. The government would defy the opposition to stay up all night if it wanted to debate the bills; some bills would generate all-night sittings, but reasoned consideration and meaningful debate were very much at a premium on legislation passed in this fashion. Government and opposition both indulge in brinksmanship over whether they will delay the legislature's work so as to prevent members' getting away for the summer or for Christmas, but it now tends to be the opposition that threatens the government with delay. This turnabout reflects several factors: the extent to which time is still at a premium; the lack of a mechanism with which the government can force late-night sessions; the general expectation on the part of MPPs that theirs is a full-time job; and the opposition's heightened sense of power, born of minority-government times, in setting the limits within which the assembly operates. The Ontario rules have no equivalent of the 'speed-up' procedure of the Manitoba legislature, which permits the government to accelerate the consideration of government business at the end of a session.[48]

HOW THE LEGISLATURE SPENDS ITS TIME

Table 3.1 shows how the legislature made use of its time in 1964, 1973, 1984, and 1986–87. The 1964 data are taken from Schindeler;[49] the 1973 data are those reported by the Camp Commission;[50] the data for 1984 and 1986–87 were derived from the tabulation of Hansard reports, which conveniently record the passage of time in ten-minute intervals. Estimates of the time elapsed on a particular item of business may be in error by a minute or two, but the overall impact of such errors is negligible. The categories are straightforward and require no explanation, except for the category 'ceremonial.' Matters ceremonial included congratulations, condolences, introduction of visitors, recognition of various 'national' days, and the like, and usually occurred at the opening of the sitting. By far the largest proportion of 'ceremonial' time was taken up by tributes to deceased members, former members, civil servants, and other noteworthy figures.[51] Inevitably, unanimous consent is given or assumed for a representative of each party to speak on such occasions. The speech from the throne is considered to be ceremonial.

A high degree of similarity is evident in the distribution of time in 1984 and in 1986–87. This congruence is noteworthy in that the 1986–87 session was conducted under a new set of rules, during a minority Liberal government, whereas in 1984 a majority Conservative government held sway. This similarity between the two sessions reduces the possibility that the contrasts with earlier times simply reflect peculiarities of individual years. And contrasts there are. If important changes are apparent between 1973 and the 1980s, the differences from 1964 to the 1980s are nothing short of staggering. More than half of the assembly's time in 1964 was given over to estimates; by 1973 this had declined to about one-sixth, and by 1986–87 barely one-twentieth of sitting time was devoted to estimates. In 1964 only 8 per cent of House time was consumed by the various phases of the legislative process; in 1973 this figure rose to 39 per cent, and in both sessions of the 1980s it was 33 per cent.[52] The two major set-piece debates, the budget debate and the debate on the speech from the throne, occupied 18 per cent of House time

90 The Ontario legislature

TABLE 3.1
Analysis of legislative time 1964, 1973, 1984, 1986–87 (percentages)

	1964	1973	1984	1986–87
Sitting days	69	109	94	103
Total hours	270a	NA	463	514
Members' statements	b	b	b	3.4
Ministry statements	2.0	2.0	3.1	6.3
Question period	1.6a	15.0	19.9	19.8
Petitions	d	d	0.8	0.8
First reading	1.8	d	0.9	0.5
Second readingc	4.8	25.0	15.2	14.8
Committee of the Wholec	1.4	13.0	16.1	13.1
Third readingc	0.2	d	0.6	4.7
Estimates	53.6	15.0	9.0	5.5
Throne debate	10.2	5.0	5.7	4.0
Budget debate	7.6	5.0	4.0	4.1
Emergency debates	d	1.0	2.6	3.2
Committee report	b	b	2.5	1.9
Private members' business	2.1	2.0	6.5	9.0
Non-confidence motions	d	d	1.0	0.0
Interim supply	d	d	1.2	1.8
Government motions	d	d	0.6	0.8
Adjournment debate	d	d	0.1	0.1
Ceremonial	d	d	1.8	1.3
Order/privilege	d	2.0	2.1	1.0
Bells/divisions	d	10.0	4.5	3.1

aEstimate (see text)
bNo such procedure at this time
cExcludes private members' legislation
dNot separately tabulated
NA Not available

in 1964, but only 8 to 10 per cent two decades later. Among numerous other differences between 1964 and the 1980s, the most significant is in question period: in 1984 and 1986–87 fully one-fifth of all legislative time was spent on question period, whereas in 1964 questions did not amount to as much as 2 per cent of total sitting time.[53]

The comparison between 1973 and the sessions of the 1980s is not so striking; still, significant (albeit subtle) differences may be divined. More time is now given to question period and less to estimates. Divisions consume much less time than they did in 1973. Although they do not represent great blocks of time (about 14 per cent in 1986–87), the importance of emergency debates, debates on committee reports, and, most important, private members' business is considerable. The legislature expends substantially more time now than it did in 1973 on matters that emphasize the private members' role in enhancing accountability and in policy development.

One way of categorizing House time is in terms of who determines the agenda. Members' statements, question period, private members' time, emergency debates, and non-confidence debates together constitute between 30 and 35 per cent of House time, and represent occasions when the opposition (or at least the private members) picks the topic for the House to debate. About 47 per cent of House time is devoted to dealing with matters of the government's choosing (ministerial statements, estimates, interim supply, government motions, and the different stages of the legislative process). These figures suggest that if the opposition fails to make its points or is unable to publicize issues of concern to it, it is not for want of opportunity.

The shifts in the distribution of House time since the 1960s are inconclusive on the question of evolution towards a more transformative legislature. Far less time is spent on supply, throne, and budget debates, which are characteristic of a classic arena legislature, and far more time is devoted to the legislative process. Yet if debate has little or no prospect of altering legislation, it can hardly be considered transformative. And, as is evident from the discussion in Chapter 5, bills are not usually amended in significant ways either in the House or in committee. Substantial amounts of time are now taken up by question period, an archetypal arena activity, whereas the time given over to committee reports and to private members' business at least holds the potential for important transformative elements.

Beyond the implications of the changes in the use of House time, the evidence of this chapter supports an interpretation of limited movement from an arena to a transformative legislature. A principal theme of the chapter has been the enormous significance of convention, of established ways of doing things, of unwritten but powerful codes of behaviour reinforcing the status quo. These are strong impediments to the fundamental change that would be entailed in the development of a more transformative legislature. Another critical factor reducing the prospects for greater transformative capacity is the complete absence of serious challenges to the primacy of party discipline. Any parliament marked by rigid party discipline, which both inhibits government back-benchers from exercising their potential influence and sharply restricts the contributions the opposition is willing or able to make, cannot go far towards becoming transformative.

4
The legislature at work II: Routine proceedings

Legislative business is divided into 'routine proceedings' and 'orders of the day.' Routine proceedings begin the legislative day (except on Thursdays, when private members' business is debated in the morning), and always occur in the same order. Except for ministerial statements, the government is largely powerless to affect the duration or the substance of routine proceedings. In contrast, once the orders of the day are reached, the government is, with only minor exceptions, in complete control of the choice and duration of government business. As well, orders of the day are far less subject to special rules than are routine proceedings. For all this, and with the notable exception of question period, the casual observer would be unlikely to detect many differences between routine proceedings and orders of the day (except for the much higher attendance by members during the former).

This chapter describes and analyses the components of routine proceedings in the order in which they are called by the Speaker: members' statements, statements by the ministry and responses to them, question period (with side trips into written questions and adjournment debates), petitions, reports, and motions. The final routine proceeding, the introduction of bills, is discussed in the following chapter. Strictly speaking, emergency debates are not part of routine proceedings, but since they occur or are at least requested prior to the orders of the day, they are considered in this chapter.

MEMBERS' STATEMENTS

After the Speaker's parade has entered, the Speaker reads a brief non-denominational prayer and the Lord's Prayer and the business of the

93 The legislature at work: Routine proceedings

House commences with members' statements (provided that no bogus, or genuine, points of privilege or minor ceremonials intervene). This procedure, which was instituted in April 1986, was inspired by a similar reform in the House of Commons in 1984. Though the symptoms differed slightly from Ottawa to Queen's Park, the basic malady was the same: members were using questionable methods to gain attention and score points before question period. In Ottawa, MPs had taken to abusing the rule that permitted them to move motions for debate on matters of supposedly urgent public importance, which were invariably denied the requisite unanimous consent. Thus, the initial fifteen minutes of 'forty-threes' (after the standing order of that number) devolved into an alternative outlet for members to briefly raise grievances or pet proposals, or to offer congratulatory messages. In the Ontario legislature the same function was performed through members' raising specious points of order or privilege at the beginning of the day. This technique, however, lacked the official sanction of the SO43 procedure and therefore combined a flagrant abuse of the rules with uncertain and ineffective results for MPPs when the Speaker's tolerance for clearly bogus procedural ploys was overstepped. One member remarked, when members' statements were initiated, that the procedure ought to have been called 'frustration ventilation period.'[1]

Under the new rule ten minutes are set aside for members, other than ministers or party leaders, to make statements of up to ninety seconds. No limitations are placed upon the content of these statements (as is the case in Ottawa, where the Speaker may rule out of order congratulatory messages, recitations of poetry, and 'clearly frivolous issues').[2] Early on, Speaker Edighoffer warned members that he would not permit statements consisting of personal attacks on other members.[3] Sometimes members ride their own hobby-horses, or recognize events of significance to their ridings, but most of the remarks are sallies in the constant party warfare. Both opposition parties fold members' statements into their question period strategies, and statements are allocated to members in essentially the same fashion as are questions. (MPPs who do not think particularly fast on their feet sometimes prefer to make their points through statements rather than risk the rough-and-tumble of question period.) Initially, the government was slow to use the opportunity presented by members' statements; the government whip's office is now responsible for organizing Liberal members' statements. Occasionally, parliamentary assistants will make statements answering opposition attacks on their ministries.

94 The Ontario legislature

Without question this reform has been, from the MPPS' viewpoint, hugely successful, as it has been in Ottawa. Members delight in being able to say their piece without replies from other members during prime legislative time, and they have become highly adept at drafting and delivering speeches of 85 seconds' duration. In consequence, the incidence of spurious points of order and privilege at the start of the day has been markedly reduced. In the 1986–87 session, members' statements accounted for only 3.4 per cent of House time, but enjoyed a singular pride of place in the hearts of back-benchers.[4]

Ninety-second statements have not supplanted the convention by which members are permitted to make 'personal' statements of an 'explanatory' nature – for example, in response to serious charges of misconduct. Such personal statements are made with the indulgence of the House and not as a matter of right.[5] This procedure is rarely invoked; more often members will rise on an alleged point of privilege and, with the indulgence of the Speaker and their colleagues, defend or unburden themselves.

STATEMENTS BY THE MINISTRY

The scheduling of ministers' statements just before question period ensures that they receive maximum attention, since both the press gallery and the members' benches are full. In turn, this high degree of exposure means that the House is used for announcements of government policy more frequently than in other jurisdictions, such as Ottawa, where statements are made following question period to a nearly empty Chamber. In 1986–87 some 6.3 per cent of House time was given over to ministers' statements and opposition responses; on only six days were no statements made.

Until the 1986 reforms, no time limits constrained ministerial statements, except on Thursdays, when they were limited to thirty minutes so as not to cut unduly into the time for private members' business. Statements may not run beyond twenty minutes under the new rules, though this does not represent a significant restriction. In 1984 statements exceeded twenty minutes on only ten of ninety-four sitting days, and only once did they run for more than half an hour. The standing orders provide that a minister may make 'a short factual statement relating to Government policy, ministry action or other similar matters of which the House should be informed.' In effect, this allows ministers carte blanche; the only recorded instance of a statement's being ruled out of order was an attempt by a minister without portfolio to speak on a constituency matter totally unrelated to government policy.[6]

The opposition long sought the right of reply to ministry statements, as recommended by the 1969 rules committee and by the Camp Commission.[7] Conservative governments consistently refused to grant the right, but it was readily accepted as part of the April 1986 reform package. It might have been expected that granting the opposition a right of reply would lead ministers to make many statements outside the House, as happens in the House of Commons and in the Quebec National Assembly, both of which permit the opposition to reply to ministerial statements. Such fears have proved groundless, in part because ministry statements have become such an integral part of legislative life and also because they continue to enjoy a favourable position in the legislative timetable. Regardless of the number or length of statements, each opposition party has five minutes to respond; responses are usually made by the party critics. Since the critics have at best a few minutes to formulate their responses, their comments are often lacking in substance. Apparently, the government has not given much away in allocating time for opposition responses to ministers' statements. The provision for opposition responses has markedly expanded the time consumed by ministerial statements; from 1984 to 1986–87 it more than doubled as a proportion of total time (from 3.1 per cent to 6.3 per cent).

Since 1976 the rules have required that the opposition leaders and the party critics be provided with copies of statements before they are made. In addition, a 'policy statement,' which is not defined, is to be accompanied by the tabling of a 'compendium of background information.' The content of these compendia is left to the minister's discretion; rarely are they more than copies of publicly available documents, and they are thus of little use to the opposition. A major brouhaha in the fall of 1981 culminated in the temporary refusal of interim supply, when the opposition attempted to force the government to table more comprehensive information about its purchase of an oil company than the skimpy material that comprised the official compendium.

The statement process is co-ordinated by the premier's legislative assistant, and it has changed little since the Liberals took power. Statements are reviewed by the policy unit in the Premier's Office, usually on the day before they are to be delivered, to ensure that they conform to cabinet's intent and to the understanding of others involved, such as Management Board or the government caucus. Since the premier's legislative assistant, who is a member of the policy unit, is often consulted about the content of the statements as they are being drafted, they are rarely sent back to the ministries for revision. Simple logistics, such as ministers' availability or the need to limit the number of statements on a given day, are the principal determinants of the schedule, though the degree of urgency attaching to a particular statement is also taken into account. The insistent demands of more than two dozen ministries make it difficult to do much by way of orchestrating the timing and juxtaposition of statements to yield a coherent political strategy.

Roughly an hour before the House opens, the opposition is told how many statements will be made, but not usually which ministers will be making statements, let alone their content. At this time the opposition is also told which ministers will be absent that day. Copies of statements are usually given to the opposition a few minutes before routine proceedings begin.

QUESTION PERIOD

In terms of members' attendance, media attention, and overall political import, question period is arguably the most significant proceeding of the Ontario legislature. Until 1970 question period enjoyed no formal status and effectively owed its existence to the sufferance of Premier John Robarts. Questions had to be submitted in advance to the Speaker, who might edit them severely or disallow them entirely. In the early 1960s an average of only slightly more than one oral question was asked per day; barely four minutes a day were taken up by oral questions and their answers in 1964.[8] In short, prior to the 1970s, question period was both unofficial and unimportant.

The chief characteristics of question period identified by the Camp Commission were its unruliness, its excessive wordiness, and its domination by party leaders: in 1973 roughly 45 per cent of the forty-five-minute question period was consumed by questions put by the opposition leaders and the answers to them.[9] In 1976, in an attempt to enhance back-benchers' opportunities to ask questions, party leaders were limited to two questions apiece plus supplementaries in an hour-long question period. This change was, at best, marginally successful in reducing the leaders' dominance.

The standing orders offer an incomplete if not a misleading account of how question period operates. The Speaker is directed by the rules to disallow 'any question which he does not consider urgent or of public importance'; this is an invidious burden and all recent Speakers have sensibly ignored it. On very rare occasions questions have been ruled out of order because they addressed ministers' personal views[10] or focused on the activities of the government party rather than on the government,[11] but in essence members are allowed to ask whatever they want. The standing orders proscribing arguments and opinions as well as extraneous facts are simply not enforced. The Speaker does attempt, with very limited success, to eliminate the worst excesses of over-long, argumentative questions and answers; in comparison with other Canadian jurisdictions, though, particularly the House of Commons and the Alberta and British Columbia legislatures, members of the Ontario legislature enjoy remarkable leeway in the ways in which they are permitted to frame questions and answers. For example, by convention and by rule supplementary questions are to be supplementary to the original answer, not to the original question, but this stricture is almost never enforced. Some half-dozen times a year questions are ruled out of order by the Speaker as not being supplementary;[12] invariably, they lack even the flimsiest connection with the original question or answer. The final misleading aspect of the rules is the provision that, when authorized by the premier, parliamentary assistants may answer questions for their ministers; in fact, no parliamentary assistant has ever answered a question.

Ontario's standing orders are unusually precise in setting out the rules for the allocation of questions. In part this reflects the fact that few Canadian legislatures are required to deal with the presence of more than one substantial opposition party, though the rules in Ottawa, which has had three (and sometimes four) parties for decades, are silent on the dividing of time among parties. Under the Ontario rules, the first two questions are asked by the leader of the opposition; the next two are asked by the leader of the third party. Questioning then proceeds in the normal debating rotation: official opposition, third party, government. Although the rules afford the Speaker discretion to permit a 'reasonable' number of supplementaries, in practice he applies a rigid formula to determine supplementaries by which leaders are permitted two supplementaries and back-benchers one.[13]

The formula was altered substantially with the spring 1986 rule changes. Before that, three supplementaries had been permitted to leaders' questions and two to back-benchers' questions; the additional supplementary went to the other opposition party. Thus, the opposition

98 The Ontario legislature

parties had to be well prepared and attentive to one another's questions so as to be able to ask good supplementaries on the spur of the moment. Reducing the number of supplementaries has indeed increased the average daily number of original back-bench questions from 5.7 in 1985 to 11.2 in 1986–87, but at a considerable loss in spontaneity and in the liveliness of the exchanges between the opposition parties.

Still, the Ontario question period is characterized by an unusual degree of interplay between the opposition parties. More than in any other Canadian House, the dynamics of question period are shaped by competition between them. Through the 1970s the Liberals and the New Democrats had caucuses of similar size. From 1981 to 1987 the NDP contingent was only two-thirds or one-half the size of the other opposition party, but the rotation required by the rules treated them as virtual equals (in 1986–87, despite their having more than twice as many MPPs, the Tories out-questioned the New Democrats by a ratio of only 1.03 to 1). Each opposition party must prepare a strategy that anticipates what questions the other will ask, how it will ask them, and on what information they will be based; questioners must weigh the benefits of trying to get further or better information on a prospective issue against the possibility of their being scooped on it by the other party. They must also consider the likely media reaction to their questions in comparison with the issues likely to be raised by the other party: for example, if one party has been attracting the lion's share of press attention with a particular issue, should the other party risk challenging it with its own issue, or should it attempt to compete on the same issue? Finally, the alteration in questioning makes it difficult for one party to mount an extended, focused attack against a specific minister or policy. This is very much to the government's advantage, since the two opposition parties expend tremendous time, energy, and invective in attacking one another.

To a degree probably unique in Canada, question period in the Ontario legislature is dominated by the party leaders. Elsewhere in Canada opposition leaders tend to make sparing use of question period, presumably on the theory that they can attract press attention at will and thus can afford to let other party members share the question period spotlight. The formal allocation of a set number of questions to opposition leaders in 1976 was an attempt to limit their domination, as the Camp Commission had recommended, as was the reduction of supplementaries in 1986. An analysis of question period in 1979 found that just over half of all time was taken by leaders' questions and answers.[14] In 1984 some 40.9 per cent of all original questions were asked by leaders. The 1986 changes reduced to 27 per cent the leaders' share of original questions in 1986–87. This reduction was less significant than it might appear, since leaders were accorded more supplementaries and since their questions and the responses they engendered tended to be very much longer than back-benchers' questions. The leaders' pride of place at the beginning of question period and their ability to appropriate the best questions and issues for themselves also contribute to their domination. The most common rationale for emphasizing the leader in question period is that the media will not pay attention unless a question is asked by the leader; of course, basing question period tactics on this perception creates a self-fulfilling prophecy.

In recent sessions leaders have increasingly permitted other members to ask their questions, original as well as supplementary, but this has not fundamentally altered the fact of the leaders' domination. Back-benchers frequently complain about their limited opportunities to ask questions, though those complaints have lessened somewhat now that the alternative of making a ninety-second statement is open to them. Such complaints are periodically made to the Speaker in public, but it is clear that so long as the party caucuses are prepared to accept their leaders' predominance in question period, it will continue. Moreover, incorporating the priority accorded leaders under the standing orders, though designed to reduce their pre-eminence, has in certain ways institutionalized it.

Question period is leader-dominated in another way. As Table 4.1 illustrates, one question in every five in 1986–87 was directed to the first minister, a much higher proportion than is generally found in Westminster-type legislatures.[15] Moreover, it tends to be the opposition leaders rather than back-benchers who question the premier. Both opposition leaders directed one-third of their questions to the premier, whereas only 20 per cent of Conservative and 13 per cent of NDP back-bench questions were addressed to the premier. This concentration on the premier, which also characterized the Davis years, stems in large part from the opposition's belief that involving the premier brings extensive media coverage, whereas more successful attacks on ministers tend to go unreported. Again, this perception is at least partly self-fulfilling, for the media assume that 'if they (the opposition) have anything good they'll go after the premier with it.' At any rate, question period strategies are clearly premised on a recognition of the relatively low salience of provincial politics in Ontario and the difficulty of generating media interest.

The opposition parties prepare for question period rather differently.

TABLE 4.1
Leaders' and back-benchers' questions 1986–87 (percentages)

	Conservative		NDP			
	Leader	Back-bencher	Leader	Back-bencher	Liberal	Total
To premier	34	20	33	13	1	20
To minister	66	80	67	87	99	80
N	213	531	211	510	113	1579

Both devote disproportionately large amounts of their caucus researchers' time to it, but organize their attacks in ways reflective of the nature of their parties. In 1986–87 the Conservative leader's questions were thoroughly researched and developed by party researchers and by the leader's staff; the content and the approach of the leader's questions were determined by the leader in consultation with his personal advisers. Questions by back-benchers were handled in a less systematic manner. A daily meeting was convened at 8:30 AM to discuss possible questions; theoretically, all MPPs were invited to attend, but in the main only members' staff turned up to propose ideas for question period. This meeting tended to be a pro forma exercise with little real influence on question period. A more formal question period committee, comprising the House leader and three or four of the more active and astute MPPs, with a representative from the leader's office (who usually took only an advisory role), met at 9:00 AM. The leader would attend meetings of this committee on an irregular basis, sometimes to dictate the questions for the day, sometimes to listen to the committee's advice on strategy. At any rate, the committee usually settled only the first few questions, and tended to take a laissez-faire attitude to indications from MPPs that they wished to ask questions. Conservative questions thus often lacked an overall tactical thrust, and co-ordination between leader's and back-benchers' questions tended to be uneven. Now, in the much smaller Tory caucus, the process of organizing question period – leaders' and back-benchers' questions – has become substantially more collegial and informal.

When the Liberals were in opposition their preparation for question period was even more haphazard. The leader's questions were carefully prepared and researched, but back-bench questions were often decided by a small committee that met shortly before question period to review members' suggestions. The committee would not always know what questions the leader planned to ask, and often MPPS knew that they would be asking a question only when they received the question period list at their desks in the House.

If these accounts of Conservative and Liberal preparations for question period can be seen as characteristic of the individualistic nature of Tory and Grit MPPS and of their leaders' independence from caucus direction, the NDP approach can be seen as typifying the party's more disciplined, programmatic, and communal nature. Senior caucus staff hold a preliminary meeting at 8:30 AM and at 9:00 AM, the leader meets with them to discuss possible questions. At 9:15 they are joined by the caucus research staff in preparation for a 9:30 meeting at which all NDP members and researchers are invited to assist in formulating the day's questions; usually, about half the caucus is present. The entire question period strategy – leader's as well as back-benchers' questions – is discussed, and suggestions are invited. At this meeting the leader's questions are first decided, usually by consensus, though the leader retains the authority to make the final decision. Other members' ideas and requests are then discussed and arranged by order of priority. An attempt is made to orchestrate all questions into a coherent plan of attack on the basis of short- and long-term tactical objectives. For example, in the fall of 1986 the caucus accepted a recommendation from its Planning and Priorities Committee that it stress seven priority issues in the run-up to the election expected for 1987; this framework was a key determinant of day-to-day question period tactics.

Table 4.2 is a compilation of all of the original questions asked in 1986–87 arranged by subject and party. The subjects are defined in terms of ministry structure, and the questions are, with two exceptions, categorized according to the minister at whom they were directed; so that, for example, a question on transportation in the north is considered a transportation question if it was asked of the minister of transportation and communications, but a northern affairs question if it was put to the minister of northern affairs and mines. There are two exceptions: first, the relatively small number of questions directed to a minister in the absence of the intended target ('since the attorney-general is not here today, perhaps the solicitor-general could explain ...'), along with all questions asked of the premier, were included with those asked of the absent minister. Second, questions that were essentially aimed at the government's management practices rather

TABLE 4.2
Original questions by subject and party 1986–87 (percentages)

Subject	Conservative	NDP	Liberal	Total
Health	14.0	11.7	1.7	12.1
extra-billing	7.5	5.7	0.0	6.1
Environment	5.1	9.7	17.6	8.1
Labour/WCB	2.8	13.4	1.7	7.6
Consumer and commercial	3.2	11.7	6.2	7.3
Industry and trade	10.6	3.2	0.8	6.5
Government management	11.0	2.4	0.0	6.3
Housing	5.4	7.2	0.8	5.9
Economy	5.6	5.7	4.4	5.6
Community and social services	3.9	6.5	4.4	5.1
Attorney-general	5.8	1.9	10.6	4.4
Agriculture	5.6	1.5	10.6	4.1
Education	3.0	3.1	1.7	2.9
Women's issues	2.0	3.3	0.0	2.5
Northern affairs and mines	1.3	3.7	0.8	2.4
Municipal affairs	3.1	1.6	1.7	2.3
Solicitor-general	3.1	1.0	4.4	2.2
Transportation	3.4	1.0	1.7	2.2
Colleges and universities	2.0	1.8	2.7	2.2
Energy/Ontario Hydro	1.5	2.9	0.8	2.1
Natural resources	1.7	2.1	1.7	1.9
Citizenship and culture	1.2	0.3	11.5	1.5
Tourism and recreation	1.5	0.4	2.7	1.1
Senior citizens	1.1	0.1	5.3	0.9
Intergovernmental affairs	0.1	1.8	0.0	0.9
Revenue	0.7	0.4	3.5	0.8
Correctional services	0.4	0.9	0.8	0.7
N	744	721	113	1579

than at the policy area involved were coded as 'government management.' A few of these questions, directed at the chairman of Management Board, centred on routine personnel and administrative practices, but the majority of them were clearly scandal-mongering, and related to allegations of impropriety, conflict of interest, patronage, and political favouritism. One-half the health care questions in 1986–87 were directed to the rancorous issue of extra-billing, which culminated in a twenty-six day doctors' strike in the summer of 1986; these questions are shown on a separate line in the table. The Ministry of Consumer and Commercial Relations is the repository of much of the government's

103 The legislature at work: Routine proceedings

regulatory powers over the private sector; most of the questions asked in this category related either to pension reform or to insurance (particularly auto insurance).

That questioning is concentrated in a relatively few policy areas is clear from the table. In 1986–87 six of twenty-six categories accounted for nearly one-half of all questions: health, environment, labour and workers' compensation, consumer and commercial relations, industry and trade, and government management. Similar findings emerged from analyses of questions asked in the fall of 1980 and in the 1984 session. In 1984 the five most common topics, which accounted for virtually half the questions, were, in order, labour and workers' compensation, health, environment, the economy, and education.[16] In 1980 the results were roughly similar; the environment was the most popular single subject (17.8 per cent).[17]

Of the top six subjects, only health was not characterized by a marked imbalance in the relative proportion of questions asked by the opposition parties. The NDP asked twice as many questions as the Tories on the environment, three and a half times as many questions on consumer and commercial relations (there were almost entirely on pensions and auto insurance), and nearly five times as many questions on labour and matters relating to the Workers' Compensation Board (WCB). Conversely, the Tories paid far more attention to agriculture in their questioning than did the New Democrats, asked more than four times as many questions on government management, and three times as many questions on industry and trade. The NDP emphasis on labour matters and the Conservatives' greater concern with agriculture reflect fundamental differences in the parties' constituencies; but the other differences are also significant, for they reflect the programmatic nature of the NDP in contrast to the Conservatives' concentration on portraying the government as incompetent and guilty of impropriety (most of the Conservative industry and trade questions were essentially aimed at demonstrating government mishandling of various sectors of the economy). A similar pattern distinguished the Liberal opposition from the NDP in 1984: the Liberals devoted substantially more attention to agriculture and government mismanagement than did the NDP, which concentrated far more than did the Liberals on labour and workers' compensation issues, on health, and on women's issues.[18]

The focus of the leaders' questions was not always the same as that of the back-benchers'. In both opposition parties the leaders asked most of the questions on extra-billing (73 per cent for the Conservatives, 78 per cent for the New Democrats). Larry Grossman, the Conservative leader, asked substantially more labour/WCB questions (2.7)[19] and questions on the economy (2.5) than did his back-benchers, who in turn were far more likely than their leader to put questions on agriculture (0.25) and municipal affairs (0.1). The NDP leader, Bob Rae, asked proportionately more questions than his back-benchers on government management (3.4), the economy (1.9), and community and social services (the principal welfare ministry) (1.7), and proportionately fewer questions on the environment (0.5), labour/WCB (0.6), housing (0.4) and education (no leader's questions).[20] The specifics of the differences in emphasis between the leaders' and the back-benchers' questions are not nearly so important as the explanation of those differences: leaders concentrated more heavily on high-profile issues and basic policy questions, and left their back-benchers to ask questions of detail and on matters of local or limited interest.

Although the premier received questions on almost all topics, they were much more concentrated in specific areas than were questions asked of his ministers. One-quarter of all questions to the premier were on government management, nearly 19 per cent were on health (15 per cent were on extra-billing alone), and 15 per cent were on the economy; nearly three-fifths of the questions put to the premier fell into these three categories. On only a few subjects was the premier asked more than 20 per cent of the questions (the overall proportion of questions he answered): 77 per cent of all questions on government management went to the premier, as did 53 per cent of the questions relating to the economy, 31 per cent of the health questions (and 49 per cent of extra-billing questions), and 21 per cent of the energy questions. Since the premier served as minister of intergovernmental affairs and for several months as minister of northern development and mines, it is not surprising that 93 per cent of the intergovernmental questions and 55 per cent of the northern affairs questions went to him.

The extent of members' participation in question period differed greatly between the two opposition parties, as can be seen from Table 4.3, which sets out the distribution of back-benchers according to the frequency of their questions. (Since the NDP had only twenty-five members to the Tories' fifty, an 'average' NDP member asked 4.2 per cent of his party's questions, whereas an 'average' Conservative member asked only 2.0 per cent.) The table demonstrates that questioning was much more evenly spread among New Democrats than among Conservatives. Seventy per cent of NDP members asked between 2 and 6 per

TABLE 4.3
Distribution of back-benchers questions by party
(percentages)

Percentage	Conservative	NDP	Liberal
More than 10	4.0	0	8.0
6.0–9.9	4.0	16.6	12.0
4.0–5.9	12.0	41.6	12.0
2.0–3.9	12.0	29.1	16.0
1.0–1.9	14.0	0	32.0
0–0.9	38.0	8.3	32.0
0	16.0	4.2	16.0
N	50	24	25

cent of their party's questions, none asked more than 8.5 per cent, and only 13 per cent (three members) asked less than 1 per cent each (two of the three members defected to the Liberals late in the session). In contrast, two Tory members each asked in excess of 10 per cent of their party's questions, but 54 per cent asked less than 1 per cent of back-bench Conservative questions; this means that in a session of 102 sitting days, twenty-seven of fifty Tory back-benchers asked either one question or no questions at all. The high proportion of Tories inactive during question period reflects in part the inability of some former veteran ministers to develop an 'opposition mentality' after losing power in 1985, but some of the variation between the NDP and the Conservatives can also be attributed to the more egalitarian, co-operative ethos of the NDP compared with the more hierarchical Conservative party.

Some 7.1 per cent of questions came from the government back benches, a slightly higher proportion than Conservative back-benchers asked in 1984 (4.5 per cent). As Table 4.3 shows, a few Liberals asked a substantial number of questions (one asked 30 per cent of all Liberal questions, and accounted for more questions than all but five Tories and four New Democrats), while a large proportion asked few or none. Questions from government members typically fall into three classes. First, some questions are designed to indicate publicly the member's concern with a (usually local) problem. Second, government back-benchers engage in questions referred to derisively by the opposition as 'set-ups' or 'lobs' ('Can the minister indicate what steps he is taking to solve the problem of ...'; answer: 'I'm so glad the member asked that question, for I am pleased to announce ...'). Finally, on rare occasions government MPPS ask tough, embarrassing questions. In 1984 a disgruntled Conservative who had recently been dropped from the cabinet, asked a series of hard questions on government purchasing practices, which, he alleged, were discriminating against a firm in his riding. On balance, however, in contrast to Westminster, the ministry has little to fear from questions put by its own members; indeed, the planting of questions by friendly back-benchers is a standard ministerial ploy. Only 1 of 113 Liberal questions in 1986–87 was directed to the premier.

In evaluating question period it is critical to recognize that whatever it may be, it certainly is not an exercise in seeking and providing information on public policy (though this will occur on occasion). First and foremost it is a political battlefield on which the parties mount attacks on their opponents while trying to protect their own political flanks. The structure of the situation fosters an expectation that the opposition will attack and the government will defend, but an adroit government can take the offensive itself by criticizing the woolly-minded, impractical, or ideologically blinkered policies of the opposition parties, their misunderstanding or distortion of the facts, their irresponsibility, their political venality, their internal divisions, and the peccadilloes of their federal brethren.

The primary objective of the opposition is to embarrass or undercut the government by drawing attention to the inadequacies of its policies or to the mismanagement of public resources. Though question period is mainly an exercise in criticism, an adroit opposition will also use it to present itself as an alternative government. The opposition may try to pressure the government into taking action on specific problems, or it may use its questions as a way of putting forward its own nostrums. Finally, questions can be used to put the government on record in ways which may prove politically harmful in the future. The underlying intention is always to score political points. Despite noble rhetoric, most opposition MPPS are not really interested in the classic question period function of calling the government publicly to account for its exercise of power. However intended, though, opposition probing and criticism of the government, together with press follow-up, does constitute an important accountability mechanism.

In Ontario the opposition parties have consciously adopted a strategy of raising many different issues rather than concentrating on a few; '[they] seem to believe that they can increase their press coverage by increasing the number of topics available for coverage.'[21] When it becomes apparent that one issue has seized the press's attention, the opposition will devote a substantial proportion of its questioning to exploiting that issue. One notable illustration was the extensive opposition concentration in late 1982 and early 1983 on the Conservative government's handling of the so-called trust company affair.

More than in other spheres of legislative activity, opposition efforts in question period are aimed at attracting media attention. In one sense they are successful, for press coverage is disproportionately focused on question period: it has been estimated that as many as four out of five stories filed by the Queen's Park press gallery originate in question period.[22] As one media analyst has explained, 'The question period provides the essential elements of news as understood in Canadian journalism: immediacy, brevity, conflict between identifiable individuals, and, of course, potential significance.'[23] Still, questions fail to generate press coverage far more often than they succeed. In the fall of 1980 the two major Toronto newspapers, the *Globe and Mail* and the *Toronto Star*, both of which play a key role in setting province-wide media agendas, ran stories arising out of only 11.1 and 9.1 per cent of questions asked. Most of these stories were fairly minor, and were not featured in prominent positions in the paper.[24] Just under 60 per cent of the questions reported were asked by the party leaders. Non-Toronto media undoubtedly would have covered other questions of local interest, but the overall message is clear: most questions fail to generate media coverage.

Question period in the Ontario legislature 'provides little ... in the way of reasoned argument, long term perspective or concern with underlying social and economic conditions or conflicts. The philosophical differences among the three parties emerge only rarely in question period.'[25] It is difficult to deny that question period generates more heat than light, yet it can be of great political consequence. Performance in question period can make or unmake ministers' and party leaders' reputations. 'Abject failure in parliament,' as one observer-turned-participant has noted, 'has a way of being transmitted to the public at large.'[26] In addition, question period can on occasion be an effective means of bringing relentless public attention to important issues.

ADJOURNMENT DEBATES

Members dissatisfied with the answers they receive to oral (but not written) questions may so notify the Speaker and thereby trigger an 'adjournment debate' within the next few days. When the House adjourns at 6:00 PM the aggrieved member is permitted up to five minutes to vent his spleen; his speech is followed by a rebuttal of equal length from the minister or his parliamentary assistant. As many as three such 'late shows' may take place at one sitting. Since the House is deemed to have been adjourned, no motions or other procedural manoeuvres are possible.

The 'late show' continues to be popular in Ottawa, but has largely fallen into disuse at Queen's Park. In 1984 (when they were held at 10:30 PM), only nine adjournment debates took place; in 1986–87 there were three. Given that the press gallery is invariably empty and that virtually no non-participating MPPS are present, it is not hard to see why the number of late shows has declined. Ministers usually make an effort to attend, but it is not unknown for an opposition MPP to harangue empty government benches for five minutes.[27]

The scheduling of adjournment debates is a prescription for irrelevance. As a means of pursuing an 'unsatisfactory' answer it is all but useless. A more effective approach might be modelled on the 'interpellation' procedure of the Quebec National Assembly, in which minister and critic debate an issue at length under the full glare of television coverage on a day when the House is not sitting.[28]

WRITTEN QUESTIONS

The use of written questions ranks far below the oral question period in the opposition's arsenal. Owing to the limitations on back-bench participation in question period, a few MPPS use written questions as an alternative to the oral questions they are unable to ask, but most written questions are aimed at eliciting information for later use, most often in question period or in estimates.[29]

Members may ask any number of questions. Many of their questions are prepared by caucus staff, and may not even be seen by the members in whose name they are submitted. Questions are sent to the Clerk's Office, which, unlike its Ottawa and Westminster counterparts, edits them only for form and grammar, not for content, and publishes them in the Order Paper. The cabinet office co-ordinates the mechanics of forwarding questions and answers to the appropriate ministry or MPP. The content of each answer is determined by the individual ministry, and is not subject to any central approval process.

The standing orders provide that all questions are to be answered

109 The legislature at work: Routine proceedings

within two weeks, although, since the phrase 'more time is required' constitutes an answer, in practice few questions are answered so expeditiously. This is in sharp contrast to the quick response characteristic of the United Kingdom, where most questions are answered within three working days.[30] Ontario has no 'starred' written questions designated for oral response, as do the Canadian and British Houses of Commons. Answers to written questions are tabled by the government House leader and are normally printed as an appendix to Hansard; long or bulky answers are not printed, but are treated as sessional papers and are publicly available in the Clerk's Office, the Legislative Library, and the Archives of Ontario.

The use of written questions has varied substantially in Ontario. In some years prior to the Second World War, more than one hundred questions were tabled, but by the early 1960s fewer than two dozen written questions were being asked annually.[31] By the late 1970s and 1980s, MPPs were asking several hundred questions a year, still not a large number when compared with the thousands of written questions posed yearly in Ottawa and Westminster.

An analysis of written questions submitted in 1983–84 concluded that the Liberals tended to ask 'scandal-mongering' questions on such topics as patronage appointments, government advertising, and public-opinion polling, whereas the NDP tended to ask more technical, less controversial questions (for example, on the numbers of injured workers treated at WCB rehabilitation facilities).[32] Not surprisingly, questions of the latter type are more likely to receive fuller, quicker answers; indeed, many of the most politically pointed questions are never answered. Of course, this may be turned to advantage; as the Liberal deputy House leader put it, 'Part of the game is to rise in the House to complain; you don't always want to get what you ask for because you can score more political points with a government's refusal to answer.'[33] A perusal of the questions submitted by the opposition parties during the 1986–87 session suggests that a substantial proportion of the Conservative inquiries were of the scandal-mongering genre; the NDP members continued to seek policy-related information in their questions.

The exponential growth in the number of written questions led the Conservative government to announce that while it 'endeavoured to fulfil its obligations' in responding to written questions, it could no longer afford the time and resources necessary to answer the increasingly complex questions posed by the opposition. Instead, opposition MPPs were directed to consult public documents, to utilize the facilities of the Legislative Library and their caucus research groups, and to put their questions during estimates debates.[34] Perhaps more significant than the merits of the government's position on responding to questions is the telling point it makes about the rights of parliament in Ontario. In the wake of the government's statement the opposition sputtered ritualistically and the press made brief, mildly critical comment; but in comparison with the uproar that might be expected in the United Kingdom should the government announce that it would no longer answer troublesome questions from members, this reaction was slight indeed.

The Liberals came to power on a pledge of open government, and at least in their initial term have been more forthcoming in their answers to written questions than their predecessors. In tabling a two-hundred-page answer to a Tory question on the purchase of computer equipment, Robert Nixon, the government House leader, noted that preparing a response to the question had cost more than $100,000.[35] By mid-1988, however, the Liberal administration was becoming less accommodating. In refusing to answer 123 Conservative questions about details of government spending, the chairman of Management Board suggested that the questions could be asked either in Public Accounts Committee meetings or during estimates review. Providing responses to these written questions would not only be costly and time-consuming, but would, according to the minister, 'be undermining the established procedures for the conduct of business in this House.'[36] Still and all, substantial amounts of information are provided in response to written questions; MPPs tend to believe that written questions are more effective in eliciting information than letters or phone calls to ministers' offices.[37] It would be premature to speculate upon how written questions will rank in members' eyes compared with use of freedom of information procedures, although it is clear that MPPs and their staff have been quick to take advantage of the Freedom of Information and Protection of Privacy Act.

PETITIONS

Although the right of the people to petition for the redress of grievances is one of the most ancient of parliamentary principles, the petitioning procedure had all but atrophied in the Ontario legislature by the mid-1970s.[38] By the mid-1980s, however, petitions were back in vogue. Two hundred and eighty-one petitions were tabled in 1986–87 on

111 The legislature at work: Routine proceedings

sixty-eight separate topics, topics as diverse as Sunday racing, abortion, the rights of naturopaths, the sale of beer and wine in grocery stores, energy prices, and the need for a traffic light in Fowlers Corners. Since petition campaigns are occasionally organized by interest groups and by the opposition parties, large numbers of identical petitions may be brought forward on the same issue. In 1986–87 more than 60 per cent of all petitions were concerned with one of five topics; forty-seven other topics were the subject of single petitions. The number of signatories to a petition can range from a handful to many thousands; three petitions received in 1986–87 carried over 10,000 signatures. Just under 1 per cent of the House's time was given over to petitions.

Members are no longer required to have petitions vetted by the clerk of the House before presentation, as was the case until 1975. Now they simply rise in their places, read the petition, usually add a word on the number of signatories, and (presuming they are in agreement) note their support for the cause. Since most petitions are critical of the government, a practice was developed under the Conservatives whereby petitions received by government members were presented, usually in groups, by one of the deputy government whips. Liberal back-benchers have usually presented their own petitions; petitions forwarded to ministers are brought to the House by a whip.

Petitions may not pray for 'any expenditure, grant or charge on the public revenue.' This stricture is of limited practical significance, not so much because the rule is interpreted generously but because the member presents the petition before the Speaker rules on its admissibility, and thus gains whatever political credit is to be had even if the petition is subsequently ruled out of order.[39]

The government is required by the standing orders to 'provide a response to a petition within two weeks of its presentation.' Invariably, these responses, which are reproduced in Hansard, are tabled without oral comment; they are usually brief, and either they are non-committal or they present a low-key restatement of government policy. Whatever practical political significance attaches to petitions derives from the process of mobilizing the public on an issue or from the publicity value to the opposition parties, not from the government's response.

Members will happily table petitions on behalf of constituents or interest groups, but most believe the effort required to organize a petition campaign is not worth the small political payoff. In consequence, they tend to be passive with respect to the petitioning process. One notable exception occurred in November 1979, when NDP

112 The Ontario legislature

members, with considerable fanfare, tabled petitions on the quality and cost of health care signed by more than 300,000 people. More recently, in the spring of 1988, the opposition brought business in the House to a standstill for more than a week by reading hundreds of petitions condemning the government's proposed Sunday shopping legislation. In this instance the petition process was in equal measure a device for bringing forward popular greivances in a highly visible manner and the functional equivalent of a filibuster.[40]

Standing order 31(h) provides that petitions complaining of 'some urgent personal grievance requiring immediate remedy' may be taken into account at once. The essentially ritualistic nature of the petition process is underlined by the failure of the opposition even to attempt to force a debate on any of its petitions. The Camp Commission, among others, suggested that a committee be charged with the responsibility of considering petitions referred to it by the House,[41] but members have shown little enthusiasm for this notion.[42] No Canadian legislature seems to possess a functioning mechanism for considering petitioners' complaints, but other Westminster-style parliaments (notably those of India and New Zealand) do regularly inquire into and act upon petitions, usually through committees.[43]

REPORTS

During the routine proceeding of 'reports,' only legislative committee reports are dealt with. Most government reports are tabled simply by forwarding copies to the Clerk's Office; should the minister wish to comment on the report or to draw attention to it, he will do so by way of a ministerial statement. Committee reports on bills are disposed of immediately; such reports are debatable and subject to amendment, but only very rarely do debates arise or amendments come forward. In contrast to Westminster, Ottawa, and other parliaments, the report stage in the Ontario legislative process is almost invariably pro forma. The procedure involving substantive committee reports – those other than on bills or estimates – is discussed in Chapter 6; for present purposes, the salient fact is that during the report phase of routine proceedings, the most that will normally transpire is that the chairman will move adoption of the report, make a brief statement, and adjourn the debate. Little time is consumed by reports.

MOTIONS

The only motions permitted under this rubric are routine in nature and pertain to House business – meeting times, committee membership, and authorization of committee travel, for example – and may be moved only by the government House leader. More substantial motions, such as motions for striking committees, referring business to committees, or setting out time allocation on bills, require notice and are considered during the orders of the day. Although the 'housekeeping' motions dealt with at this time do not require notice, they are always cleared through the opposition house leaders; though they are debatable, they are invariably passed on the nod. The time taken on these motions is negligible.

EMERGENCY DEBATES

The Camp Commission reported that the infrequency of emergency debates demonstrated 'the disinclination of Members of the Ontario legislature to use tools available to them.'[44] As is apparent from Table 4.4, this criticism is no longer valid; in most recent years, as many motions have been made as in the entire twenty-five years after the Second World War. In 1986–87 seven emergency debates were held; these consumed 3.2 per cent of the House's time.

Schindeler explains that in the 1960s prospective motions to hold emergency debates (then called 'adjournment debates,' since, technically speaking, they were motions to adjourn the House 'for the purpose of discussing a definite matter of urgent public importance') had to be submitted in advance to the Speaker, who ruled on them in private and rarely even permitted the member to move the motion in the House.[45] Until the rule was changed in 1970, a highly restrictive interpretation of the standing orders was used to prevent emergency debates.[46]

The current procedure requires that notice of the intention to move for an emergency debate be given to the Speaker two hours before the afternoon sitting of the House (that is, by 11:30 AM). Copies of the intended motion are then forwarded to the House leaders. Just before orders of the day are called, the member moves his motion and speaks in support of it for up to five minutes. Representatives of the other parties each have a similar amount of time to put forward their parties' positions. A vote is then held on whether the debate should take place.

This procedure represents a tremendous improvement over its predecessor. Until the 1986 rule changes, the Speaker, having heard the arguments for the debate, ruled whether the matter was indeed one of 'urgent public importance'; the standing orders required the Speaker to determine that the matter was 'a genuine emergency, calling for

TABLE 4.4
Emergency debates 1945–1988

Period	Motions for	Debates held
1945–59	2	0
1960–69	11	0
1970–79	17	9
1981	9	3
1982	13	3
1983	16	4
1984	14	5
1985–86	5	5
1986–87	7	7
1987	3	3
1987–88*	8	4

SOURCE: 1945–82, Office of the Clerk of the House, *Precedents of the Legislative Assembly of Ontario*; 1983–1987/88, *Journals*
*To end of June 1988

immediate and urgent consideration.'[47] If the Speaker ruled against the motion as being out of order, his ruling was invariably challenged. The process was at once unnecessary (for the parties decided on political grounds whether the debate would go forward) and harmful to his office (since it put him in the difficult position of evaluating the opposition's claim that an issue of political significance to them was indeed of 'urgent public importance'). Moreover, the procedure virtually invited the opposition to challenge the Speaker's ruling for political rather than procedural reasons, thus forcing the government to support his ruling on the same basis; this was hardly conducive to the opposition's perception of the Speaker's independence from the government. Now, the Speaker is called upon only to rule on whether motions comply with a small number of relatively clear-cut requirements; in the first two years of the new procedure, no motion was ruled out of order.

If the debate does go ahead, each speaker is limited to ten minutes; the debate concludes, without a vote, at 6:00 PM. Some emergency debates are lifeless charades, conducted before an empty press gallery, with the political impact of a soggy order paper; others generate substantial media attention or serve to maintain a high level of intensity on a continuing political controversy, and thus are of some significance. Clearly, the opposition parties consider emergency debates effective because they resort to them frequently. Emergency debates are almost exclusively the province of the opposition; only one has ever originated on the government back-benches.

In addition to the startling increase in the frequency of motions for emergency debates, Table 4.4 reveals a remarkable recent development: during the Liberal minority, every motion for an emergency debate resulted in a debate. No doubt this reflects the minority complexion of the House and the conduciveness to debate of the new procedure; but it also demonstrates the extent to which emergency debates have become accepted as routine. As a matter of course, when the government is planning its legislative timetable, it will make provision for losing several days to emergency debates. During the Conservative majority of 1981–85 the government was far more tolerant of demands for emergency debates early in the session, when time was not at such a premium as it is later in the year; in 1984 four of the five debates that took place occurred prior to the summer recess. The early days of the Liberal majority were characterized by a fairly open attitude towards emergency debates: of eight motions for debates made between November 1987 and June 1988, four were allowed to go forward. The government's decision to accede to a request for an emergency debate is not always based on altruism and sympathy for the opposition's need to express its views. For four days running in May 1988 the NDP pushed for emergency debates on problems in the health care system; the first three motions were rejected by the government, but the NDP called for recorded votes and wasted a good deal of time responding to the bells. Finally, the government relented and the debate went forward.

Among the topics that were the subject of emergency debates during the 1986–87 session were a strike by the company that provides transportation to the disabled in Toronto, the closing of a large manufacturing concern in Hamilton, a major lay-off at the Algoma Steel plant in Sault Ste Marie, the imposition by the United States of a countervailing duty on Canadian lumber, difficulties in the liability insurance industry, and violations of the law against Sunday shopping.[48]

The account of the various components of routine proceedings in this chapter brings to mind Lewis A. Froman's observation about the U.S. Congress: 'Few rules and procedures are neutral, politically, in their effects.'[49] With respect to routine proceedings, as with the procedures relating to the legislative process and to financial matters, almost any question one cares to ask about the way in which the Ontario legislature operates can be answered in two very different ways. First, there is the technically correct, procedurally proper answer. The second answer may be quite different but more informative about the reality of the legislature; this is the answer that looks to the politics of the situation – the political gains and losses, the threats and opportunities to or for the parties or the individual members. This is not to suggest that the formal rules can be ignored; rather, they need to be interpreted within the political context of the legislature. Procedural wrangles are almost never pursued for their own sake; the question of partisan advantage is usually the root cause. Despite the formal trappings and the apparent intent of the rules, the legislature is not so much a debating society as a political battlefield.

Although the material in this chapter does not specifically address the extent to which the Ontario legislature has become more transformative, it does offer support for the view of the legislature as still primarily an arena. For most practical purposes, routine proceedings comprise members' statements, ministerial statements, and question period. All three of these proceedings are strongly 'arena-like' in nature, and feature the clash of party positions, the debating of the political issues of the day, and the ventilation of diverse viewpoints; but they offer very little in the way of policy formulation or decision-making. The other principal aspect of routine proceedings is that, in attendance, press coverage, public attention, and intensity of cabinet and opposition effort they constitute the main focus of the House day. Thus, some of the central activities of the Ontario legislature are characterized by overwhelming dominance of arena over transformative elements. The conclusion regarding emergency debates is similar: when an emergency – genuine or contrived – occurs, the legislature permits members and parties to air their views, but does not allow so much as a non-binding vote by way of concrete action.

5

The legislature at work III: Legislation and finances

In common with other legislatures, the Ontario Legislative Assembly does much more than deal with bills. Yet the public perception, which tends to be shared by newly elected MPPs, is that its primary activity lies in the legislative realm. This chapter describes and analyses the processes by which bills are considered and passed in Ontario – government bills, private bills, and private members' (public) bills. In understanding these processes, it must be recognized that, as with other Westminster-style parliaments, the Ontario legislature is not so much a law-making body as a law-passing one. In Nelson Polsby's terminology, it lacks transformative capacity – that is, the ability to transform policy proposals into law independent of other institutions, such as the cabinet.[1] This does not mean that the legislature is simply a rubber stamp for the actions of the cabinet; as will be seen, the legislative process can assume a life of its own.

This chapter also contains an analysis of financial procedures – the budget and the estimates.

GOVERNMENT LEGISLATION

Given the range of modern-day government involvement in all spheres of activity, it is scarcely surprising that a very substantial part of the Ontario legislature's time is given over to the consideration and passage of government legislation: some 33.1 per cent – 171 hours – in 1986–87, compared with only 8.2 per cent in 1964. Government bills are those introduced by a cabinet minister; they represent official government policy with the full force of the cabinet behind them.

Even a cursory examination of the figures on government bills over the past fifteen years reveals two clear trends: fewer government bills are being introduced, and the proportion of those that are passed is declining. Table 5.1 presents data on government bills introduced and passed since 1970, summarized for four periods (1970–74, 1976–80, 1981–84, and 1985–87). The first and third of these periods were majority governments (1975, an election year, is excluded, as are the aborted spring 1977 and 1987 sessions, which ceased prematurely when elections were called). The average number of government bills introduced in a session has declined from more than 150 in the early 1970s to fewer than 100 in the early 1980s, and, even more significantly, the proportion of government bills actually passed has fallen from 19 out of 20 to 3 out of 4 or 5 in the same period. Particularly noteworthy is the fact that the rate of passage of government bills was substantially higher during the minority government years (1976–80) than during the subsequent majority government. (The low proportion of government bills passed in 1985–86 and 1986–87 is partially an artefact of the extraordinary number of bills carried over from the first session to the second; if these bills are counted only once, the figure rises to 70 per cent.)[2] A similar pattern is evident when the focus shifts to the number of pages of government legislation enacted in the four periods. During the minority years, on average, just over half as many pages of legislation were produced as in the early 1970s, but the return to majority government did not have the effect of increasing the total amount of legislation passed by the House. The conclusion would seem to be that the more thorough, less expeditious approach to government legislation that developed during minority government has become ingrained in the legislative process. If the government has had to get used to not enacting as much legislation as in the past, it has clearly found an alternative in its regulatory power. The volume of regulations (which do not have to be tabled in the House, let alone approved by it), rose by nearly 50 per cent in the minority years, continued to rise in the subsequent majority period, and rose slightly during the 1985–87 minority.

I do not want to suggest that the consideration of legislation by the Ontario legislature is anything like ideal; none the less, it is clear that a balance exists between expeditiousness and the adequacy of members' opportunity to speak on and inquire into the merits of proposed government legislation. Time limits on speeches or on stages in the legislative process are all but non-existent, and yet the government usually has little trouble in seeing its bills passed within a reasonable time. In 1986–87, of 121 government bills introduced, 71 became law, which in itself is an impressive record in a busy legislature. Even more

TABLE 5.1
Government legislation and regulations 1970–87 (average per session)

	Government bills		Pages of acts passed	Pages of regulations
	Number introduced	Percentage passed		
1970–74	152	95.9	1164	1332
1976–80	109	85.3	632	1923
1981–84	96	75.8	646	2109
1985–87	85	58.4	453	2206

tellingly, of the 50 that did not pass, 35 were never called for second reading, so that their demise can hardly be attributed to roadblocks in the House. Moreover, as is discussed below, an additional dozen were given special dispensation so that they could be studied by standing committees in the interval between sessions.

Table 5.2 provides a breakdown of the time required for the passage of the 71 government bills in 1986–87.[3] The first column shows the total length of time between first reading and third reading. Since the House was adjourned for more than three months in the summer and nearly a month over Christmas, these figures could be misleading; accordingly, the second column recasts the data by counting only the time when the House was in session. The final column contains data on the length of time from the beginning of the second reading debate to third reading (in 'legislative weeks'). Nearly half the bills took more than four months to make their way through the system, and a substantial proportion took more than half a year. Much of this time, however, is accounted for by the long adjournments in the summer and at Christmas, for, as the second column demonstrates, more than half the government bills in 1986–87 went through all stages of the process in six sitting weeks or less, and only 11 required more than four sitting months for passage. The data in the final column are more revealing still, for they confirm that bills spend far more time on the order paper awaiting the government's decision to commence second reading debate than they do in all subsequent stages of the process (when opposition- and committee-induced delays occur). In other words, the length of time a bill takes to be passed is primarily a function of where it stands in the government's scale of priorities, and in particular how eager the government is to bring it on for second reading. Two conclusions emerge

120 The Ontario legislature

TABLE 5.2
Time taken for passage of government bills 1986–87
(number of bills)

Weeks	First reading to third reading		Second reading to third reading
	Calendar	Legislative	legislative
1–3	17	19	60
4–6	4	17	2
7–10	10	9	5
11–15	7	15	3
16–20	9	10	1
21–30	16	1	0
31+	8	0	0

'Calendar' weeks refer to the actual amount of time elapsed; 'legislative' weeks refer only to the time during which the House was in session.

clearly from this analysis: first, the government can normally count on having its legislation passed with remarkable speed; second, in most cases the length of time that elapses during the legislative process is determined more by the government than by the opposition.

To be sure, a direct relationship exists between speed of passage and complexity. Short, straightforward bills of a 'housekeeping' or otherwise non-controversial nature tend to pass in a few weeks, whereas complex, controversial bills entailing major policy thrusts take substantially longer. In part because the government has relatively little difficulty getting legislation passed, the device of the 'omnibus bill,' which incorporates a number of essentially unrelated legislative proposals, is little used at Queen's Park.

When Schindeler wrote about the Ontario legislature in the 1960s, and indeed until 1975, a common government strategy was 'legislation by exhaustion.' Large numbers of important bills would be introduced late in the session, and if the opposition balked at quick passage, it found itself debating until the small hours of the morning.[4] This approach, which was hardly conducive to the serious consideration of proposed legislation, could not survive in a minority House, and significantly was not revived during the Conservative majority of 1981–85. In 1984, the last session of the Conservative majority, only 22 government bills were introduced in the fall sitting; 9 of these were not called for second reading. Except for the Supply Act, only 3 bills were introduced in the last month of the session, and for none of these was a second reading debate begun. Similarly, although 17 government bills were given first reading during the final month of the 1986–87 session (in January and February 1987), only 7 (including the Supply Act) were called for second reading; none were major pieces of legislation.

Only infrequently are opposition parties absolutely determined to delay a bill with every procedural tactic available. Should this be the case, though, many delaying tactics are possible, even aside from prolonged debate. If more than twenty members object, a bill cannot pass more than one 'stage' a day; with six possible stages (first reading, second reading, standing committee, report, Committee of the Whole, third reading), a five-day wait before standing committee proceedings begin, and one-day delays in the case of reasoned amendments at second reading and for bills going from standing committee to Committee of the Whole, twelve sitting days could be taken before delays arising from filibusters, divisions, procedural wrangles, and the like are even considered.[5]

As in other parliamentary systems, the most important stages in the legislative process in Ontario are pre-parliamentary; that is, the basic policy decisions are all taken before first reading, as are most of the background studies and interest group consultations. The roles of the government caucus and of individual back-bench MPPS vary according to the specifics of the bills involved, but in general they are limited. Although most draft bills are brought before the government caucus prior to their introduction, this usually takes place just before their introduction in the House and is rather more of an information exercise for the benefit of government back-benchers than a genuine attempt to seek their advice and approval. With limited advance notice, little time for discussion, and a disinclination on the part of ministers to accord caucus a genuine share in decision-making, it is difficult for caucus to develop sufficiently organized opposition to a proposed measure that will force its reconsideration or withdrawal by the sponsoring minister. On occasion caucus has been successful in blocking legislation or in delaying its introduction until substantial amendments were forthcoming.

Until 1970 the anachronism of requiring two days' notice of intention to introduce a bill prevailed, though it served little purpose in that members had only to give notice of the bill's title, which gave almost no idea of its content or purpose. Current practice simply requires a member to stand in his place when the Speaker calls 'Introduction of Bills' and move that 'leave be given to introduce a bill entitled ... and that the same be read a first time.' The member then hands the draft bill to a page to take it to the Speaker, who puts the question to an entirely oblivious House, assumes a positive verdict, and passes the bill to the clerks at the table.

After one of the clerks announces the bill's first reading to the House, the member is permitted to make a brief statement explaining the main idea behind the bill.[6] Recent Speakers have been rigorous in enforcing the rule that introductory statements be brief, and will usually cut a member off if he speaks much more than a minute. Accordingly (and given the sparseness of attendance in the House and gallery at this juncture), ministers with important legislation to introduce usually make a detailed statement about the bill during the time allocated for ministerial statements. Most statements given at the time of introduction are little more than a recital of the explanatory notes prepared by the Office of Legislative Counsel, which are printed with the bill. The standing orders require that the introduction of a government bill be accompanied by a 'compendium of background information.' As with compendia accompanying 'policy statements,' the information they contain tends to be limited and already publicly available, and is of limited value to the opposition.

No amendment or debate is permitted at first reading. Divisions are unusual, though in recent years the opposition parties have sometimes been sufficiently exercised about a proposed government measure to force a recorded vote on its first reading. Most often it is tax bills that are so greeted, but the wage restraint bill in 1982, the Conservative government's 1984 freedom of information bill, and a 1986 bill to end a transportation strike also occasioned enough opposition wrath to require a division for their introduction. The only recorded instance of a bill's being defeated at first reading occurred in 1981. Piqued by a division on first reading of a tax bill forced by the opposition, the Conservative majority defeated the motion for first reading of an NDP private members' bill. This heavy-handed retaliation was severely criticized, and the next sitting day saw the reintroduced bill pass first reading without incident.

The Quebec National Assembly and several European parliaments permit bills to be sent for committee study and hearings after first reading so that the committee deliberations may extend to both the principle and the detail of the bill. No such provision exists in Ontario; if the government wished, it could easily receive all-party agreement to suspend the normal rules and hold committee hearings prior to second reading, but this virtually never happens. On occasion, government reports on position papers incorporating draft bills are referred to standing committee; this has happened recently with proposed legislation dealing with workers' compensation and social services for children. Conversely, the government will sometimes introduce a bill with no intention of taking it beyond first reading; instead, the bill is widely circulated among affected or interested groups for comment (but not via a legislative committee).

Standing order 58(a) provides that the bill may not be called for second reading until it has been printed and so denoted on the order paper. Normally, two or three sitting days are required for the bill to be printed and distributed to members, but a more significant time constraint is the convention that legislation will not be called for second reading until the opposition parties have had an opportunity to 'caucus' on it. In practice, more time than this usually passes before the second reading debate is begun; in 1986–87, of 78 government bills which went beyond first reading,[7] only 5 were called for second reading within a week of their introduction, 7 more were called within two weeks, 7 were not called until three or four weeks after first reading, and 59 waited five or more weeks.[8] Accordingly, the one day's delay in calling a bill for second reading required by standing order 58(b) if notice of a reasoned amendment is received by the Clerk's Office by noon of the day after first reading comes into play only in the rare instances in which one or both opposition parties are engaged in an all-out campaign of delay. Once a common tactic, the reasoned amendment has largely fallen into disuse in the Ontario legislature.

The second reading debate is begun by the minister, or, in the case of fairly routine legislation, by his parliamentary assistant. The opposition critics speak next, followed, in the usual party rotation, by any members who have something to say on the matter (or who have been persuaded by the whip to have something to say). A strong tradition holds that any MPP who wishes to speak on a particular bill is entitled to do so. Late in the session, however, pressure may be exerted on the parties to limit the number of their speakers. This tradition and the lack of time limits on speeches notwithstanding, few serious delays are encountered at second reading for most government bills. To illustrate this point, we need only consider the 78 bills on which second reading debates were held in 1986–87: 52 were debated for less than an hour (38 for less than thirty minutes); only 4 were debated for more than four hours, and none for more than six hours. Only 17 bills did not pass second reading on the day they were first called; only 1 required three days' debate. This relatively modest amount of debate at second reading nevertheless represents a substantial growth from the 1960s; Schindeler reports that only 24 of 135 government bills that received second reading in 1964 were debated, and the average time for those debates was just thirty-three minutes.[9]

Second reading debates are supposed to be confined to the principles of the bill, but the chair tends to be indulgent of members whose remarks stray across the nebulous line between principle and detail. Once all other MPPS have had their say, the minister or the parliamentary assistant winds up the debate. Only the minister is permitted to speak twice at second reading.

The only amendments permitted at second reading are not really amendments at all. A reasoned amendment is an attempt to substitute for second reading an agreement by the House that, for specified reasons, the bill is defective. The Camp Commission pointed out that this 'does not entail outright rejection of the bill'[10] and, if this is technically true, reasoned amendments tend to be functionally equivalent to complete repudiation of the bill. The other type of permissible amendment at this stage is the 'hoist' amendment, which takes the form of an amendment to the second reading motion 'that the bill be not now read a second time but be read a second time this day six months.'[11] Hoist and reasoned amendments have fallen into disuse in the Ontario legislature. Short of employing one of these procedures simply for the sake of doing something different, the only possible reason for recourse to them would be to create delay, since members who had already spoken in the second reading debate could also speak in the debate on the amendment.

If a division is to occur anywhere in the legislative process, it will be at second reading; yet by no means are all bills divided upon even here.[12] In 1986–87, 71 of 78 government bills called for second reading did not occasion a division. Clearly, the more contentious the bill or the more significant the policy involved, the more likely will be a division. Two government bills were lost on division in 1986–87; both related to the Liberals' controversial proposal to permit the sale of beer and wine in corner stores. Such defeats mark the end of the bills, at least until the next session.

Immediately after the bill has received second reading, the Speaker asks whether it shall be ordered for third reading. A substantial proportion of government bills (straightforward and non-controversial ones, to be sure) go directly onto the order paper for third reading: some thirty-nine, or 46 per cent of those which gained second reading, did so in 1986–87. Since unanimous consent is required to bypass the committee stage, all it takes is one 'no' in response to the Speaker's query to send the bill to committee. The initial decision whether the bill should be considered by the Committee of the Whole or by a standing committee is made by the minister or parliamentary assistant in charge of the bill.[13] An important rule change in 1976 gave twenty members – in effect, any party – the ability to override the minister and to force the bill before a standing committee. The standing orders are silent as to the mechanism for deciding which standing committee will consider the bill; in point of fact, this issue has usually been agreed upon beforehand by the House leaders.

Contrary to the rules in the House of Commons, where government bills are automatically referred to standing committees, most Canadian provincial legislatures (Ontario and Quebec being the principal exceptions) hold the committee stage on legislation in Committee of the Whole and use standing committees sparingly, if at all. The purpose of committee consideration of a bill is the clause-by-clause analysis and possible amendment of detailed provisions of the bill, whether the venue is the Committee of the Whole or a standing committee. This purely procedural equivalence belies important differences in political significance as well as in parliamentary tactics. First, referral of a bill to committee entails additional steps (and thus potential delays) as compared with consideration in Committee of the Whole. Meetings on bills referred to standing committees may not be held for five days after second reading unless all three parties agree (technically, twenty members). Moreover, if a party is intent on maximizing delays, it can force a Committee of the Whole stage on bills already studied in standing committee.[14] This has occurred only a very few times in recent years. During every session several bills are considered in both standing committee and Committee of the Whole, but in most cases this is done to permit amendments not raised in standing committee, or to serve as a vehicle for resolving an impasse encountered in the standing committee.[15]

A second difference is more fundamental, though it becomes of real significance only in times of minority government. Unless the House directs otherwise, which it rarely does, standing committees are free to order their own business and (within broad limits) to determine their own procedures. Committees typically have a number of diverse matters before them at any given time; thus, a committee may decide not to begin the study of a bill referred to it until several sets of estimates or one or two special studies are completed. A committee could decide to call for public hearings before its clause-by-clause treatment, and also to hold further public hearings on specific clauses.[16] In short, unlike the Committee of the Whole, in which business is called at the discretion of the government House leader, the government can lose control of the timetabling of its legislation once it is referred to standing committee. In a majority House the government can use its majority on the committee to give the bill whatever priority it wishes.

The most important difference lies in the possibility – indeed the expectation – that standing committees will hold public hearings, call for expert witnesses, and hear directly from ministry staff. In Committee of the Whole, only members are allowed to speak; a small table may be brought into the Chamber and placed directly in front of the minister's desk so that two or three civil servants may directly advise him during the debate, but those civil servants cannot take part in debate. The civil servants who accompany the minister or parliamentary assistant to standing committee are regularly called upon to explain technical points to the committee or to comment on substantive policy concerns. All such interventions by civil servants are nominally made only by consent of the Minister but in practice, the minister's approval is rarely sought, and is even more rarely refused; an informal relationship usually prevails between committee members and ministry staff when committees are reviewing bills, to the point that casual observers might be forgiven for assuming that the civil servants were committee staff or even committee members.

If it is useful for MPPs to be able to speak directly with civil servants, of far more political consequence in terms of permitting 'strangers' (non-members) to address standing committees is the submission of briefs and oral presentations from experts, interest groups, and private citizens.

Whether to hold public hearings, how they are to be advertised, and whether meetings are to be held outside Toronto are decisions left to the committee.[17] Since bills referred to committee are almost by definition controversial (otherwise they would have stayed in Committee of the Whole), an expectation exists that public hearings will be held. That expectation is almost invariably met; hearings on bills are usually widely advertised through notices in the daily newspapers of the province's major urban centres calling for written or oral presentations. Most of those who ask to appear before a committee are organized interest groups that probably were already aware of the bill and would have submitted a brief regardless of the advertising. The notices attract some correspondence from private citizens, but few requests to make presentations in person. When dealing with important or controversial bills, committees will frequently hold meetings throughout the province to accomodate groups and individuals without the time or wherewithal to travel to Toronto. The typical itinerary for committees engaged in such an exercise is Ottawa, Windsor, Thunder Bay and Sudbury, or North Bay. Depending on the nature of the bill and the expressed level of interest, cities such as London, Kingston, Hamilton, and Sault Ste Marie may also be visited.

Public hearings, wherever held, are significant in that they enhance the legitimacy of the legislative process and of the political system generally by fostering a sense of participation in the policy-making process among those affected by or interested in the legislation. Though it is true that, in general, public involvement through committee hearings promotes legitimacy, some people and groups come away from public hearings with less respect for the process and faith in the system as a consequence of their realization that the government's position would not be altered by any evidence or argument presented to the committee. This was certainly the case for many of those who appeared before the Social Development Committee to oppose the separate-school funding bill in 1985–86.

The substantive policy impact of public hearings is uncertain. Many illustrations could be cited of bills that were changed not a whit despite repeated and vociferous criticism from interest groups during extensive public hearings. Other bills were amended in response to suggestions put forward during public hearings, sometimes by the government, sometimes (in minority settings) by the opposition over government objections. In the case of government amendments, one can never be sure to what extent they were occasioned by the public hearing process or to what extent they would have been made anyway as a result of other channels of pressure and advice. Even though it may be difficult to determine how effective public hearings are in changing government legislation, their political impact can be substantial. The government may choose not to act in accordance with the wishes of those who appear before committee, but it must be prepared to offer some sort of response or rebuttal, and, ultimately, to suffer the political consequences of refusing the demands of the groups and individuals who take part in the public hearing process. Accordingly, the opposition parties will sometimes encourage groups to become involved in committee hearings, not because they hope to mobilize enough opposition to a bill to bring about significant amendments, but because they sense that the government will remain steadfast, and they know that potentially favourable groups can be politicized by their frustration in encountering an immobile government.

Once a bill has received second reading, any proceeding in a committee aimed at altering its fundamental principle is out of order. Many of the groups appearing before the committees studying the Inflation Restraint Act in 1982 and the separate-school funding bill in 1985 (among others) argued strenuously that those bills were fundamentally wrong and should be rejected by the committee. Technically, such comments should not be permitted, but political exigencies obviously dictate otherwise. In 1979 the Administration of Justice Committee told the House that it would not report a government bill referred to it after second reading. The tactic was, of course, entirely improper, but no attempt was made to challenge it by the government, presumably because the bill would probably be defeated at third reading. The bill in question was a routine bill to amalgamate the Ministry of Education with the Ministry of Colleges and Universities, which was the subject of a month's public hearings during which group after group criticized every aspect of the province's educational system. (A few presentations actually did address, at least briefly, the proposed amalgamation.) This episode illustrates the political uses of committee hearings as well as the way in which procedure can fall victim to politics.

Especially in the case of long, complex bills, large numbers of amendments may be made in committee. Even during minority situations, most successful amendments originate with the government, in part because the government is accorded the first opportunity to move amendments, and in part because the government frequently pre-empts the opposition parties by moving amendments they favour. However, the opposition can and does successfully initiate and carry amendments over the government's objections, or at least against its preferences, in minority Houses; the exceedingly controversial addition of the words 'sexual orientation' to the Ontario Human Rights Code in late 1986 is a case in point. Successful opposition amendments are unusual during majority government. One of the more interesting impasses of minority

129 The legislature at work: Legislation and finances

government occurs when the opposition parties combine in committee to pass amendments unacceptable to the government. The government cannot remove the offending amendment, but it can threaten to refuse to call the bill for third reading once it returns to the House. In these stalemates the opposition must weigh the risk of killing the whole bill should it insist on its amendments, while the government must decide whether the offending amendments are so unpalatable that it is prepared to abandon the bill altogether. Many such stand-offs are resolved by mutual compromise, but some bills (for example, the 1980 Pits and Quarries Bill) expire if the two sides remain intransigent. In the fall of 1986, the Liberal government warned the opposition that if they amended the rent control bill the legislation would be withdrawn. The opposition ignored this threat and proceeded with numerous amendments (few of which passed, owing to disagreements between the NDP and the Conservatives).

In 1986–87, 44 government bills had committee stage; 20 bills were dealt with entirely in the Committee of the Whole; and 24 were referred to standing committee. When the session ended 11 were still before standing committees; of the 13 that were reported back from the standing committees, 7 were subsequently referred to the Committee of the Whole.[18] Most legislation that goes straight to Committee of the Whole is dealt with expeditiously: 13 of the 20 bills that travelled this route were debated for less than half an hour, 4 took as much as an hour, and none required more than four hours' debate. Those bills that went to Committee of the Whole after study by a standing committee tended to take rather more time: none was completed in less than an hour; 5 required between one and four hours' debate. Two were the subjects of opposition filibusters: the extra-billing legislation, which consumed nearly thirty hours, and the bill extending the protection of the Human Rights Code to homosexuals, which took eighteen hours. Clearly, this reflects the more controversial nature of the legislation that is referred to standing committee. Thus, while only about one-quarter of the government bills that pass second reading are sent for study to standing committee, these are inevitably the most contentious and most significant in the government's program. As is the case in Ottawa, though its effects are highly variable, committee review of legislation does enhance the influence of private members, and of the opposition parties, in the legislative process.[19]

Committee of the Whole consists of all members sitting as a committee in the Chamber. The Speaker is not in the chair (and therefore the mace is placed beneath the table); the deputy Speaker, in his capacity as chairman of the Committees of the Whole House, presides from the clerk's chair at the table. Aside from these trappings, the principal distinguishing features of the Committee of the Whole are the relaxation of the rules of debate, principally the provision that members may speak any number of times on a motion (thus permitting a question-and-answer format or an attack-counterattack approach), and the ability of the Committee of the Whole to make detailed amendments. The dividing line between amendments to the detail of the bill and those to its principle is imprecise at best, and rulings on admissibility of amendments depend on the good judgment of the chairman.[20] Recent rulings have tended to allow a good deal of latitude, though obvious offenders are unhesitatingly struck down, particularly if they attempt to add to a bill clauses unrelated to any existing clause, and, in the case of bills amending existing acts, if they attempt to change parts of the act not affected by the bill. As well, so-called money amendments, which would raise taxation or directly allocate public funds, may not be moved by private members. Until fairly recently, the definition of what constituted a money amendment was rather restrictive, but rulings by chairmen over the past two decades have allowed some leeway to private members. Particularly significant were rulings that permitted amendments to bills moved by back-benchers to reduce expenditure,[21] to reduce taxes or to widen tax exemptions,[22] and to increase the number of persons eligible for government payments (provided that the payments were not mandatory).[23] The old procedure whereby the Committee of the Whole was required to pass financial resolutions to accompany money bills was done away with in 1970.

Whether in Committee of the Whole or in standing committee, most successful amendments are proposed by the government. If the government is prepared to accept an opposition criticism or suggestion, it is more likely to put forward its own amendment than to support one from the opposition. A large proportion of government amendments arise independently of the committee process – that is, from the bureaucracy's refinement of the bill or from lobbying efforts directed at the government rather than at the legislature.

Since the opportunity exists for substantial debate and for moving amendments in Committee of the Whole, the report stage of bills coming back to the House from standing committee is usually a formality in the Ontario legislature. In the British and Canadian Houses of Commons, the report stage is frequently a significant hurdle for a bill, and involves large numbers of amendments and a considerable expenditure of time. No bill was subject to debate at report stage in the Ontario legislature during 1986-87. On the infrequent occasions when report-stage debates arise they are usually species of delaying tactics. In the normal course of events, the standing committee chairman simply rises in his place during the routine proceeding of 'reports' and presents the report; a table clerk indicates that the bill is reported with or without amendments; and the Speaker ascertains whether the bill is to be ordered for third reading or sent to Committee of the Whole. The whole procedure is over in seconds.

The 'report' of a committee on a bill is simply the bill itself, with or without amendments; no text explaining amendments or analysing the merits of particular aspects of the bill is permitted. In a few instances in recent years, special motions have been passed to authorize standing committees to report to the House on the substantive policy issues underlying a particular piece of legislation.

Third reading in the Ontario legislature is usually pro forma. Debate is not usual; only seven bills were the subject of any debate in 1986-87, and only three were debated for more than fifteen minutes. Divisions at third reading are rarer still: only three occurred in 1986-87. Amendments are not permitted at third reading, though it is in order to move that a bill be sent back to committee with instructions to make specific amendments. Such motions, once quite common, are all but unknown today.

Royal assent follows third reading; this is the formal approval of the bill in the queen's name by the lieutenant-governor. Theoretically, of course, the lieutenant-governor can withhold approval, but it is almost impossible to imagine circumstances in which this might occur. Far more significant than royal assent, which is purely a formality, is the question of a bill's coming into force, and the proclamation process. Most bills in Ontario provide that 'this Act comes into force on the day it receives Royal assent'; this simply means that as soon as the lieutenant-governor approves the bill and signs it, it becomes effective. Some bills mention a specific date on which they come into force (tax bills were formerly made retroactive to the date of the budget); still others '[come] into force on a day to be proclaimed by the Lieutenant Governor.' In such cases the decision as to when a bill becomes effective – or indeed whether it ever will – is left entirely to the discretion of the cabinet. The most common reason for delaying the implementation of the bill until it is proclaimed by the cabinet is the need to put the required administrative machinery into place; since it may be hard to estimate how long this will take for a complex new policy, it is useful for the government to have flexibility. On occasion a bill or parts of a bill may not be proclaimed pending the resolution of federal-provincial complications or of legal uncertainties; for example, sections of the Residential Tenancies Act in the late 1970s were not proclaimed because they were expected to be subject to a court challenge on constitutional grounds. Sometimes, however, the date of implementation is left to the cabinet because the government is uneasy over the policy underlying the bill; the tactic amounts to an escape hatch, since the government is under no obligation ever to proclaim a bill. Thus, a number of statutes that have been 'on the books' for years have never been proclaimed, owing to the government's (ultimately political) decision not to bring into effect its own legislation.[24] The question of non-proclamation, though of substantial import, is usually far too arcane and obscure to attract much attention, but the Conservative government's refusal to proclaim its 'Spills Bill' (an environmental protection measure) did become an important issue in the 1985 election.

With the end of the session, all legislation uncompleted dies on the order paper; in other words, a bill must go through the entire process, beginning at first reading, again in the next session if it is to be enacted. In recent years, though, a practice has developed that effectively circumvents this principle. At the end of each session special motions are passed, with the agreement of the three House leaders, to provide that at the beginning of the next session certain uncompleted bills will be deemed to have received first and second reading and are referred to committee for study. In addition to doing away with the need to repeat the second reading debate, this procedure permits committee study – usually public hearings – of the bills in the interval between sessions, and thus expedites passage by several weeks. Though procedurally irregular on several grounds, this practice is accepted without question on all sides as a practical means of dealing with bills in which the legislature has invested substantial time or with bills that may require prolonged committee hearings during the winter. Most important bills that have passed second reading are so treated, but this normally only represents a handful or fewer each year; nine bills that had received second reading were carried over from the first session of the Thirty-third Parliament (1985–86) to the second session (1986–87); all but one, the ill-starred freedom of information bill, were passed during the 1986–87 session. At the close of the 1985–86 session, in a departure from previous practice, nineteen government bills that had not been called for second reading were also carried over. Thirteen government bills were carried over at the end of the 1986–87 session. With the dissolution of the House, of course, all incomplete business lapses entirely.

PRIVATE MEMBERS' BUSINESS

The Ontario legislature's provisions for private members' business offer, within limits, a certain scope for its members to pursue policy objectives. Indeed, private members' business symbolizes the legislature's policy role: at first blush, the impact seems negligible, for private members' bills virtually never pass and their resolutions have little legal force; yet, on close inspection, the possibility does exist for influencing policy – subtly and slowly to be sure – through them.

Private members' business takes two forms: bills and resolutions. Private members' bills may deal with any aspect of public policy, except that they may not be 'money bills,' which impose taxes or directly allocate the spending of public funds. This 'money rule' is interpreted loosely, and does not prevent the House from dealing with private members' bills that would entail costly administrative machinery. For years one NDP member routinely introduced a private members' bill to nationalize Inco, the province's largest mining concern; the bill was allowed because it simply authorized the acquisition but allocated no funds for it. Resolutions are not bound by this restriction, since they are only abstract opinions of the House, but for this same reason (with the exceptions discussed below) they have no legally binding force.

Private members are not limited in the number of bills or resolutions they can bring forward. In 1986–87, 68 private members' bills were introduced or carried over from the previous session – 43 by the New Democrats, 20 by the Conservatives, and 5 by government backbenchers. (This last figure does not reflect pressure on government members to submit resolutions rather than bills, as was common when the Conservatives were in power.) Sixteen of the 25 New Democratic members had private members' bills on the order paper, but only 11 of 51 Tories introduced private members' bills. Two NDP members accounted for nearly one-third of all private members' bills. Fifty-nine resolutions were tabled by 17 New Democrats, 10 Conservatives, and 12 government back-benchers; few MPPs introduced more than one resolution. These figures differ somewhat from those reported in a study of the 1980 session, primarily in that the number of private members' bills was substantially higher (130).[25] The 1986–87 session resembles

1980 in the extent to which NDP members utilized this procedure more often than MPPs of other parties: in 1980 nearly three-quarters of private members' bills were introduced by the NDP;[26] in 1984, when they were still in opposition, the Liberals brought forward almost as much private members' legislation as did the NDP. A far more significant change, however, is the revival of interest in private members' business which had fallen into general disuse in the 1950s and 1960s after having been a principal focus of activity in the nineteenth century.[27]

An important step in rescuing private members' business from oblivion occurred in 1966 with an informal agreement to debate more private members' bills and resolutions,[28] but far more significant was the establishment of a radically new procedure a decade later. Under the 1976 reforms, all private members who wish to participate submit their names to the clerk, who conducts a random ballot (by party) which assigns each a priority.[29] The standing orders require a new ballot each session, but in practice no new ballot is held until all MPPs have had one item debated. Members must designate at least two weeks in advance the bill or resolution they wish to have debated. Two items of business are called for debate every Thursday morning,[30] with time divided equally between the two. Since the vote must be held at noon, and the sponsor of the bill or resolution may speak for twenty minutes and other Members for up to ten minutes, usually no more than five or six members have an opportunity to debate a particular item.[31] The usual lax procedure which permits amendment without notice does not apply, and indeed no amendments are permitted during private members' time lest the two-week notice rule be circumvented via a last-minute amendment.

The most noteworthy aspect of the 1976 reforms was the requirement that all items of private members' business debated come to some sort of vote rather than simply being 'talked out.' At the conclusion of the two debates, votes are held on whether the bill in question should receive second reading, or whether the resolution should be carried. The government protected itself somewhat in 1976 by insisting on a mechanism by which it could prevent a vote from taking place. Any twenty members may 'block' a vote by standing in their places when the question is about to be put. Procedurally, this is a useful device for a government, especially a minority government, but politically it is of less value; in one way or another the government must take a position and literally stand up and be counted. In 1984 the government blocked nine of sixteen items of private members' business brought forward by opposition members. Only very rarely has the opposition resorted to using the blocking provision. In its first three years the Liberal government refrained from blocking any private members' business, perhaps because the Liberals remembered their outrage at the Tories' blocking of their bills and resolutions. The refusal to block is also more politically astute; the government retains the power to scupper any bill by refusing to call it for third reading. The Liberals' more open attitude towards private members' business is also shown in their 'carrying over' to the new session private members' bills that were still before standing committees at session's end.

Table 5.3 details the fate of private members' bills in the 1986–87 session. In several respects they fared much better than was the case under the Conservative government. First, seven out of nine that were debated passed second reading; largely because of the government's frequent recourse to the blocking procedure, it was unusual during the Tory regime for more than one or two bills to successfully negotiate even this preliminary hurdle (in 1984 no private members' bills received second reading). Second, for the first time five private members' bills that had passed second reading were carried over at the end of the 1985–86 session. One bill, which would have prohibited smoking in public places, was the subject of a week's public hearing before the Social Development Committee; another was passed after brief consideration in Committee of the Whole. Third, though this is not shown in the table, several of the bills that passed second reading were referred to standing or select committees rather than to Committee of the Whole, as the rules normally direct, where they are called at the discretion of the government House leader. (The requirement for a government-scheduled Committee of the Whole stage represents a response by the Conservative government to its experience with a private member's bill in 1979–80. This was a bill introduced by an NDP member that would have required all Ontario employers to abide by the principle of equal pay for work of equal value. After passing second reading, the bill was referred, by the twenty-member rule, to a standing committee, which held several weeks of highly publicized public hearings. These served to politicize the issue and generally to embarrass the government. No one involved had any illusions that the bill would become law, but the opposition gained considerable political mileage in the process.)[32] Finally, two private members' bills passed into law in 1986–87.

TABLE 5.3
Private members' bills 1986–87 session*

	Introduced	Debated	Passed second reading	Considered in committee	Passed third reading
Liberal	5	1	1		
Conservative	18 (2)	4	3 (2)	(1)	1
NDP	40 (3)	4	3 (3)	(1)	(1)
Total	63 (5)	9	7 (5)	(2)	1 (1)

*Five private members' bills that had second reading in the 1985–86 session were carried over into 1986–87; they are indicated in parentheses and are not included in the figures to their immediate left (that is, the Conservatives introduced 18 private members' bills in addition to the 2 carried over from the previous session).

If the prospects for the passage of a private member's bill are only slightly better than those of a goldfish in a piranha tank, why are so many introduced? Indeed, why do any MPPS bother with them? One response is that, feeble as private member's bills may be as political weapons, back-benchers have such a limited arsenal that they can scarcely afford not to make use of them. In a more positive light, several reasons exist for introducing and promoting private members' bills. First, they can stand as symbolic affirmation for something one believes in, regardless of how unlikely its passage; the Inco nationalization bill illustrates this point. Stewart Hyson has called this the 'expressive' function of private members' bills.[33] Second, and less altruistically, a private members' bill dealing with a specific constituency concern may be good for one's reputation back home, particularly since a large proportion of the electorate is unaware of the ultimate fate of most private members' bills. Similarly, some private members' bills are introduced at the behest of interest groups that may or may not understand the legislative process.

Finally, there are several cases in which private members' bills can be influential in the policy process even if they are not passed. On occasion the government will ask one of its back-benchers to bring forward a legislative proposal as a trial balloon, thus permitting the government to gauge public reaction without making any commitment (as it might be presumed to have done if the measure were brought in as a government bill). Such a strategy was said to lie behind a Tory back-bencher's 1982 bill to abolish the mandatory retirement age. In other cases, though they may not have been 'planted' by the government, private members' bills, such as the anti-smoking bill studied in committee in 1986, are carefully monitored as possible precursors to government legislation. Thus, private members' bills may be attempts to draw attention to an idea, mobilize public opinion, and convince the government of its merits, with the intention of having the government adopt the idea as its own. For example, it is widely agreed that an important factor leading to the government's appointment of an ombudsman in 1975 was the perennial introduction by a Liberal MPP of an ombudsman bill, which not only generated interest in the concept but also won over a number of cabinet ministers. Far more common, though, is the use of private members' bills to promote party policies, embarrass the government, and generally score political points. Through the organization of support among the general public and interest groups and the publicity arising from a well-orchestrated campaign, a private members' bill can goad the government into action it might not otherwise have taken or force it into taking a stand on an issue it would rather have avoided – or both. The equal-pay bill mentioned above not only served to politicize the issue, but was in part responsible for government decisions to hire more inspectors to enforce existing legislation and to embark on an extensive advertising campaign informing the public of the law relating to equal pay.[34] Such a concrete government response is unusual, but the strategy of mobilizing supporters for party causes – and thus, it is hoped, for the party – through the vehicle of private members' bills is not. In sum, 'private members' business provided a platform for opposition party policy and for the personal concerns and interests of private members. Discussion was opened on a number of issues that would have otherwise gone untouched. Private members' bills and resolutions help the private member to criticize and scrutinize the Government as well as to carry out his role of educator.'[35]

Most private members' resolutions are couched in terms such as 'in the opinion of this House, the Government should ...,' 'this House urges ...' Accordingly, even if passed, the resolutions remain only expressions of opinion that require no action of anyone (depending on their content and the circumstances surrounding them, they may carry substantial political or moral force, but no legal force). Not all private members' resolutions are so toothless (leaving aside want-of-confidence motions, which are technically private members' resolutions). Resolutions directing the House or its committees are binding; an inquiry by the Ombudsman Committee in the early 1980s into international human rights was instigated by just such a resolution, as was a 1985 study by the Social Development Committee into the problem of missing children. Resolutions are sometimes introduced calling upon the Speaker to communicate the views of the House to an outside body, usually another government. If such resolutions pass, the Speaker transmits the message as directed. A fiercely debated 1980 resolution (which passed after a free vote that split all three party caucuses) directed the Speaker to inform the federal government of the legislature's opposition to the sending of Canadian athletes to the 1980 Olympics in view of the Soviet invasion of Afghanistan.

One possible use of private members' resolutions has the potential to be very far-reaching indeed. Under the amending formula of the new constitution, amendments are brought into force by resolution of the Parliament of Canada and of the provincial assemblies; these resolutions are clearly within the prerogative of private members. One such resolution – to entrench the right to private property in the Charter of Rights and Freedoms – was passed by the legislature in the fall of 1986. Many members who applauded or bemoaned the passage of this resolution did not realize that it was of no force in the amending process because it was not supported by a majority of the members (as opposed to a majority of the members present), as required by section 38(2) of the Constitution Act, 1982. Most constitutional amendments require far more than the agreement of the Ontario Legislative Assembly, but certain constitutional amendments that would affect only Ontario can be implemented simply by the passage of a resolution. In 1982 a Franco-Ontarian Liberal MPP had a resolution on the order paper which, had it passed, would have rendered Ontario constitutionally bilingual.

All twenty-two private members' resolutions debated in 1986–87 were passed (ten were sponsored by government members, six each by Conservatives and New Democrats). As had been the case under the Conservatives, the resolutions brought up for debate by government back-benchers in 1986 were often innocuous in the extreme – for example, resolutions favouring the enhanced promotion of Canadian food products and improved search and rescue services, or condemning cutbacks of federal transfer payments. Others – for example, on improving the provincially regulated new home warranty program or limiting court awards on liability damages – were more controversial, but were certainly not official Liberal party policy. In the 1970s and early 1980s many of the opposition bills and resolutions that came up for debate were unmistakably *party* bills rather than *private members'* bills; that is, they reflected the personal interests of individual MPPS through the prism of party policy or party-based criticism of the government. This tendency was substantially less in evidence in 1986–87, which may partially account for the unusually small number of items that did not pass (only two of thirty-one). Not surprisingly, members of the more programmatic NDP were far more likely than Tory MPPS to bring forward party rather than personal matters; NDP items covered such key party policies as northern economic policy, pension reform, labour relations, and public auto insurance. Still, several NDP members brought forward matters that were hardly key tenets of party dogma, such as improved community services for senior citizens and a marginal expansion of the mandate of the Ontario Institute for Studies in Education.

The relatively high number of non-party matters is illustrated by the results of the nine divisions that took place in 1986–87 on items of private members' business. Whereas in 1984 only two divisions were marked by anything other than unanimity within the three caucuses, 1986–87 witnessed only one straight party vote (on the OISE bill). The NDP voted en bloc in each division, but the Liberals were split six times, as were the Tories on five occasions; moreover, these splits were as likely to be 9 to 10, 21 to 6, or 13 to 8 as they were to be 17 to 1 or 22 to 2. In other words, the members – at least the Liberal and Conservative members – exercised their own judgment rather than voting according to a party line. In contrast, most of the divisions were whipped on the government side when the Conservatives held power.

Prior to the changes in the procedure governing private members' business in 1976, no private members' bill had passed for more than two decades. The number of successful bills remains, to be charitable, modest; only eight have passed since 1976: a minor amendment to the Elections Finances Reform Act permitting weekly newspapers to carry election ads the day before an election, an act that closed a minor loophole in the Family Law Reform Act, an act banning leghold trapping in urban areas, an act naming a Northern Ontario township after disabled athlete Rick Hansen, an act to adopt daylight saving time earlier in the spring, an act extending the protection of the Landlord and Tenant Act to roomers and boarders, an act permitting bookstores to open for business on Sundays, and an act requiring health professionals to report adverse reactions to a controversial children's vaccine. All but one of these were brought forward by opposition MPPS. Still, private members' business is of far greater significance than it formerly was in Ontario (and than it still is in most Canadian jurisdictions). Private members' business is regularly considered in all party caucuses; the government must reflect and decide upon upcoming bills and resolutions (often conveying its views to the House in debate via the parliamentary assistant to the minister most directly affected); and the government must take a public stand by supporting, opposing, or blocking an item.

PRIVATE LEGISLATION

Private bills are often confused with private members' bills, but differ fundamentally in content and in the procedure applicable to them.[36] In distinguishing a private bill from a public bill, be it government or private member's, origin is a better guide than substance. In both formal and informal terms private bills originate with a specific applicant, usually a municipality, corporation, charity, or religious organization, which is required to follow certain specified steps. A private member (usually the member in whose riding the applicant is located) introduces and sponsors the bill as a courtesy; the member bears no responsibility for the bill and may even make known publicly his opposition to it. In contrast, whatever its informal genesis, a public bill is the responsibility, both procedurally and substantively, of the MPP who brings it forward. The fundamental principle defining the substance of private bills is easily stated, but not so readily applied: they 'create exceptions to the general law or confer benefits in addition to the benefits enjoyed under the general law.' In practice, 'the boundary between public and private legislation has long been considered to be difficult to draw.'[37] Many of the measures relating to specific municipalities implemented by private bills might easily be accomplished, and occasionally are, by public bills. For example, in 1983 the Borough of East York sought and received authority to demolish a derelict apartment building (a power not available to municipalities under existing law). The same end could have been reached through a public bill couched in precisely the same terms as East York's private bill, or through a public bill granting all municipalities in the province power to demolish dangerous abandoned buildings; but the implications of such a broad-brush policy illustrate why private bills are often preferable for specific local problems.

Among the more numerous and significant private bills are those requested by municipalities; twenty-four of fifty-one private bills in

1986–87 originated with municipalities. Many of these are essentially technical and non-controversial, but others involve important policy concerns, such as a 1983 City of Toronto bill that would have given the city power to prohibit the demolition of apartment buildings, or a 1980 City of Brantford bill that would have exempted a contentious downtown redevelopment project from the normal Ontario Municipal Board approval process. Certain types of municipal debentures or other borrowing also require private legislation, and are referred to the Ontario Municipal Board for comment prior to committee consideration.

There are other reasons for the introduction of private legislation: religious, charitable, and cultural institutions may hope to gain exemption from municipal taxation; certain types of corporations whose charters have lapsed can only be revived by legislation; and educational institutions wishing to confer degrees must be authorized to do so by legislation (this primarily affects religious educational institutions such as Bible colleges). In 1986–87 seventeen bills could be classified as charitable or cultural; nine were corporate revivals; and two involved degree granting institutions. This listing by no means exhausts the range of matters that may be subject to private legislation; in 1984 five private bills came before the House from would-be professional associations requesting some sort of legal status.[38]

Prior to the first reading of a private bill, the applicant must publish in the *Ontario Gazette* and one local newspaper once a week for a month a notice outlining in non-technical language the purpose of the bill and giving objectors a clear idea of how to voice their opposition before the legislature. Once these notices are completed and the draft bill has been vetted by the Office of the Legislative Counsel, the bill is given first reading. At first reading the bill is referred to the Standing Committee on Regulations and Private Bills. Private bills are sent to committee prior to second reading so that the committee can consider their principles as well as their details.

At the meeting of the Regulations Committee, the applicant, his solicitor, and often but not invariably his local member appear to defend and to explain the bill. All objectors are notified of the meeting and invited to appear; in only a small minority of cases do objectors come forward. Much more significant, particularly for municipal private bills, is the attitude of the government. Early in the process the draft bill is circulated to the appropriate ministries for review. Ministry recommendations are often incorporated into the bill prior to introduction. In the case of municipal bills, during the Conservative administration the parliamentary assistant to the minister of municipal affairs and housing, assisted by ministry legal staff, took part in the meeting to make the government's views known. Under the Liberals, another parliamentary assistant served as the designated government spokesman. An unfavourable response from the government means the demise of the bill; even if the bill survives committee, the government will exercise its prerogative not to call the bill for second or third reading.

Although many private bills complete their committee stage in ten minutes or less, the passage of a private bill is by no means a certainty. Significant amendments are frequent, and in each session some private bills are not reported (that is, they are rejected) by the committee; in 1986–87 one private bill met this fate, though another was withdrawn. Committee consideration of private bills may involve substantial disagreement among members, but not usually along party lines.

Private bills seeking to vary the terms of wills or trusts are referred to the Commissioners of Estate Bills (who are justices of the Supreme Court of Ontario) after first reading. Rarely do more than two or three such estate bills appear in a session. An unfavourable report from the commissioners, which is rare but not unknown, is fatal to a bill.

Once private bills are reported to the House, second and third readings are almost invariably given as a matter of course; debate and divisions are all but unknown. The provision in the standing orders for a Committee of the Whole stage on private bills is virtually never invoked. The City of Brantford bill was the subject of a heated second reading debate and was ultimately defeated on a division marked by splits across party lines, but that was very much the exception.

Private bills consume a negligible amount of House time and place only minor demands on the committee system. Most are routine and non-controversial, so that their rate of passage is high (in 1986–87, 41 of 51 private bills were passed, and 4 more were carried over to the next session). None of this should be taken to mean that private bills are insignificant, for they are often of crucial importance to the municipalities or other institutions requesting them.

FINANCIAL PROCEDURES

As with virtually all other British-style parliaments, the Ontario legislature's ability to scrutinize, let alone control, government finance is all but non-existent. An analysis of the factors contributing to this sorry development in the once fundamental parliamentary 'power of the purse' must await a later chapter on accountability and legislative-executive relations; the discussion that follows is confined in the main to the mechanics of financial procedure.

Financial procedure in the Ontario legislature is quite straightforward: all of the cumbersome procedural paraphernalia of notices of ways and means motions and motions 'that the Speaker do now leave the chair' were abolished in the 1960s, as indeed was the Ways and Means Committee.

The budget

The budget is the cornerstone of the government's economic policy and the highlight of the legislative year. Typically, the budget is brought down in April or early May; the only formal restraint on the timing of the budget is the requirement that the throne debate be completed. Budget day is a major event; the galleries are crowded with invited guests, CBC provides complete live television coverage, and the building swarms with reporters, observers and commentators who are unlikely to return until the next budget is brought down.

The process begins when the treasurer moves 'that this House approves in general the budgetary policy of the government' and then reads the budget speech. After the speech is read, the minister of revenue introduces any tax bills necessary to implement the budget's tax changes. The House then adjourns. (The introduction of tax bills is sometimes postponed until the next day's sitting.)

After taking a day or two to work up their responses, the finance critics of the opposition parties reply formally to the budget in lengthy speeches that usually end with detailed non-confidence motions in the form of amendments to the budget motion. The budget responses from the opposition critics are made to a largely empty House and attract far less attention than the critics' off-the-cuff remarks to the press scrums on budget day. The policies announced in the budget continue to attract attention in question period, but the budget debate soon lapses into irrelevance for the rest of the session. Budget debate tends to be used as filler when no other business is ready to proceed. Back-benchers may make speeches purely for local consumption or on pet projects, but rarely on budgetary issues. In 1986–87, in addition to the critics and leaders, 28 members spoke in the budget debate: 5 Liberal back-benchers, 16 Conservatives, and 7 New Democrats.

By tradition, the budget motion and the opposition amendments do not come to a vote until the last day of the session. Indeed, the 'budget wind-up,' which usually features speeches by the party leaders, is virtually the last item of business for the year. Two implications arise from this hyperextension of the budget debate. First, issues that may have been 'hot' in April, and that therefore figured prominently in the opposition amendments, may by December seem antique. Second, although the opposition is free to devote one of its scarce non-confidence motions to the substance of the budget, it lacks the opportunity for an early division on the budget motion itself, such as that required by standing order 54 of the House of Commons. In other words, the opposition amendment that brought down the Clark government in Ottawa only days after the 1979 budget would, in Ontario, have lain on the order paper for many months before being put to the House.

Bills arising out of the budget are subject to the rules and constraints applying to any legislation, but some of their features bear highlighting, particularly in contrast with the process in the House of Commons. In Ottawa, all budgetary changes are typically consolidated into one major bill, which follows, sometimes by many weeks, the detailed notice of ways and means motion tabled on budget day;[39] long delays, sometimes of a year or more, are common before the bill is enacted. On all these points the Ontario practice differs: no notices of ways and means motions are required; separate budget measures are incorporated into separate bills, often half a dozen or more; and the bills are passed expeditiously (1986 was unusual in that only one of the six bills accompanying the treasurer's mid-May budget was passed prior to the summer break; the rest were passed by Christmas). To a substantial degree these differences are explained by the relative simplicity of most budget-inspired tax changes in Ontario in comparison with the often staggering complexity of federal tax law. In Ottawa, tax bills often involve many pages of intricate amendments to the already horrendously complicated federal tax legislation; Ontario's budget bills may simply replace one figure with another in the Retail Sales Tax Act or the Tobacco Tax Act.

By convention, budget bills receive clause-by-clause study in the Committee of the Whole rather than in standing committee; in contrast to the federal practice, however, this custom is not enshrined in the standing orders. In 1982, despite some specious government arguments that to do so was somehow unparliamentary, a contentious sales tax amendment was referred to standing committee for two weeks of public hearings. The treasurer's 1985 paper, *Reforming the Budget Process*, contemplated the routine reference of budget bills to an Economic Affairs Committee, but this has yet to transpire except on a piecemeal basis. One proposal from that paper that has been adopted is the abandonment of the practice of making tax changes retroactive to the date of the budget.

The estimates
Within a week of the budget, all of the main estimates are tabled by the chairman of Management Board.[40] The estimates of all ministries and all agencies funded out of the consolidated revenue fund are bound into four volumes according to policy field. Depending on the size of the ministry and the range of its programm, its spending proposals will be broken down into several discrete 'votes,' which in turn will be composed of a number of specific 'items,' the funds for which are set out in a standard accounting format (salaries and wages; employee benefits; transportation and communications; services; and transfer payments). The estimates documents are clear and easy to follow, particularly in comparison with the all but incomprehensible federal 'blue book'; but by the same token, the amount of useful information they convey is limited. Ontario has no equivalent to the massive 'Part III' volumes of the federal estimates books, which provide a vast range of useful data on government programs. Opposition critics and other interested MPPS are provided with more substantial briefing books containing a good deal of detailed financial data, information on staffing levels, program explanation, and the like. There is no standard format for these briefing books; each ministry is free to include or exclude whatever it wishes.

The standing orders allocate up to 420 hours for estimates consideration, though typically 40 or 50 hours remain unused at year's end; in 1986–87 estimates consumed 293 hours.[41] The rules further require that 'approximately half' the estimates be considered in standing committees, thus implying that the other half are to be considered in the House. Whether the criterion is time or sets of estimates, standing committees do far more than one-half of the estimates; the 1986–87 session was fairly typical in this respect, for only about one-fifth of the estimates debate occurred in the House. All of the estimates reviewed by the Board of Internal Economy must be referred to standing committee.

The parties, through their House leaders, take turns selecting the order in which estimates are to be taken; the location (standing committee or House) and the time allocated to them are negotiated among the House leaders. Large ministries or ministries fraught with controversy, such as Health, Labour, or Community and Social Services, may have twenty-five hours of available time; smaller or less politically significant ministries, such as Citizenship and Culture, Government Services, or Correctional Services, are typically assigned less than ten hours.[42]

On occasion the minister and the critics will establish a schedule for dealing with specific votes and items so that interested MPPS and required civil servants will know when the matters touching them will be considered. Usually, however, no such sensible arrangement prevails, and one vote and item are reached only when everyone has had his say on the preceding vote, or when the chairman's pleas to move along are heeded. This necessarily means that the last few votes and items tend to be dealt with rather less extensively than earlier votes; sometimes they are not discussed at all. Discussed or not, when the time limit is reached, the chairman puts the question on all outstanding votes and items. Thus, unlike opposition members in many other Canadian legislatures – though not the House of Commons – the opposition in Ontario cannot delay the estimates process significantly, and therefore lacks a powerful weapon in the parliamentary arsenal. Until the late 1960s, both in Ontario and in Ottawa, the supply process knew no time limits and was becoming increasingly protracted, fractious, and unproductive, and thereby a target for reform. Observers agree that the excesses of the old Committee of Supply could not have continued but they express grave doubts over the wisdom of, in effect, abolishing the opposition's power to hold up the estimates.[43]

The principal difference between the estimates procedure in the House and in standing committees relates to the participation of civil servants. When the House sits as the Committee of Supply, a small table is brought into the House and placed in front of the minister's desk; as many as three staff members sit at the desk to provide assistance, but they do not take part in the debate. In standing committees civil servants routinely answer questions and speak directly to the committee. Their participation is at the discretion of the minister, and depends a good deal on his approach: some ministers encourage the extensive involvement of their staff, while others prefer to deal personally with most questions, having conferred privately with their civil servants. One minister caused a minor stir when he categorically refused to allow civil servants who were present in the room to be questioned by the committee; in his view, the doctrine of ministerial responsibility meant that he alone should answer to the committee.[44]

Whatever the venue, each set of estimates begins with a ritual which in its predictability, pointless expenditure of energy, and lack of injury to the combatants resembles nothing so much as an encounter between male bighorn sheep in mating season. The minister reads an opening statement summarizing the ministry's accomplishments over the past year and explaining its new policy initiatives; these statements may run to two or three hours. Next, the opposition critics make opening statements attacking the ministry's record and its proposals; these are usually shorter, but often last an hour or more apiece. Following this, the minister replies at length to the critics' opening remarks, taking special pains to refute with copious statistics any detailed criticism of ministry activity. As the opposition MPPS take issue with the minister's rebuttal, the real estimates debate begins.

A discussion of the dramatis personae of the typical estimates review is instructive. The featured players are the minister and the opposition critics. In the House of Commons, the minister stays only long enough to make an opening statement before leaving his deputy minister and parliamentary secretary to defend his estimates. In Ontario, ministers remain through the entire debate; if they are unable to attend, the meeting is cancelled. The minister, who sits beside the chairman at the front of the committee, usually has his deputy next to him. As many as two dozen senior ministry officials are seated in the audience, ready to supply the minister with information or to respond to questions from committee members. The critics normally do not have researchers or other staff present during the meeting, and the committees do not have research assistance for estimates; in short, the opposition is hopelessly outgunned by the government. The turnout of government backbenchers and opposition MPPS varies with the issues under discussion, but their participation tends to be limited. Notably absent are ordinary citizens and reporters.

Interesting and important things sometimes happen in estimates, but for the most part the debates are mind-numbing exercises in tedium that serve little point. Significantly, when estimates debates are worthwhile it is because of the extended give and take between minister and critics on matters of policy; this may take the form of a co-operative endeavour to improve policy along agreed-upon lines, or it may be a sharply confrontational occasion for setting out party differences. In terms of consideration of the actual estimates – the spending projections and the financial details – the process is an abject failure. Only infrequently does the debate touch on dollar figures; questions about why a particular activity requires a given funding level or how a specific year-over-year increase is to be explained are very rarely asked. Members prefer to talk about policy issues or to bring up constituency concerns rather than to delve into the specifics of government finance. The raising of constituency cases ('Why has your ministry refused Mr X's request that ...') can be viewed as the modern-day equivalent of grievance before supply, and of course can also be of direct political benefit to the MPP. The preference for discussion of policy over money has several roots. First, most members are by nature simply less interested in financial projections than in the policy decisions underlying them. Second, given the dearth of research assistance available to MPPS doing estimates, it is hardly surprising that debate focuses not on details of finance and budgeting, which would require a substantial investment of research and preparation time on the member's part, but rather on policy issues, on which the experienced critic can hold forth at length with little specific preparation. Finally, even if members were willing to do the difficult and time-consuming preparation necessary for serious discussion of money, the political payoff, either in press attention or in possible benefit in their home ridings, is virtually nil. The press stay away from estimates in great hordes, and nothing will find its way into an editor's wastebasket more quickly than a press release from a back-bencher discussing in detail routine items of government finance.

The tenor of estimates meetings is far more often restrained and advisory than inflammatory and confrontational. This mood is symbolized by the extreme infrequency with which formal votes take place on specific estimates; when it comes time to decide on a particular item or the whole estimate, the chairman simply asks, 'Shall vote X, item Y carry?' whereupon a distracted 'Carried' is mumbled by all present. Nor do members make even the symbolic gesture of moving a reduction in particular sums. Even during minority government, attempts by the opposition to amend the estimates were very rare indeed, in part because, during the 1975-81 period at least, opposition members had been cowed by government threats that the slightest tinkering with any estimate was a matter of confidence that could precipitate an election. More fundamentally, though, MPPS of all parties have been socialized into believing that while the government should be made to defend or amend its policy in the course of estimates debates, it is entitled to have its spending requests passed completely intact.[45] In addition, of course, opposition members who take part in the estimates process are more likely to become exercised over too little rather than too much spending (though members in estimates committees are not permitted to move motions to increase spending, since only the cabinet has the constitutional authority to increase the estimates).

After all of the estimates assigned to the House are completed, a concurrence resolution consolidating all the earlier individual resolutions from the Committee of Supply is passed in a pro forma fashion. The procedure for House approval of estimates considered in standing committee is more involved. The committee chairman reports the estimates to the House, and an order is automatically placed on the order paper for concurrence in supply for that set of estimates. The orders for concurrence are not called for debate until very late in the session, principally to afford the opposition another 'kick at the can' in instances of estimates considered months earlier: issues of concern to the opposition may emerge after the completion of the particular set of estimates. Concurrence debates may last up to two and a half hours each, but few do; most are discharged in a few perfunctory minutes, but the opportunity for haranguing the government for an extra sitting is available should the opposition care to exercise it. Divisions are all but unknown for concurrence debates.

Following the completion of all concurrences, the way is clear for passage of the Supply Act, which provides the final legal authority for government spending. Although there is no legal requirement to do so, it has become traditional to pass the budget motion before introducing the Supply Act, which receives all three readings in a matter of minutes. In order that the government be able to spend money in anticipation of the Supply Act (which is not usually passed until nine months into the fiscal year it covers), the treasurer will, two or three times a session, present a motion for interim supply. In 1986–87, 1.8 per cent of the House's time was given over to debate on motions of interim supply (which may not be for periods longer than six months). Interim supply debates tend towards hollow ritual, though in 1981 the government brought forward its interim supply motion only one sitting day before it was required, and the Liberals' refusal to pass it in one day precipitated a minor panic, since for roughly seventy-one hours (mostly over a weekend) the government lacked the legal authority to spend money or issue cheques.[46]

Since the estimates are compiled months before the start of the fiscal year, it is often necessary for the government to obtain authorization for spending beyond that set out in the main estimates. Three methods are available to it: supplementary estimates, special warrants, and Management Board orders. Supplementary estimates for a few ministries are tabled in the fall. If the main estimates have yet to be completed, the supplementaries are simply folded in with them; otherwise, they are usually allocated a brief review in the Committee of Supply. Special warrants may be used only in restricted circumstances: the House must be prorogued (not merely recessed); the money must be urgently required; and the expenditure must fall outside existing votes and items in the estimates.[47] Only infrequently are special warrants issued: a senior treasury official described the issuance of two warrants in early 1981 as the first 'in current memory.'[48] In the wake of the 1981 election, the entire operation of the government for the first three months of fiscal 1981–82 was funded with warrants for $4.7 billion. The Liberal official opposition argued in the House that this represented a serious and possibly illegal diminution of the legislature's financial powers, but Speaker Turner ruled that it was not for the Speaker to decide on the legality of special warrants, and the issue died.[49] In 1985, owing to a May election, the House did not convene until two months of the fiscal year had passed, so that special warrants totalling $7.2 billion were required to fund government operations; because of the September 1987 election, $2.7 billion of special warrants were issued.

Management Board orders are cabinet directives authorizing expenditures beyond those set out in the estimates, where the money does fall under an existing vote and item. The legislature has absolutely no role in approving these moneys, and indeed is not officially informed of them until the provincial auditor's report is issued many months later. The standing orders require that Management Board orders be printed in the weekly *Ontario Gazette*, but even the most diligent MPPS or researchers rarely examine the bulky *Gazette* thoroughly. In 1986–87 eighty-one orders were issued for some $921 million (just under 3 per cent of total expenditure); the great bulk of orders, both in number and in dollar terms, occur within a month of the end of the fiscal year.[50]

Management Board orders may not represent so much of a threat to parliamentary control of finance as might first appear. First, a former director of legal services at the treasury has noted that 'it is the policy of Management Board of Cabinet, except where very small amounts of money are involved, not to issue an MBO when the House is sitting.'[51] The chairman of Management Board has stated that few orders actually represent new spending, and that most simply authorize the transfer of funds already included in the estimates. Most of these transfers represent either salary revisions, the precise impact of which on specific votes and items is not known when the estimates are compiled (a substantial item for salary contingencies is therefore included in the Management Board estimates), or personnel shifts within a ministry from one program to another. On a more fundamental level, since the normal estimates process in the legislature is hopelessly inadequate, it is hard to argue that in escaping legislative approval Management Board orders are significantly more of a travesty of parliamentary control.

If the estimates process is an abject failure in its ostensible purpose, which is the legislative scrutiny of government spending plans, why has reform been so slow to come? Certainly, it has not been for want of dissatisfaction with the existing process, for MPPS, ministers, and ministry staff alike regard estimates as a burdensome, futile duty. Nor has there been a shortage of reform proposals, usually variations on the theme of referring all estimates to one specialized committee, which would thoroughly examine a few sets of estimates and permit the balance to go through as a matter of course.[52] By mid-1988 momentum for a revamping of the estimates process had become formidable; a highly critical analysis had come from the provincial auditor, a special report was issued by the Public Accounts Committee recommending the creation of a new estimates committee, and a package of estimates-related reforms was presented by an informal all-party group.[53]

There are several possible explanations for the persistence of the estimates format. First, since the cost of estimates, measured in time and resources, is much higher for the government than for the opposition, the opposition is loath to allow the government off the estimates hook without substantial concessions in return. Second, the comfortable predictability of inertia and routine should not be underestimated; estimates are not the only aspect of legislative life that might be dismissed as hollow ritual that survives only because it offers a structure for members' activities. Third, a number of opposition critics are unwilling to do away with estimates because they present the critics with an ego-bolstering opportunity to be front and centre for an extended period, with the minister, deputy minister, and senior ministry officials responding to their demands and criticisms. For critics of low-profile ministries, who may participate only infrequently in question period, estimates, dreary as they may be, are the highlight of the legislative year. Finally, though it would be over-generous to attribute to MPPS a knowledge of other jurisdictions' lack of success in dealing effectively with estimates (for example, the failure of the

British Expenditure Committee of the 1970s), they do have an essentially accurate sense that no structural reforms will restore genuine parliamentary scrutiny – let alone control – of government spending.

On a more positive note, the significance of estimates in the accountability process should not be entirely discounted. It is true that no threat exists of MPPS' altering government spending; moreover, one-half to three-quarters of the money supposedly approved in estimates has often been spent before the debate begins. The real value of estimates lies in the preparation that ministers and civil servants must make for them: no one is certain what the opposition will ask, and the government must be prepared to explain and justify its policies at length in a very public forum before its principal political enemies. As is generally the case with parliamentary accountability, the estimates debates themselves are normally far less effective in fostering accountability than the fear engendered in government by their mere existence. If this seems to be damning with faint praise, so it is intended, for the estimates fall far short of any reasonable expectation of proper procedures for accountability.

With few exceptions, the evidence in this chapter demonstrates just how limited is the Ontario legislature's ability to transform policy proposals into authoritative policy decisions independent of cabinet. The legislature's almost complete lack of control over government spending and financial policy is especially noteworthy. In times of majority government the legislature's normal role in the legislative process is not much greater. To the extent that the legislature can influence the essentials rather than the details of legislation, it is by way of opposition intransigence, which forces the government to shift its position or to re-evaluate its priorities. Instances of the legislature's taking the initiative in policy development and passing the requisite legislation of its own volition are rare indeed.

Committees reviewing bills can develop a modicum of independence, certainly more than would have been normal in the 1960s and earlier, and do influence policy outcomes. The power of committees, as of the legislature generally, is obviously at its apogee under minority government. In practice this power has been tempered, since minority governments of both Liberal and Conservative stripe have become adept at minimizing the opposition's clout by successfully playing off the two opposition parties against one another.

In minority or majority governments, private members' business does

153 The legislature at work: Legislation and finances

offer a certain scope for opposition members and government backbenchers to affect policy. The limits are obvious, but, as this chapter shows, a number of instances can be cited of policies, mostly minor but some of consequence, having been shaped in some important measure by private members' bills or resolutions. This constitutes a significant advance, since for decades prior to the 1970s, private members' business was all but entirely irrelevant to the policy process.

6

Committees

Members of the Ontario legislature rightly believe that their most interesting and effective work takes place in committees. Over the past two decades many of the most important improvements in the legislature, be they carefully thought out reforms or unplanned evolutionary changes, have occurred in the realm of the committee system. Moreover, as is common elsewhere, would-be reformers tend to focus their hopes and schemes for future progress on committees. A strong committee system is the hallmark of a transformative legislature; indeed, most transformative activity in modern legislatures occurs in committees.

This chapter describes and evaluates the committee system of the Ontario legislature. It demonstrates the truth of the proposition that in many ways the real work of the legislature is done in committee, whether that work entails scrutiny of the executive and fostering of governmental accountability, the development and refinement of policy, the representation of individual and group interests to government, or the legitimization of the entire political system.

THE SETTING AND ATMOSPHERE OF COMMITTEE MEETINGS

Upon entering a committee room, the observer passes an open telephone booth, probably occupied by an MPP checking in with his office or returning phone calls. Except at the small number of committee meetings where political pyrotechnics are expected, spectators, other than prospective witnesses or civil servants involved in the work of the committee, are few; seldom are more than a dozen of the eighty or so spectators' seats filled.

Although other arrangements are sometimes used, the standard configuration of desks is E-shaped, with the open side facing the audience (and the door). Members sit on the outside of the top and bottom bars of the E and on both sides of the middle bar; witnesses are usually seated with their backs to the audience at a table at the end of and perpendicular to the middle bar of the E. The chairman sits at the centre of the vertical bar of the E (that is, directly facing the audience); to his right are the committee clerk and the Hansard interjectionist,[1] to his left the committee researchers.[2] If a minister or parliamentary assistant is taking regular part in the committee proceedings, he is seated beside the chairman, with one or two ministry staff on his left and the committee researchers beyond them. Seats are not assigned, but by custom government members occupy the seats to the chairman's right, the NDP members sit on the chairman's left, and the Liberals or Conservatives, whichever are in opposition, sit in the middle. Name-plates may be used to identify members and staff, but they are of limited assistance to spectators, who are often uncertain of the identities of the people before them. At the side of the room, between the committee and the spectators' chairs, are small tables reserved for the press.

The atmosphere of a committee meeting is more informal than that of the more dignified, controlled setting of the Chamber. The desks along which the members are arrayed are piled high with documents and coffee-cups.[3] Members do not stand while speaking, and frequently break into one another's remarks with questions or comments; they engage in sotto voce conversations (which are often not all that sotto), read newspapers and work through their correspondence seemingly oblivious to committee proceedings.[4] MPPS, committee staff, spectators, and the odd television cameraman wander freely about during meetings. During routine hearings and debates several members of the committee may be absent for extended periods, and it is not uncommon for only two or three to be actively participating in the proceedings.

Meetings almost invariably begin ten or fifteen minutes late. The chairman rarely waits for a legitimate quorum, but calls the meeting to order as soon as all three parties are represented. Indeed, one of the most important unwritten rules of committee behaviour is that nothing of any consequence is done unless members from all parties are present.[5] No limits of any kind restrict members' speaking and questioning, and pressure from fellow members or chairmanly admonitions are not always effective in curbing loquacious speakers. The rotation of speakers among parties followed in the House is not observed in committee; one simply catches the chairman's eye to be put on his list. It is open to any member to move that the committee meet in camera, but save for deliberations on reports (as discussed below), and very occasionally for exceptionally sensitive testimony, members see no need for privacy.

Partisan clashes may be every bit as rancorous and seemingly pointless as in the House, but in general the atmosphere in committees is more harmonious and conducive to co-operation. Issues are more likely to be amicably discussed on their merits. Party leadership, through a combination of benign neglect and faith in its members, allows them fairly free reign in committee without issuing detailed or explicit directives. On non-controversial matters or issues not central to party policy, it is not uncommon for members of one party to support opposing sides of a question. Because (and as a result) of this, recorded divisions in committee seldom occur.

Other explanations may be advanced for the lower degree of politicization in committee work. Reporters assiduously avoid the more tedious routine meetings, and their absence undoubtedly reduces the incentive for posturing and rhetoric. As well, the detailed nature of committee work can often admit of compromise, whereas the great debates in the House, such as those on second reading, on the budget, and on the throne speech, are generally structured along clearly defined partisan lines; moreover, unlike many committee decisions, their outcomes are foregone conclusions which no amount of reasoned argument can affect. The physical proximity of the members is certainly a factor. Though it is true that being five or ten feet away from a political opponent rather than, as in the Chamber, forty or fifty feet away, with a great no-man's-land between, can add fuel to already fiery exchanges, it is more often the case that members are less confrontational in the more intimate committee setting.[6]

Committee work, particularly that carried out over an extended time, engenders a camaraderie among members which in turn fosters a more harmonious approach and a willingness to compromise. Especially noteworthy in this context is the effect of committee travel, which throws members together for long periods, in often unfamiliar settings, and results in cross-party friendships (or at least greater mutual understanding).[7] Finally, members, particularly those who are in opposition, recognize that it is in committee that they have the greatest opportunity to influence the development of governmental policy; this inclines them to leave bluster aside and get on with serious discussions.

157 Committees

HISTORY OF THE COMMITTEE SYSTEM

From its first session the Ontario legislature has employed committees to lighten the burden of work on the House and to permit the detailed examination of particular problems. Although both existed from the outset, the select committees (temporary, with a mandate limited to a single question or policy issue) were for many years more important than the standing committees (permanent, with broad terms of reference).[8] Oliver Mowat frequently turned to select committees of the legislature for advice and ideas on policy; so too did Leslie Frost and John Robarts,[9] though it must be added that one of Frost's motives for establishing select committees was to keep his many back-benchers occupied. In many of the these select committee studies, the government was not committed to a particular policy and was genuinely seeking guidance. Accordingly, many reports from select committees over the years have had a significant influence on subsequent government policy. Select committees were also struck on occasion to inquire into charges of corruption or malfeasance against members. (Many other such allegations were referred to judicial inquiries or royal commissions, as legislative committees were often ill-suited for the dispassionate and unbiased investigation of politically controversial charges.) An indication that select committees were intended for serious business was their small membership; often they were composed of only half a dozen members, and on occasion of as few as three members.

Throughout the nineteenth century and until the 1960s, standing committees were of rather less consequence. Typically, they were very large (from forty to fifty members); they met infrequently and had relatively little business referred to them. The busiest and most important standing committees were those that dealt with private bills and railway bills. Except for such committees as Public Accounts, Private Bills and Standing Orders, standing committees were constituted according to policy areas, such as agriculture and mining. In 1964 the number of standing committees was reduced from eighteen to ten, and some were substantially reduced in size; each committee typically encompassed more than one government department. Still, these changes made little difference, for the committees were given little to do.

The workload of standing committees increased during the 1960s, as did the business of the legislature generally, and took a quantum leap in

1969 when committees began to consider departmental spending estimates. By 1970 the number of standing committees had grown again to sixteen, though the average membership had fallen to twenty-seven. In 1971, in anticipation of the reorganization of the executive into policy secretariats, the sixteen standing committees were consolidated into Procedural Affairs, Regulations, Public Accounts, and Estimates, and the three policy field committees of Legal Administration (more recently Administration of Justice), Human Resources (now Social Development), and Natural and Physical Resources (now Resources Development). Procedural Affairs and Legal Administration sitting together constituted the Private Bills Committee. No member could serve on more than one policy field committee, or on more than one of the remainder. An important change occurred at this time, when years of pressure from the opposition finally induced the government to permit the temporary substitution of members on committees by notification of the chairman rather than by order of the House. This was a great boon to the opposition parties, which were often left unrepresented in a committee if one or two of their members were ill or otherwise occupied (often in another committee).

As the policy field committees became more heavily involved in estimates, the Estimates Committee became 'Miscellaneous Estimates' and then disappeared altogether, to be replaced with the General Government Committee. This committee was given jurisdiction over ministries that did not fall under other committees (for example, Treasury and Government Services), as well as the provincial auditor, the ombudsman, and the Office of the Assembly. A Members' Services Committee was established in 1977. In 1976 the Private Bills Committee was abandoned, and for several years private bills were assigned to the appropriate policy field committee. This approach proved unsuitable, and by the mid-1980s the Regulations Committee had in effect become the new private bills committee. (It is a telling illustration of the nature of legislative change that the Regulations Committee acquired the private bills remit not through any connection between regulations and private bills, but because it simply had more time on its hands than any other committee.)

The Camp Commission proposed far-reaching reforms to the committee system. It recommended doing away with select committees, the reference of legislation to 'largish' (twenty-to twenty-five-member) ad hoc committees, the creation of small (seven- or eight-member) specialist committees to scrutinize estimates and to carry out special investigations, and the establishment of eleven-member committees on procedure and on administration.[10] These drastic proposals were greeted with hesitation. The Morrow committee, which examined the two final reports of the Camp Commission, rejected its proposals for fundamentally restructuring the committee system. Instead, it recommended that the policy field committees be increased to twenty members and that subcommittees be struck to conduct special investigations. In addition, it made a number of detailed recommendations to improve committees' effectiveness, such as granting them the authority to determine their meeting times.

In the late 1970s the Procedural Affairs Committee inherited the task of revamping the assembly's committees. In 1980 it produced a report entitled 'Proposals for a New Committee System,' which called for revolutionary reforms. Among the more important recommendations were suggestions for reductions in the size of committees, the establishment of ad hoc bills committees on the British standing committee model, open terms of reference for all committees, and the creation of an Economic Affairs Committee that would review budget documents and economic forecasts and conduct a serious if limited examination of spending estimates. The principal benefit held out to the government in the report was the proposal to establish specific bills committees, which would have substantially reduced the committee logjams that played havoc with the government's legislative program. This might have appealed in a minority setting, but was of limited interest to the majority Conservative government of 1981–85. Accordingly, the report languished unimplemented until the advent of the Liberal administration in 1985.

The strengthening of legislative committees was a key item in the May 1985 Liberal-NDP accord. The litany of reports began anew, but this time there was a widespread expectation that they would lead to genuine change. Treasurer Robert Nixon, who was government House leader and the strongest 'House-man' on the government side, issued a discussion paper, entitled 'Reforming the Budget Process' with his first budget.[11] The paper was aimed at establishing a more public budgetary process with more participation by MPPs; its central recommendations included a proposal to create a legislative committee on economic and fiscal affairs, very much in the mould of the Finance and Economic Affairs Committee suggested by Procedural Affairs in 1980. The committee would hold public pre-budget hearings, conduct the committee stage for any budget bills, review an annual government statement on the province's economic outlook, and make recommendations on the overall level of provincial revenues, expenditures, and net cash requirements, and perhaps play a role in the estimates process.

Within a month the Procedural Affairs Committee released an omnibus report on changes to the standing orders and procedures; the report contained a section on committees that was principally inspired by the 1980 report of the committee's predecessor. As is described in Chapter 9, the report was studied by the party whips, who agreed to a package of reforms that was implemented on a provisional basis in April 1986. In numerical terms most of the committee's ideas were accepted, but two of its most important proposals were rejected: the ad hoc bills committees and the reference to the Economic Affairs Committee of all estimates, six sets of which were to be reviewed every year (with the addition of six Ottawa-style 'opposition days' a year).

Structurally, the new committee system was not all that different from the old: the four policy field committees, Public Accounts, and the Regulations and Private Bills committees were continued, as was the Ombudsman Committee; the Members' Services Committee was folded in with Procedural Affairs to form the Committee on the Legislative Assembly; the agency review function was taken from Procedural Affairs and lodged in a new Government Agencies Committee; and a Standing Committee on Finance and Economic Affairs was established 'to consider and report to the House its observations, opinions and recommendations on the fiscal and economic policies of the province and to which all related documents [were referred].'[12]

The informal all-party committee that had been struck late in 1987 to negotiate a solution to the estimates imbroglio proposed a number of substantial changes to the committee system, including the establishment of an estimates committee and extensive committee review of ministry and agency activity. As of the end of 1988 these proposals had yet to be accepted by the government.[13]

TERMS OF REFERENCE AND POWERS

As was recommended by the Procedural Affairs Committee, the terms of reference for all standing committees are now incorporated into the standing orders. This is not a particularly significant advance over the old custom of appointing committees afresh at the beginning of each session with terms of reference unchanged from year to year. The same could be said of the formalization in the standing orders of the procedure by which committee substitutions are made – that is, notification in writing within thirty minutes of the beginning of a meeting (this had previously been renewed by motion every session).

The new rules provide for a maximum of eleven members on either a standing or a select committee (Procedural Affairs had recommended eight), with the proviso that membership 'shall be in proportion to the representation of the recognized parties in the House.'[14] The old standing orders limited select committees to fifteen members but made no mention of limits on standing committees or of principles of representation. In practice, however, committees have always been appointed in rough approximation to the party balance in the House, and the size of committees has usually been determined by a complex set of calculations. In recent years the number has been that which offers the best basis for dividing membership evenly in proportion to representation in the House (exclusive of the non-voting chairman) and for ensuring that the third party has at least two members on all committees, that the official opposition has more members than the third party, and that the majority or minority complexion of the House is maintained in the microcosm of the committee. Thus, in the Thirty-third Parliament, to which were elected 52 Conservatives, 48 Liberals, and 25 New Democrats, committees had 11 members (4 Conservatives, 4 Liberals, and 2 New Democrats plus the chairman); in the Thirty-second Parliament committees had 12 members (6 Conservatives, 3 Liberals, and 2 New Democrats, plus the chairman), reflecting a House of 70 Conservatives, 34 Liberals, and 21 New Democrats. It may thus be confidently predicted that the standing order specifying the maximum number of MPPS will regularly be amended in tandem with changes in the composition of the House.[15]

No formal proscription exists, but it has been some years since ministers served on committees. From time to time a minister is substituted in a committee in order to move a money amendment to a bill.

The 1980 Procedural Affairs report proposed that all committees have open terms of reference, along the lines of those given British select committees in 1979, so that, without approval from the House, committees might inquire into any matter within their jurisdiction. (The specialist committees, such as Public Accounts and Members' Services, already enjoyed the freedom to look into anything within their ambit.) Curiously, given the example of the federal government, which had already agreed to the McGrath Committee's recommendation that committees be free to instigate inquiries without authorization from the House,[16] the 1986 Ontario reforms, which followed the 1985 Procedural Affairs report, came at this key issue in a sideways, half-a-loaf manner. In 1977 the Liberal opposition discovered that it could place an issue of its choosing before a committee by using a standing order (which was never designed for such a purpose) that allowed a petition of twenty members to refer a ministry's or agency's annual report to a committee. The annual report reference was simply a vehicle for an opposition party to circumvent the House and legitimize a committee inquiry into a specific policy issue. During the 1978 revision of the rules, the government was successful in stipulating that only 'statutory' annual reports would be subject to this procedure. Statutory annual reports were construed to be those required by statute (or, later, mentioned in a statute).[17] Since many agencies, boards, and commissions and some ministries are not required by law to table their reports, this had the effect of restricting somewhat the scope of the annual-report gambit. The new standing orders provide for automatic referral to the appropriate committee of statutory annual reports, and thereby eliminate the need for a formal petition while leaving the policy field committees no closer to having open mandates than before. The Procedural Affairs Committee recommended that the government bring in legislation requiring all ministries and agencies to present annual reports to the House, but the government has so far taken no such action.[18]

One of the new standing orders empowers committees to travel within Ontario and to hire staff subject to the budgetary approval of the Board of Internal Economy. Previously, formal orders of the House were required for such undertakings, though these were routine; if committees were prevented from travelling within the province or from hiring staff – a rare if not unknown occurrence – it was because the board balked, not because there was no proper motion in the House. Another of the new rules gives committees the power 'to send for persons, papers and things' in accordance with section 35 of the Legislative Assembly Act, 'except where the House otherwise orders.' Save this last proviso, the intent of which is obscure,[19] this is the formula that was regularly approved by motion in the House before the new rules were put into place, and merely confirms existing procedure.

In utilizing this power, committees normally request that witnesses – ministers, civil servants, or others – appear or ask for certain documents. Most such requests are granted. A committee whose request is not honoured is usually satisfied with the explanation proffered for non-attendance or non-production of papers, or else is not inclined to pursue the matter. A committee does, however, have the option of requesting a Speaker's warrant compelling attendance. This is a powerful weapon, since failure to comply with a warrant is a contempt of the House under section 45 of the Legislative Assembly Act, and is punishable by the House. The issuance of a Speaker's warrant, which is more than slightly out of the ordinary, normally follows a report from the committee and its adoption by the House.[20] Committees that sit while the House is recessed could be seriously handicapped in their attempts to secure warrants by this procedure, and they are sometimes empowered to go directly to the Speaker with a request for a warrant. This power to make direct requests of the Speaker for warrants was formerly given willy-nilly to all committees that were to sit during a recess,[21] but recently it has been bestowed more sparingly; for the summer recess in 1986, for example, of the ten committees authorized to meet, only two were so empowered. During the 1975–81 period of minority government, and particularly in the last two years, the opposition made effective use of Speaker's warrants to ensure the appearance of recalcitrant witnesses, to obtain confidential financial statements from private corporations, and to force the government to produce documents (such as public opinion polls and seized records of failed trust companies) it wished to keep secret.

Although Speaker's warrants have no force outside the province, within Ontario they can compel the production of highly sensitive documents from private citizens and corporations as well as from government, and can be employed to force the attendance of virtually any witness before a committee.[22] This sweeping power applies only to the documents and witnesses that are relevant to a committee's terms of reference; this limit scarcely constrains a determined committee, however, for by long-standing parliamentary convention the committee itself interprets its terms of reference.[23] In this as in other important ways, legislative committees, which may (especially to the legal fraternity) appear quasi-judicial in their proceedings and terminology, are not at all like courts of law. Legislative committees can simultaneously act as prosecuting attorney, judge, and jury, with no necessary presumption that anyone will pay heed to the precepts of justice or fairness. Circumstances calling forth committees' inquisitorial tendencies are not common; when they do arise, however, it may well be true that, in the words of one aggrieved lawyer representing a client who was questioned by a committee, 'they call themselves the highest court in the land, but you get more justice in small claims court.'[24]

Although several pages of the standing orders are now devoted to committees, almost none of the legislature's formal rules speak to the way in which committees are actually to operate. Standing order 94 states, with magnificent ambivalence, that the rules of the House are to be observed in committee 'so far as may be applicable.' Thus, within rather broad limits, committees are free to determine their own procedures. It is always open to the House to specify in which order a committee is to deal with the various items of business before it, or the way in which it is to approach a given reference (for example, limits on the time devoted to public hearings), but such mandatory directions are rare. Among the procedural questions that are left to committee's discretion are decisions to limit or altogether forgo public presentations; to set limits on time allocated to members' questions; to meet in camera; to offer honoraria or expenses to witnesses; to permit witnesses' legal counsel to take part in committee proceedings; and to permit MPPS who are not members of the committee to participate in debates. Given this substantial potential for variation, it is an indication of the force of convention and the power of established folkways that very few differences are evident in these or other procedural matters within the committees' province.

One organizational matter within the committees' discretion does vary substantially from one committee to the next: the use of subcommittees. The most frequent use of subcommittees is in the organization of committee business, most commonly for special studies. Recourse to subcommittees is far from uniform, however. Subcommittees may be called upon to draft reports and to hear evidence outside Toronto. On one memorable day the Social Development Committee split, amoebalike, into four subcommittees which were dispatched to far corners of the province to hold public hearings. Subcommittees are usually composed of the committee chairman and one representative of each party; their business tends to be transacted in an informal fashion.

SELECT AND STANDING COMMITTEES

The once-clear distinction between standing and select committees has become decidedly blurred. Some minor points of difference remain, but in all essentials one may speak of 'committees' without concern for the appropriate adjective. In the recent past, select committees had limited mandates to study specific policy areas or to investigate particular allegations; occasionally they reviewed legislation, but never estimates. Once their tasks were completed, they reported and disbanded. Further, select committees met only when the House was not in session, and they often had professional staff, usually a committee counsel. Substitution was not permitted, and they tended to be small (in the 1940s and 1950s, select committees of three or five members were not uncommon). In contrast, standing committees were large, were more or less permanent, dealt only with bills and with estimates, met only when the House was in session, had no research staff, and were characterized by wholesale substitution. Now, however, all committees conduct special inquiries, engage expert staff, meet extensively when the House is not in session, are of similar size, and are subject to the same substitution rule. Even the most astute observer would be unable to detect any differences between meetings of standing or select committees, for the very good reason that there are none.[25] Almost all the standing orders dealing with committees are couched in terms of 'standing and select committees.' Still, a few differences persist. Select committees are almost never asked to review estimates or legislation, and only infrequently meet while the House is in session; unlike the chairmen of standing committees, who according to standing order 88 are appointed in proportion to party standings in the House, the chairmen of select committees are usually specified in the motion establishing the membership of the committee; and, finally, chairmen of select committees do not receive the extra allowance paid to chairmen of standing committees. Although it may be premature to offer definitive judgments, the day of the semi-permanent select committee appears to be over (the life of the Select Committee on Economic and Cultural Nationalism extended over four years in the early 1970s; the Select Committee on Ontario Hydro spanned most of the 1975– 81 minority government period, and the Select Committee on Company Law existed in one form or another from 1965 until the 1980s).

Five select committees existed during the 1986–87 session. The Select Committee on Economic Affairs completed its examination of the province's stake in and strategy with respect to free trade with the United States. The Select Committee on Energy was primarily concerned with the question whether to proceed with the massive Darlington nuclear power station. The Select Committee on Health reviewed commercial health services. Select committees on the environment and on Sunday shopping were struck late in the session, and held only organizational meetings before the session ended.

166 The Ontario legislature

COMMITTEE ACTIVITIES

Like Caesar's Gaul, all committee activities are divided into three parts: legislation, estimates review, and special studies. Special studies, which are examined in detail below, encompass any work done by committees not specifically tied to estimates or to specific bills. Table 6.1 presents data on committee activities for the 1986–87 session, and shows not only the overall extent of committee work but also the time devoted to various committee functions. The table covers all committee meetings during the second session of the Thirty-third Parliament and the interval between the second and third sessions – in effect, a year (from 22 April 1986 to 16 April 1987). The entry in the first column indicates the number of days on which a committee met. The next six columns show the number of (average) two-hour sittings devoted to various pursuits;[26] the totals of these columns invariably exceed the number of meeting days, since on many days committees held two or (exceptionally) three sittings. The final column shows the mean number of substitutions of members per meeting-day. Sessions identified as public hearings were those principally given over to presentations by and the questioning of witnesses, whereas 'other' sessions were devoted to organization, to deliberation on reports, or to discussions entirely within the committee. Sittings at which legislation was considered on a clause-by-clause basis are also indicated separately (all meetings of the Regulations and Private Bills Committee dealing with bills combined public hearings with clause-by-clause scrutiny). Subcommittee meetings, which would have numbered two or three dozen, are not included in the table.

The picture that emerges is one of intense activity: close to 600 meetings constituting nearly 1,700 hours of committee work. The lion's share of committee time, roughly 53 per cent, was devoted to public hearings on legislation and special studies. 'Special studies' were defined to include everything other than legislation or estimates; if the hearings conducted on routine matters and on the conflict-of-interest inquiries by the Public Accounts, Ombudsman, Legislative Assembly, and Government Agencies committees are removed, just under 28 per cent of all committee activities involved the study of policy issues other than those arising out of legislation or estimates. Far more time was devoted to legislation than to estimates; less than 12 per cent of committee meetings were spent in estimates review, whereas 31 per cent of meetings dealt with legislation.

The table shows substantial variation in the extent and range of

TABLE 6.1
Committee activity in the 1986–87 session

	Meeting days	Sittings					Estimates	Subs
		Special studies		Legislation				
		PH	O	PH	CC	O		
Economic Affairs*	20	20	13	–	–	–	–	2.6
Energy*	3	–	3	–	–	–	–	1.0
Environment*	13	21	3	–	–	–	–	2.9
Finance	45	50	13	2	–	–	–	1.8
General Government	44	2	5	35	6	2	13	1.7
Government Agencies	29	19	17	–	–	–	–	1.6
Health*	20	21	8	–	–	–	–	2.6
Justice	62	–	–	37	31	4	12	2.5
Legislative Assembly	69	24	66	11	4	–	2	2.4
Ombudsman	20	15	15	–	–	–	2	1.4
Public Accounts	55	63	20	–	–	–	–	2.6
Regulations	21	–	3	–	16	2	–	1.6
Resource Development	95	33	21	59	7	1	25	2.1
Social Development	77	–	1	14	27	2	43	1.4
Store Hours*	15	21	2	–	–	–	–	1.8
Total	573	289	188	158	91	11	97	2.1
Percentages	–	34.6	22.5	18.9	10.9	1.3	11.9	–

PH, public hearings; O, other; CC, clause by clause; Subs, average number of substitutions per meeting
*Select committee

committee activity. The select committees were the least busy, followed by the specialist standing committees (Ombudsman, Regulations, Government Agencies, and Finance), and the policy field committees (Justice, Social and Resources). Normally, the workload of the Public Accounts and Legislative Assembly committees would have been similar to that of the other specialist standing committees, but in the summer of 1986 both met extensively to consider conflict-of-interest allegations against former ministers. The Resources Development Committee met on 95 days over the course of the year, a remarkable figure considering that when weekends and statutory holidays are removed, there are only about 250 working days in a year. The only committees that handled more than a trivial amount of estimates were the policy field committees, which also did most of the work in relation to legislation. Of the four policy field committees, only the Resources Committee also found the time to engage substantially in special studies.

The table also reveals the extent of substitution: the average committee meeting had 2.1 substitutes; certain committees averaged almost 3 substitutes. Even on the doubtful assumption of full attendance, this represented nearly one-quarter of the committee, though it is true that it was common for the same members to be regularly substituted on particular committees for extended periods. Substitution has come to be looked upon as a necessary (indeed, an immutable) evil required by the overlap of committee schedules and the conflicting demands on MPPS' time. Its drawbacks are as obvious as its benefits, however: the need to repeat previous discussions for the substitute members; impediments to the development of a committee's corporate identity and to the prospect of its assuming a consensual approach to a problem; and the frequency with which committee decisions are reached by members who may not have been present for key testimony or discussions (a situation likened by one member to having a trial with several different judges presiding). The ease of substitution and its effective control by the party whips render it a useful device for removing troublesome committee members, particularly government members, when they might embarrass the party; it is not unknown for members to turn up for a meeting only to discover that more 'reliable' members have been substituted for them.

While the House is in session a formal schedule determines when the committees meet during the week. The policy field committees are entitled to meet two or three times a week; the other committees are given only one block of time. With authorization from the House, committees may meet evenings (or at any other time, for that matter), but this happens only a few times a year, usually close to the summer adjournment or the Christmas prorogation. Fridays are kept clear of committee meetings, as are Monday mornings, in deference to out-of-town members, and Tuesday mornings are reserved for the party caucuses. By convention, committee meetings are called for 10:00 AM or after routine proceedings (approximately 3:00 PM); it is almost unheard of for meetings to begin on time. Most meetings last from two to two and a half hours.

A day or two before the House adjourns or prorogues, a motion is passed authorizing various committees to meet for specific purposes.

169 Committees

Spurred on in part by the per diem payments and allowances payable for attending committee meetings when the House is not in session, committee members are often eager to meet extensively during recesses. Simple logistics, among other things, requires that, after consulting the committee chairmen, the party whips and House leaders work out a schedule for committee meetings, which is then made binding on the committees by an order of the House. With the agreement of the whips and House leaders additional meetings may be scheduled, but this is not a regular occurrence. During recess, committee sittings are scheduled for Tuesday, Wednesday, and Thursday at 10:00 AM and 2:00 PM, with the lunch break beginning anytime after noon. Monday and Friday meetings are not unknown, and except when committees are travelling to hear submissions, evening meetings are rare.

SPECIAL STUDIES

Perhaps the greatest strength of the Ontario committee system lies in its special studies. Anything done by committees that is neither legislation nor estimates is categorized as 'special studies.' A useful distinction may none the less be drawn between what might be termed routine studies (carried out by the standing specialist committees, flowing directly out of their mandates, often focusing on administrative concerns, and retrospective in nature) and studies of particular policy issues by select committees or policy field committees (aimed at developing future government policy). Among the former can be counted the review by Public Accounts of matters raised in the provincial auditor's report, the examination of the operations of particular agencies, boards, and commissions, by the Government Agencies Committee, and the Legislative Assembly Committee's consideration of the rules and practices of the House. The latter category includes the inquiry by the Standing Committee on Economic Affairs into free trade, the Social Development Committee's studies on family violence, and the reviews of workers' compensation policy by the Resources Development Committee.

Special studies of policy issues may have their genesis in government-initiated orders of reference, in the use by opposition parties of the annual-report ruse, or in the activities of private members. Often, committee references authorized by government motion represent in some measure an acquiescence to opposition pressure; the establishment of the Select Committee on Plant Shutdowns and Economic Adjustments in 1980 and the two 1986 committee inquiries into ministerial conflicts of interest are cases in point. Other government-initiated studies reflect a genuine desire on the government's part to have a legislative committee take hold of an issue; the reference to the Finance and Economic Affairs Committee of the question of corporate concentration, the General Government Committee's review of provincial legislation relating to teachers' strikes, and the establishment of the Select Committee on Health to look into commercial health services are all examples from the 1986–87 session. Several major committee inquiries have taken the form of reviews of reports of royal commissions or government-commissioned task forces; among these are the Select Committee on Pensions, the Resources Development Committee's studies in the early 1980s of the Weiler reports on workers' compensation, and the review in 1983 of the Child and Family Services Act draft legislation and background paper issued by the Ministry of Community and Social Services.

To say that the government is eager to have a legislative committee conduct a special study into a policy question is by no means equivalent to suggesting that the government is thus turning the policy-development function over to committees of MPPs. To be sure, this does sometimes happen when the government has no firm direction in mind and wants the advice of practical politicians who can work through a problem with the benefit of public participation. Liberal and Conservative governments have proved themselves adroit at using committee inquiries for their own political purposes. These may include involving opposition members in the policy process to thwart possible future criticisms, or to get them to commit themselves to a clearly defined position on a controversial issue; legitimizing a potentially unpopular decision by appearing to defer to the recommendations reached by an all-party committee after a detailed public hearing process (such is the interpretation often placed upon the Liberal government's delaying its decision on the completion of the Darlington nuclear station until the Select Committee on Energy reported); and using a committee to mobilize support behind a government objective (the committee studying the Canada-U.S. free trade agreement served as a useful foil in the Ontario government's confrontations with the federal government over this question).

Opposition-initiated committee studies combine a desire to embarrass or discredit the government with attempts at promoting causes and policies. Particularly in times of minority government, when the government loses almost all control over committee activities, the opposition parties have a chance to gain political mileage on issues of their own choosing.

As with most other aspects of legislative life in Ontario, the instigation of committee studies largely reflects the wishes and the priorities of the parties; yet some scope does exist for individual members to initiate committee inquiries. No private member could be successful in mounting a committee study over the objections of his party, but some members have had pet projects realized in studies to which their parties would not likely have given high priority. Some of the most effective committee studies conducted in recent years were the inquiries into aspects of family violence, particularly wife-battering and child abuse, held by the Social Development Committee, which were sparked by the enthusiasm and perseverance of Richard Johnston, an NDP member. The mechanism he employed was the annual-report referral, but this was clearly an individual rather than a party project. Private members' resolutions have been used by both government and opposition members to authorize committees to hold inquiries into such topics as the role of the assembly in protecting international political rights and the problem of missing children.

The format of special studies strongly resembles the public-hearing phase of committee consideration of legislation. The committee calls for briefs and expert testimony through advertisements and selective invitations, holds public hearings, and, if appropriate, travels throughout the province or elsewhere to receive briefs or to meet with experts or practitioners in other jurisdictions. Depending on the nature of the subject at hand and the degree to which the committee's thinking has crystallized, the committee may issue an interim report containing particularly urgent recommendations or setting out its preliminary views and calling for public reaction to them.[27] The length of special studies varies according to the complexity of the issues involved, the demand by interest groups for hearings, the press of other business before the committee, and of course the political motivations of the parties and committee members. Exceptionally, the studies may last for only a week or two, but several months is more typical, and time spans of over a year from the initial reference to the final report are not uncommon.

Unquestionably, some committee inquiries have had a substantial effect on government policy. Though they were not accepted in their entirety, the reports of the Social Development Committee on family violence affected not only the content of government policy, but also the priority accorded the issue on the government's agenda and in its spending decisions. Other committees whose reports have directly influenced policy in recent years are the select committees on company law, on Ontario Hydro, and on highway safety; the General Government Committee, which succeeded in thwarting the government's plans to integrate the Ontario Institute for Studies in Education into the University of Toronto; and the Resources Development Committee, which examined workers' compensation policy in depth. Not all committee inquiries enjoy such success. The Select Committee on Plant Shutdowns and Economic Adjustment had little discernible impact on government policy; the same can be said for the report of the Ombudsman Committee on international political rights. With few exceptions, the inquiries that leave the greatest mark on policy outcomes are those that focus on issues on which the parties have no established positions, or on naturally non-partisan issues such as family violence or child welfare. In such inquiries it is often difficult to discern from behaviour in committee or from views on specific proposals which members are government and which are opposition; the government tends to treat these serious attempts at working towards improved policy seriously. In contrast, when committees become partisan battlegrounds over issues of party dogma, the government is much less receptive to ideas coming from any members other than its own.

Persuading the government to adopt their recommendations by force of argument is not the only way in which committees can influence policy. By bringing to public attention policies the government is uncomfortable defending, committee inquiries can effect changes in policy which the government might not have otherwise made. Nor should the educational function of legislative committees be ignored; the private members serving on committees engaged in special studies can develop formidable expertise in policy as well as an understanding of problems, which may become important when they move into cabinet. In terms of having a direct affect on government policy, the Select Committee on Plant Shutdowns and Economic Adjustment was an abject failure;[28] however, it may have had a more subtle influence. One of the Conservative members of the committee, who went on to become the minister of labour, attributed his interest in a number of policy initiatives addressing the plight of workers who lose their jobs through plant shutdowns to his experience on the committee.[29]

One strategy for influencing policy that is seldom used by committees is a thorough follow-up of earlier recommendations. The Ombudsman Committee uses this technique to good advantage, and brings officials before it, year after year if need be, to report on their progress in implementing past committee recommendations. The Public Accounts Committee has recently instituted more vigorous follow-up procedures, and the Government Agencies Committee publishes government responses to previous recommendations. Rarely, though, do other committees even attempt to keep track of the government's acceptance or rejection of their proposals, let alone ask for formal progress reports or call ministers or officials before them to discuss their reaction to past reports. Select committees, which often disband after reporting, may not be able to monitor the fate of their recommendations, but other committees could certainly enhance their influence through judicious follow-up procedures.

THE COMMITTEE CHAIRMAN

Conventional wisdom portrays the chairman of a u.s. congressional committee as a feudal baron holding unrivalled sway over his fief, and the chairman of a British committee as a neutral arbiter who does little except keep order. Both views are oversimplified and increasingly inaccurate, and neither is analogous to the key position of committee chairman in the Ontario legislature. The chairman has a substantial array of subtle yet effective powers. Though his impact may be much less evident than that of an opposition chairman, a chairman from the government side can be quite effective in keeping contentious issues out of harm's way and in expediting the government's program.

In formal terms the chairman's powers are sharply limited: except in the event of a tie, he is not entitled to vote; all of his rulings are subject to appeal; and he cannot discipline members of the committee, but must rely on his committee to report to the House any grave breaches of order. His influence is in part a reflection of his skill in running a meeting – knowing how and when to cut members off, how to steer debate towards or away from certain topics, how to draw consensus out of disparate viewpoints. The chairman's power stems principally from the fact that he is, by default, left with the responsibility for organizing the committee's affairs. Other committee members lack the time and the inclination to take the lead, and are usually content to react to proposals as they are presented to them. This is not to suggest that committee members will not take an active and keen interest in the approach taken to important or controversial issues. On less crucial matters, however, the chairman's guidance of committee business tends to prevail, and the cumulative effect of small, unseen decisions may be very significant.

The chairman directs the preparation of the committee budget by the clerk, and is responsible for presenting and defending it before the Board of Internal Economy. The chairman also has signing authority for committee bills and members' expense accounts. A more important chairmanly prerogative is the responsibility for setting committee agendas: topics and witnesses set down by the chairman for consideration will be discussed and heard, whereas those he omits will not. To be sure, a member's desire to examine a particular topic or to hear a particular witness usually will be accommodated, but most members on most committees tend to accept the agendas put before them.

Though the chairman is by no means given carte blanche, he is often the key figure in the acquisition of committee staff. Moreover, although committee staff are responsive to requests from all members, in practice they take their instructions from the chairman. Committee reports are usually prepared under his direction, and though draft reports are subject to keen scrutiny and often to wholesale revision by committee members, they can nevertheless be a powerful device for structuring discussion, merely in terms of the issues they highlight or fail to mention.

To a certain extent these subtle sources of influence have been reduced by the use of subcommittees, particularly steering committees that set schedules and subcommittees that oversee the preparation of draft reports. Not all committees employ such subcommittees, and even on those that do the chairman can exert a disproportionate influence. One potentially important source of such influence is the chairman's style in leading the questioning of witnesses or in guiding discussion. Some chairmen to take a very active role during meetings; others are content to remain passive. Active participation in committee proceedings by a chairman may conflict with his responsibility as a neutral presiding officer. Most chairmen are sensitive to this dilemma and strive to be fair, if not always perfectly neutral.

One of the great innovations of minority government in the 1970s was the appointment of a large number of committee chairman from the ranks of the opposition. Before this, only the chairman of the Public Accounts Committee had been a member of the opposition, a tradition begun in the late 1960s. The return of majority government put an end to opposition chairmen, except on that committee. Following the recommendation of the Procedural Affairs Committee report, the 1986 rules institutionalized opposition chairmanships: committee chairs are to be distributed in proportion to party standings in the House. As is the case in Quebec, the mechanics of allocating chairmanships among parties is not left to interparty negotiation, but is spelled out in the standing orders. The polite fiction is maintained in standing order 89 that committees elect their own chairmen, but in fact the House leaders orchestrate the chairmanships. Standing order 88(b) formalizes the custom of an official opposition member's chairing the Public Accounts Committee; the chairmanship of the Finance and Economic Affairs Committee is reserved for a supporter of the government. The standing orders are virtually silent on vice-chairmen, an indication of their minor role: they usually come from the same party as the chairmen, and do little beyond filling in for absent chairmen. They receive no extra pay.

Though it is crucial to the effective operation of the committees, the position of committee chairman carries little of the prestige that characterizes chairmanships in Britain and the United States; nor is a chairmanship viewed as part of a parliamentary career structure, as some have advocated for Ottawa.[30] Thus, though merit undoubtedly plays a part in the selection of chairmen, baser motives are also at work. With an entitlement of an extra $4,600 a year, plus an extra $10 per diem, an element of patronage inevitably attaches to the distribution of chairmanships. Accordingly, some MPPS are chosen by their parties (which is to say by the party leadership) to chair committees for their ability and their interest in the committees' business, but others are chosen because they are owed a favour. There is a high turnover in chairmen, and a chairman with more than two or three years's experience at the helm of the same committee is something of a rarity. All of this contributes to the very uneven quality of committee chairmen. Nor is there much by way of training to compensate for lack of experience or ability; periodic meetings have been convened by the Speaker or the clerk to instruct chairmen and to discuss common problems, but they have proved largely unsuccessful.[31] On a positive note, if some chairmen lack competence or effectiveness, and few shed their partisan stripe entirely, virtually none may be fairly accused of overt or blatant partisanship, a statement that could not have been made fifteen or twenty years ago.

RESOURCES

The most important resource of a legislative committee is its staff. Until the late 1970s, with the exception of select committees, which often engaged their own counsel (often lawyers who were friendly to the government) or seconded civil servants, most committees had no research staff. All committees had clerks, but their functions were and are administrative and procedural: they keep the committee's records, organize the paperwork and the travel, and advise the chairman and the members on procedure. Moreover, as late as the 1950s, newspaper reporters were often hired as clerks to committees; not the least of the reasons why this was unsatisfactory was the journalists' propensity to abandon the committees if a good story broke.

By the mid-1970s it was becoming apparent that the committees' new activism and the members' heightened expectations required a higher level of staff assistance. The Procedural Affairs Committee hired a full-time researcher to assist it in finding its way through the thicket of semi-independent agencies it was to examine, and the Regulations Committee hired a retired registrar of regulations, on a part-time basis, to vet regulations for it. The most significant step, however, was the establishment in 1979 of the Legislative Library's research service, modelled on the research branch of the Library of Parliament. Initially hesitant about getting involved with committees, in part because the four researchers were hard-pressed to keep up with requests from individual MPPS, the research unit was soon providing staff to several standing and select committees. As much as half the time of the twelve researchers (political scientists, lawyers, economists, urban planners, and other professionals) in the research unit is now devoted to committee work. Specialist committees such as Public Accounts and Government Agencies have researchers assigned to them on a permanent basis; the policy field committees and select committees make requests for research help for particular bills or studies and are assigned a researcher or two on a temporary basis. Committees rarely take on a special study or a major piece of legislation without arranging for a library researcher, but they do not use them for estimates review.

To describe the work done by committee staff as 'research' is to use that word in a somewhat limited sense. Committee researchers do very little original or primary research; instead, they summarize and codify oral and written presentations; they prepare briefing notes on particular issues on the basis of secondary sources or information culled from authorities in the civil service, academe, and elsewhere; they locate and distil publicly available data requested by individual MPPS; and they draft and redraft committee reports under the direction of the chairman. These are invaluable services without which no committee could function effectively, and which are beyond the abilities or resources of most members. As servants of the assembly whose work has come to be recognized for its high quality and political neutrality, committee researchers avoid the suspicion of partisan taint that would inevitably accompany research provided by MPPs' or party staff.

The researchers from the library research unit have made a tremendous difference in the professionalism and effectiveness of committee work, but they do suffer from a serious limitation. They are for the most part passive and reactive, and respond to the wishes and directions of the committee and its members rather than taking an active role in suggesting lines of inquiry or guiding the committee along new paths. To some extent this reflects their lack of expertise in the areas under consideration; but more fundamental is their status as permanent employees of the assembly who must be careful about taking too active a role lest their neutrality be called into question. This style contrasts markedly with the approach characteristic of the lawyers in private practice who worked for select committees, and who were aggressive, confrontational, and activist. Whereas library researchers rarely speak during committee meetings, and do so guardedly if called upon, committee counsel often led evidence as if they were before a court or a royal commission; spectators (and MPPs themselves) could be forgiven for wondering on occasion whether the counsel were working for the committee or vice versa. Since the advent of the research service, committees have rarely engaged their own outside counsel, not least because of the staggering legal bills run up by some committees in the late 1970s, which provoked a vigorous reaction from the Board of Internal Economy. One committee that continues to retain outside counsel is the Ombudsman Committee. As is discussed in Chapter 8, this committee's singular mandate requires of its staff not only considerable expertise (the current counsel has been with the committee since its creation in 1976) but also the ability and the inclination to confront forcefully – and in public – senior civil servants and representatives of the ombudsman. It is not realistic to expect assembly staff to take on such a role.

The old custom of seconding civil servants to work for committees (as opposed to giving formal testimony and providing information to committee staff) has been almost entirely abandoned. In 1981–82 the Select Committee on Pensions seconded the province's superintendent of pensions as an expert adviser, but this was an unusual arrangement. Aside from the substantial demands on the civil servants' time that secondments can entail, they tend to create awkward situations that border on conflict of interest: civil servants work for the government, but committee staff work for all three political parties.

The 1985 report of the Procedural Affairs Committee proposed that an alternative source of committee staff be established in a new committees branch within the Clerk's Office. In addition to supervising committee staff on short-term contracts, this bureau would supply lawyers, economists, and other professionals to House committees. To tie committees entirely to the legislative research service for their staffing needs would, in the words of the report, 'limit flexibility and reduce opportunity for innovative staffing alternatives.'[32] Though this may be true, the recommendation, which has yet to be acted upon, holds the potential for destructive bureaucratic infighting if two similar organizations find themselves in competition for the limited trade in committee research.

As committee activities have grown in scope and complexity, the duties of the committee clerk have become increasingly administrative. It is now not uncommon for especially busy committees to have two clerks, and the offices of the committee clerks have in effect become the committee offices. The committees have clerical assistance and access to photocopying and word processing services through the clerks. Other assembly personnel who serve committees, such as Hansard reporters and, more recently, translators, are assigned to committees on a pool basis and are not considered committee staff. The same may be said, though for slightly different reasons, of lawyers from the Office of the Legislative Counsel who may be present in committee when legislation is being considered; except in the case of private bills, counsel attend in the capacity of the government's legal draftsmen and not as servants of the committee.

Other committee resources tend to be routine and unexceptional – meeting rooms, coffee service, and the like. An important resource that is now taken for granted but that was either unknown or rudimentary a decade ago is the transcription of committee proceedings. Only the proceedings of committees reviewing estimates are regularly printed in the typeset format of the House Hansard; on other occasions the House may order that such full service be provided for other committees. Virtually all committees exercise their option to have their meetings transcribed. The transcripts are produced in a word-processed format. These documents are unofficial and do not carry the imprimatur of the formal Hansard. When several committees are sitting at once during recesses, it may be days before transcripts are available; in urgent situations they can be produced in a matter of hours. Committee transcripts, often erroneously referred to as 'instant Hansard,' are not widely distributed; only about fifty copies are usually printed for the committee's use. They are public documents, available to anyone who requests them, but they are not included in the package of House and estimates committee Hansards offered to the public on a subscription basis, nor are they distributed to libraries or other institutions on the government's depository list. The Hansard service and the assembly generally are loath to authorize the extra money that would be required to print and distribute committee Hansards. The low demand for committee documents is often cited as justification for their limited distribution, though it would be fair to add that individuals and organizations cannot demonstrate an interest in documents of whose existence they are unaware.[33] Questions of distribution notwithstanding, the value to committees of their having a permanent record of the evidence before them and of their deliberations cannot be underestimated; serious committee work without transcripts is all but unimaginable.

REPORTS

Committee reports are of two varieties: routine and substantive. Routine reports are those on estimates and legislation. No standing order or ruling from the chair prohibits committees from incorporating into their reports on estimates observations and commentary, as has been the case in Ottawa. Doubtless owing to the generally accepted futility of the committee review of estimates, no committee has ever thought to go beyond the formula approval of estimates in its reports. With respect to legislation, it is widely accepted that it would be out of order for committees to offer in their reports anything beyond the text of the bill being reported back. (On rare occasions, a committee is permitted by special order of the House to make an additional report on the subject-matter of a particular bill.) Reports on bills are dealt with immediately, and reports on estimates are automatically placed on the order paper to await concurrence.

Substantive reports, which is to say all other reports, take a number of forms and may come before the House in several different ways. Some are no more than a line or a paragraph; others run to hundreds of pages. Some contain no recommendations; others may contain dozens of recommendations, with or without considerable explanatory verbiage. The days of hardcover reports with glossy photos of the committee members are long gone; most reports are inexpensively produced word-processed texts with cerlox binding. In the early 1980s the Social Development Committee issued several of its major reports on family violence in both French and English, but most reports are issued in English only. The format and content of a report are left entirely to the discretion of the committee. Similarly, deadlines for the issuance of reports are in most cases generated within the committee, though occasionally the House will set a specific deadline in its order of reference for a committee; and, of course, the government may informally press for committees to report sooner rather than later.

For many years committees routinely met in camera to deliberate on their reports, but recently it has become common practice to conduct these sessions in public. One approach has the virtue of avoiding unnecessary posturing and promoting genuine give and take among committee members; the other avoids the appearance of secrecy. Most committees still prefer to write their reports behind closed doors, but the choice is up to the committee. When reports are considered in camera, it is considered irregular – indeed, a breach of privilege – for anyone to make public their contents before they are tabled in the House.[34] None the less, reports with any news value are often leaked to the press. Such leaks occasion much breast-beating and the odd investigation by a committee, which inevitably fails to unmask the culprit; none of this halts the practice.[35] Of course, for committees that deliberate in public, the issue of leaks does not arise.

In Ontario as elsewhere, the proper procedure is for the chairman, and only the chairman, to sign a report on behalf of the committee. By custom however, all members of a committee may sign the report. Procedural purists frown at such an impropriety, in which not all committees engage, but there are two good reasons for its continuation. First, many members take considerable pride in their committee work and like to emphasize their participation by signing the report, particularly if their committee has been successful in obtaining a unanimity. In a less noble vein, members can effectively pillory their opponents by pointing to the opponents' signatures on controversial reports (which may not have seemed controversial at the time).

The standing orders clearly state that no minority reports are to be countenanced, although 'dissenting opinions' are permitted. This distinction is lost on most MPPs, who rightly recognize that written dissents can be used as minority reports; comprehensive fifteen- to twenty-page dissents are not common, but neither are they unknown. Although, so far as is known, no committee had refused to permit a member to include a dissent in its report, the new rules make it mandatory for committees to include in their reports the dissenting opinions of any members who care to register them. By their very nature dissents are unpalatable to all, and committees may expend substantial effort in arriving at a set of recommendations that all members can support.

Until the mid-1970s the standard procedure was for substantive reports to be presented to the House and then left to languish. Even reports that succeeded in affecting government policy usually received no treatment in the House. During the minority government era, however, it became common for committee chairmen to attempt to have the House concur in their committees' reports. Although traditionalists objected that the very notion of calling on the House to approve a committee report was irregular, a formal procedure was eventually developed. A committee now has three options in reporting to the House, and will instruct the chairman as to its preference. First, as in the past, a report may simply be presented to the House with no call for further action. Second, the chairman may present the report and ask that it be placed on the order paper for consideration. This entails a subsequent debate, to be called at the discretion of the government House leader, which ends without a vote. The third possibility has become the favourite of modern committees: the Chairman presents the report and moves for the adoption of the report or of the report's recommendations. Lest over-exuberant members attempt to force the issue and call for the House to pass judgment on a document it has not seen, the standing orders require that after making his motion, and a short explanatory statement, the chairman move adjournment of the debate. An order for resuming the adjourned debate is then placed on the order paper 'to be called by the Government House Leader in the same manner as Government Orders.'[36] This rule is also intended to maintain the government's control of matters to be brought before the House, since the opposition has no procedural way of forcing the government to call a particular item for debate.[37] When a formal motion is before the House, a question (or questions) is put to the House on completion of the debate; this creates the opportunity formally to approve or reject the committee's proposals. Debates on committee reports tend not to rank highly in members' priorities, and months may go by before time is found for a debate. Though it often lacked enthusiasm for them, even during the majority government years from 1981 to 1985, the government eventually permitted debates on committee reports (when the government did not want to see a report come to a vote, it permitted debate but ensured that the debate was again adjourned).

The debate on a committee report is rarely enlightening, and tends to attract few contributors apart from the committee members. Clearly, the importance of the procedure lies not in the debate but in the decision of the House and in the implications for the government of that decision. Save with respect to internal House proceedings and in a few other special cases (such as rule-making under the Ombudsman Act), the decision of the House to adopt or concur in a committee report or recommendation has no binding legal force. Nevertheless, substantial political or moral force may attach to committee proposals or judgments backed by a vote of the House. It is not uncommon for the government to be faced with a committee report it dislikes yet does not wish to be seen to oppose; it may in this way be possible for a committee to pressure the government into taking action it would rather avoid. The new standing orders contain a provision that has the similar effect of forcing the government to declare itself on the work of committees: a committee may now require that the government table a 'comprehensive response' within 120 days of the presentation of the report.

CONCLUSION

Judgments as to the effectiveness of special studies by committees depend on the criteria brought to bear. Influence on policy is certainly the most obvious, and perhaps the most important, but by no means the only criterion. Encouraging public discussion of policy questions, promoting clarification of party positions on key issues, educating MPPS, involving interest groups in the policy process, and legitimizing both government actions and the political system itself are further functions of the committees engaged in special studies.

The primal reality of legislative committees is that they are composed of party politicians engaged in political work. What has been styled the 'dilemma' of such committees in Ottawa applies with equal force in Ontario: 'On the one hand they have been expected to be non-partisan and develop a corporate identity of their own, while on the other, most of the work has been on the Government's programme, which is a natural focus for partisan controversy.'[38] Any number of examples could be cited of committees racked by bitter confrontation in which the result of every debate and every vote was a pre-ordained certainty with no semblance of compromise or accommodation. Any evaluation of the

Ontario committee system must seek the balance between those committee activities which are extensions of the electoral battle and those in which all members work towards influencing and improving public policy. Both are legitimate, and both serve important purposes.

According to Nelson Polsby, an effective committee system is a principal prerequisite for an independent, transformative legislature 'in placing its imprint upon public policy.'[39] In this context, this chapter has offered extensive evidence of the validity of the two principal theses informing this book: that the Ontario legislature has made notable advances towards becoming more transformative, and that such advances are subject to sharp limitations owing to the structural and behavioural constraints inherent in the parliamentary model. Committees of the legislature are far more effective in their work, are taken far more seriously by the government, and serve as a much more important conduit into the policy process for the views of the public and of interest groups than was the case two decades ago.

The influence of committees on legislation usually is not pronounced, and their impact on policy through estimates is nil. Committees' policy influence derives mainly from the special studies they conduct. These special studies are being undertaken in substantial numbers, and the reports they engender are usually accorded a high degree of credibility by the government and by other key players in the policy process. Special studies can and do effect policy, not simply through their recommendations, but also by the very act of publicly examining a policy issue in a tripartisan political setting assisted by professional, independent staff.

The limits to the enhancement of the legislature's transformative capacity through committees are equally evident. Committees (or the legislature) have no means of ensuring that the government will act upon their recommendations; their influence arises from the quality of their work and from the political support they can generate. Moreover, committees have only limited scope for producing effective special studies. The government is unlikely to be swayed on policies close to its heart or on politically supercharged issues, so that only certain subjects are suitable for effective committee review. In addition, the press of business – estimates, legislation, and other routine matters – severely restricts the time available to committees for special studies. Similarly, only a limited number of members are available to serve for extended periods on committees engaged in policy studies.

7
Services to members

An evaluation of the services available to the members of the Ontario legislature depends, to a degree, on whether one views the glass as half empty or half full. In comparison with the situation in the 1960s, and with the services enjoyed by most other Canadian provincial legislators, Ontario MPPS are well served indeed. In comparison with the aspirations of many opposition members and with the impressive range of services provided to American legislators, however, the Ontario member's position calls for substantial improvement. Ontario MPPS tend to compare themselves longingly with U.S. congressmen rather than with state legislators, many of whom are not nearly so well served as their Ontario counterparts.

Important as the procedural advances have been over the past two decades, they are far less dramatic than the truly staggering improvements made to members' services and facilities during the same period. In the 1950s Donald MacDonald, who was the leader of a party (the three-member CCF), shared with his two caucus colleagues a small office and one assistant. Long-time MPP Robert Nixon, who entered the House in 1962, recalls being shown the facilities available to him: his desk in the Chamber and the pay telephone in the hall.[1]

This chapter examines the resources and services available to members of the Ontario legislature to assist them in their duties as legislators and as 'constituency caseworkers.' The chapter also discusses members' indemnities and allowances, television coverage of the House, and the Board of Internal Economy; none of these are 'services' to members, though their funding and operation are closely linked to the administration of legislative services.

185 Services to members

PHYSICAL FACILITIES

For a building constructed in the 1890s, that has not undergone more than piecemeal renovation since the north wing was completed in 1913, the Legislative Building serves the needs of its occupants reasonably well.

The Legislative Building and the attached north wing (which houses the Legislative Library and opposition offices) both have four usable floors, plus a basement (the fifth floor of the main building has been closed because of inadequate fire escape routes). In addition to the Chamber and offices for MPPS, legislative staff, and members of the press gallery, the Legislative Building contains a large dining-room, a small cafeteria, a cramped media studio for press conferences and party broadcasts, four committee rooms capable of holding up to eighty spectators each, and several lounges and small committee rooms under the control of the parties or the government.

The Speaker maintains a small apartment in the west wing of the building, directly above a large two-storey suite of offices and reception rooms used by the lieutenant-governor. The spacious lobby, the first-floor corridors, and the grand staircase are frequently used for receptions, awards ceremonies, and similar occasions. For an old building, the legislature is remarkably open to persons in wheelchairs; principally as a result of judicious placement of elevators and ramps, few parts of the building are inaccessible.

For several years MPPS turned down offers of good-quality office space in nearby government office buildings; they preferred to stay in inferior facilities in the Legislative Building in order to preserve their sense of immediacy and collegiality. After the 1985 election, a substantial proportion of the Conservative caucus agreed to move to the Whitney Block, a building located across the street from the legislature and connected to it by tunnel.

A major symbolic advance occurred in 1982 when the final member secured an office with a window; as this milestone suggests, many MPPS' offices tend toward the cramped and slightly tawdry rather than the opulent. Under the Conservatives, government back-benchers clearly enjoyed offices more spacious and better appointed than those of their opposition colleagues. More recently, members' location (inside or outside the Legislative Building) has been a better indicator of the quality of their offices, though a relatively small proportion of the Liberal caucus is housed in the legislature. Few ministers or parliamentary assistants retain offices in the legislature; for the most part their offices are located in the government complex just to the east, though a few are two or three miles distant.

A number of grandiose plans have been mooted over the years to renovate the building thoroughly or to rehouse many of its functions in nearby government buildings. All have come to naught in the face of the substantial costs involved, which would be well into the tens of millions (a wholesale restoration in the 1970s of the British Columbia Legislative Building, which is similar in size and vintage, cost in excess of $10 million). Significant upgrading and refurbishing of facilities has taken place over the last fifteen years; but these renovations were piecemeal and failed to come to grips with the problem of an aging, inadequate structure. During the Tory years it was not only the Government that balked at allocating the necessary funds; some of the older, more traditional Liberal members were reluctant to spend money on the building.

In March 1988 the minister of government services and his senior staff appeared before the Legislative Assembly Committee to discuss the renovation of the Legislative Building. Seasoned observers experienced a strong sense of déjà vu as the minister emphasized the unique and historic nature of the building, pledged to bring it up to modern standards while retaining its essential character, and explained how the ministry was developing plans for renovation, which would be discussed with the members in due course – just as his predecessors had done for at least the previous decade. The principal new element in the minister's presentation was his suggestion that costs could reach or exceed $100 million.[2]

It is something of an anomaly that until very recently an otherwise substantially independent legislature enjoyed only limited control over its own building. A 1978 order in council passed pursuant to the Legislative Assembly Act granted the Speaker control over roughly half the building: the Chamber and its lobbies and galleries, MPPs' offices, assembly offices, and most of the public areas.[3] The remaining space, used in the main by the Premier's Office and the Cabinet Office, remained outside the jurisdiction of the legislature until October 1988. At the same time the first two floors of the Whitney Block came under the Speaker's control as part of the legislative precincts. The trend has clearly been away from governmental uses and towards legislative uses (as late as the mid 1970s some ministry offices were housed in the building), and the pressure from expanding legislative requirements continues unabated.

Services to members

Even with the expansion of members' offices into the Whitney Block, and with the assignment of some library and administrative staff to rented office space as much as ten minutes' walk from the legislature, space in the Legislative Building remains at a premium and is jealously fought over. It is the Speaker's responsibility to allocate office and meeting space among the parties, a process that entails the most delicate interparty negotiations and, inevitably, bruised egos. From time to time members flatly refuse to vacate offices their parties have relinquished claim upon; some are permitted to stay, thus adding further complications to the endless 'space wars' in the legislature.

MEMBERS' INDEMNITIES AND BENEFITS

Let us turn to a discussion of the matter of foremost concern when legislators from different jurisdictions compare notes: indemnities, benefits, and allowances. Until the 1970s members of the Ontario legislature were paid on the presumption that theirs was not a full-time calling.[4] The reports of the Camp Commission signalled the end of that practice and the beginning of a new era in financial munificence for MPPS. In 1986 the basic indemnity was $37,567, with an additional tax-free allowance of $12,616; this was virtually equivalent to the level of payment in Quebec, which was in turn well below that of federal MPS but substantially higher than in other provinces. Ontario MPPS receive per diem payments of $68, and non-accountable meal allowances of $27 a day for attending committee meetings when the House is not in session (plus all travel and accommodation expenses);[5] most MPPS collect about $2,000 a year in these tax-free payments. On the cautious assumption that the marginal tax rate for MPPS is 50 per cent, the effective value of the basic indemnity and the tax-free allowances is roughly $67,000 per annum. To put this in context, in July 1986 the average industrial wage in Ontario was $23,027,[6] and the salary range for assistant deputy ministers in the Ontario government as of 1 November 1986 was from $64,200 to $79,200. Some 56 per cent of Ontario members, principally those on the government side, enjoyed additional emoluments in 1986 for serving as Speaker, minister, parliamentary assistant, party leader, whip, House leader, or committee chairman.[7]

Members have their own pension plan, the Legislative Assembly Retirement Allowances Account, which offers one of the better retirement schemes available to Canadian legislators.[8] In contrast to most similar plans in Canada, its benefits are not automatically indexed to inflation; however, periodic adjustments are made by the Board of Internal Economy, as are substantial capital injections, since, despite the assembly's matching of the members' contributions, the fund chronically faces an actuarial deficit.

It is, of course, a matter of opinion whether the members' precarious lot justifies their generous pensions. Clearly, though, the provisions of the plan impinge somewhat on political questions, in that the requirement of five years' service for eligibility affects MPPS' eagerness for elections in direct proportion to their faith in their ability to win re-election. For example, there is no doubt that the large number of MPPS of all parties first elected in September 1975 exerted pressure to prolong the Thirty-first Parliament beyond the fall of 1980. (In the event, the legislature was not dissolved until the spring of 1981.)

A severance allowance equal to six to twelve months' sessional indemnity (depending on length of service) is paid to MPPS who lose their seats in the electoral wars or through redistribution. Members from outside Toronto enjoy generous allowances for maintaining a residence in the capital and for travel between Queen's Park and their ridings. Finally, on a culinary note, the Members' Dining Room offers good fare at reasonable, unsubsidized prices, but rates at best a star and a half in comparison with the three-star facilities of the Parliamentary Restaurant in Ottawa, or le Parliamentaire in Quebec City.

Since 1978 the Legislative Assembly Act has enjoined the Commission on Election Finances to review and to report annually on Members' pay and benefits. In recent years the commission's recommendations have been for greater increases than the government has been willing to countenance; the increments that have been implemented have been at or below the rate of inflation. In its 1987 report the commission lamented the fact that the assembly had not seriously debated expenses and indemnities for some years, and that its proposals were being implemented piecemeal; it called for a formal mechanism for members to adopt the commission's recommendations by resolution. The government has not responded to this idea, which was reiterated in the Commission's 1988 report.[9]

MEMBERS' SUPPORT SERVICES

Support services for MPPS can be categorized as relating primarily to constituency concerns or to policy and legislative matters. By statute all members are entitled to a personal assistant (variously styled 'secretaries' or 'legislative assistants').[10] Few assistants can escape spending a large part of their time on constituency business, despite the provision, since 1976, of publicly funded constituency offices. Members in 1986 could spend up to $14,700 on rental and similar expenses for constituency offices (rural MPPs often have two or three part-time offices in separate communities).

A 1974 amendment to the Legislative Assembly Act guaranteed a personal secretary (a 'legislative assistant' in the NDP caucus) for each MPP. Members became entitled to a second staff person when public funding of constituency offices began in 1977. For some years the NDP lobbied vigorously for the public funding of a personal researcher for each MPP. As with other demands for costly extensions of services, the Conservative government balked, though, over the course of repeated discussion, its attitude shifted from hostile rejection to a cautious willingness to negotiate proposals of one researcher for every two or three MPPs. Very soon after assuming power, the Liberal government agreed, though not without misgivings, to add an extra person to each MPP's staff. Although it is premature to make definitive pronouncements about the uses to which this third staff member is put,[11] it is apparent that most of them are primarily doing constituency work, though a substantial number are engaged in policy research and more 'legislative' activities. Whereas virtually all secretaries or legislative assistants are women, many the 'executive assistants' are men. Most constituency assistants are women. Members have a global staff allowance ($94,625 in 1986) which they may spend as they see fit, provided they do not exceed the maxima for various positions (executive assistant, $34,611; legislative assistant/constituency assistant, $28,026; special assistant, $26,276) or put their relatives on the payroll. Members' allocation of their staff resources varies somewhat according to caucus; as of late 1986 virtually all Liberal and Conservative private members maintained two staff members at Queen's Park, whereas only about half the New Democrats did so; they preferred to have their additional staff work directly in the ridings.

The assembly pays all the members' long-distance and postage charges, and provides supplies and equipment. Each MPP is entitled to print and mail yearly, at public expense, three 'householders' (folders detailing the member's work on his constituents' behalf, summarizing policy developments at Queen's Park, and providing extensive evidence of the member's photogeneity). The official guidelines require that the content of these mailings be non-partisan in nature,[12] but in practice the householders are filled with all manner of blatant party propaganda that stops just short of proclaiming, in 20-point type, 'Vote for Bloggs.' In addition to communications specialists who design and write householders and who often ghost-write the columns that many rural members produce for their weekly newspapers, each caucus has a research unit of roughly seven to ten professionals plus support staff.

The Legislative Library is an increasingly important source of research support for MPPS. The library has extensive holdings of government documents and newspapers; it has a large professional staff (ninety-five in 1986) and offers a wide range of services. Of greatest significance to the back-bench MPPS is the library's research unit, which consists of a dozen professionals (including lawyers, economists, and scientists) who prepare non-partisan papers and oral briefings for MPPS on a confidential basis. As in other jurisdictions with similar bodies, the library research officers also serve as staff on committees, but their availability to all MPPS regardless of status and their independence from internal party intrigue render them particularly valuable to ordinary members.

MPPS can also call upon the services of the legislative draftsmen in the Office of the Legislative Counsel. The senior legislative counsel and his staff are employees of the Ministry of the Attorney-General, and in that sense are clearly governmental rather than legislative in nature. None the less, both the standing orders and long-established tradition require them to serve committees in a neutral fashion and to provide assistance to all members on a confidential basis, primarily in drafting of private members' bills.

Public funding of caucus research and leaders' support staff dates only from the mid-1960s, and only since the 1970s has the amount of money involved become significant. Money is allocated on a per-member basis. In 1986 the parties' research offices were funded as follows: Liberal, $923,500; Conservative, $954,700; New Democratic Party, $558,500. These sums are in addition to the funding for caucus administration ($348,300 for the government caucus, $636,500 for the Conservatives, and $306,200 for the New Democrats), and do not include money for the opposition leaders' offices ($692,000 for the Conservatives and $527,600 for the NDP).[13]

An insight into the nature of this funding is offered by a Board of Internal Economy decision of May 1981, which altered the funding formula so that the twenty-one New Democratic members were treated as if they numbered thirty.[14] This was a blatant attempt by the

Conservative government to prop up the NDP, which had faltered badly in the 1981 election, so as to avoid having one opposition party eclipse the other and emerge as the clear alternative to the government. The formula was not rescinded when the Liberals came to power.

A service of fundamental importance to MPPS is the transcription of House and committee proceedings. Ontario has had the official Hansard report of House business since the early 1940s, but only in the 1970s did coverage of committee meetings become routine. A staff of fifty transcribers and editors prepares rough transcripts of House proceedings within an hour of their taking place; these 'instant Hansards' are produced in limited numbers for ministers, leaders, caucus research units, and the press gallery. After correction and further editing, the transcripts are printed by a commercial firm and are available within three or four days.[15]

The Ministry of Government Services maintains a slightly cramped media studio in the Legislative Building which is made available to all MPPS. The studio is used mostly used government press conferences, but opposition members hold press conferences there as well. A few members make use of direct radio feeds to stations in their ridings; the studio has the necessary lighting, wiring, and backdrops for television, but tends not to be used much by individual MPPS for the production of television shows. Until it was forced by high costs to drop the service in 1982, a private cable television firm assisted members in producing television programs for distribution through local cable-TV facilities.

Most MPPS, and certainly all those who represent large urban centres, have their own cable television shows on the local community programming channel. The cable companies welcome such shows because they are inexpensive and boost the companies' quota of local content and community-service programming. The quality of the shows in production values, styles and content tends to be low but according to eports from the MPPS, the shows attract a surprisingly high audience and add substantially to the member's visibility in the riding. Individual members' cable shows usually are generally produced by the local cable operator. Each caucus has recording and editing facilities that are used for free-time party broadcasts.

In the mid-1980s a massive computerized office system was installed in the legislature at a capital cost slightly in excess of $4 million (this was somewhat higher than it might have been had the parties not insisted on separate central processors for security reasons). Although

192 The Ontario legislature

the system has the capacity for data manipulation, links into extensive data banks and information services, and electronic mail, its principal use has been in word processing and office automation. In addition to an intelligent work station, which includes a high-quality printer, in each MPP's office, the system is linked to caucus research and administrative offices and to the administrative office of the assembly. By late 1988 more than 250 offices were linked to the system, with the expectation that the constituency offices would also eventually be integrated into it. The system offers all manner of sophisticated possibilities, though it was primarily designed on the understanding that members' staffs rather than members themselves would be the primary users and that its principal benefit would be improved routine correspondence management, file management, and related functions.

Members of the Ontario legislature receive all manner of minor perquisites and services, most of which fall into the constituency-service category. For example, MPPS are provided with an endless supply of impressive official plaques conveying congratulations to constituents on fiftieth wedding anniversaries, ninetieth birthdays, and other notable occasions; a professional photographer records for posterity the member welcoming visiting schoolchildren, church groups, and scout troops on the grand staircase, and provides copies for everyone in the group; the assembly pays for the translation of members' correspondence and other documents; and members are annually issued 1,900 lapel pins and 20 large Ontario or Canadian flags to distribute as they see fit.[16]

THE MEMBER AS CONSTITUENCY CASEWORKER

A question of great interest to MPPS is whether the greatly extended range of services at their disposal confers a significant electoral advantage on incumbents. The heightened visibility of incumbents through cable television shows and household mailers, together with the individual services provided by the constituency office, might be expected to give sitting members an advantage at election time. The widespread view among MPPS that this was indeed the case received considerable support in the results of the 1977 election. In that election, the first held after the establishment of publicly funded constituency offices, only 9 of 113 sitting members standing for re-election were defeated. In the 1981 election, which was marked by a larger turnover in both seats and votes, only 15 of 112 incumbents lost their seats; in 1985

85 of 104 incumbents were returned; in the 1987 cataclysm 78 of 103 incumbents won re-election.[17] These figures confirm the findings of other researchers that incumbency is a factor of some import in Ontario elections,[18] but they are not conclusive on the role of publicly funded services in the incumbency advantage. The inability to demonstrate a causal relationship between members' services and the incumbency effect is less significant than the members' firm belief that a strong link does exist.

This perception is related to what has come to be known as the 'constituency casework' syndrome – the tendency of members to devote great amounts of time and energy to problems brought to them by constituents. The Camp Commission recommended that MPPS be relieved of the burden of casework so that they could attend properly to their other legislative duties. A good many long-term members are of the view that the additional resources now available to MPPS have at best allowed them to keep up with their burgeoning caseload, and that they have no more time to devote to their legislative role than they did in the early 1970s.

A distinction can be drawn between constituency service aimed at securing benefits for groups of constituents – funding a community centre, obtaining grants for local industry, improving roads – and constituency service aimed at rectifying the problems of individual constituents, which cover a vast range of matters, not all governmental, and certainly not always the responsibility of the provincial government. The morning mail and telephone messages might typically seek an MPP's assistance in obtaining workers' compensation or welfare benefits, finding a job, resolving a relative's immigration plight, rezoning a property, fighting a rent increase, rectifying an injustice at the hands of a private company, or solving other problems ranging from the bizarre to the mundane to the heart-rending.

The increasing number of problems brought to MPPS reflects the growing intrusiveness of government, the difficulties faced by citizens in dealing with the complexities of the modern administrative state, and a tendency to seek governmental solutions to what used to be thought of as private problems. In addition, the members have themselves to blame for much of the growth of their constituency service caseloads. Rare indeed is the MPP whose household mailers and cable television programs do not prominently offer the help of his constituency office in resolving all manner of problems.

Purists sometimes decry this 'glorified social worker' role as an unseemly exercise in vote-grubbing that seriously detracts from the member's capacity to act as a legislator. Certainly some MPPS spend inordinate amounts of time signing congratulations-on-your-new-baby letters, delivering anniversary plaques, and personally chasing down WCB cheques gone astray. Still, the member's ombudsman function should not be lightly dismissed. In the first place, it is important that citizens have an easily identifiable person to whom they can turn when they are bewildered by bureaucracy, and that this person be knowledgeable, effective, and not bound up with red tape and buck-passing.[19] MPPS fill this need admirably; they are experienced, they possess a certain clout, they are unlikely to be stymied by formalities, and they have a clear incentive to solve problems – the electoral support of the aggrieved. Second, it is important to understand how constituency work can fill the member's needs – and not just the need for votes. Most MPPS bring with them, in addition to many other goals and motives, a fair degree of altruism and a genuine desire to help people. Further, most find that whether they sit in opposition or on the government back-benches their ability to help people by contributing to policy or by influencing major government decisions is sharply limited. Accordingly, one of the few areas in which ordinary members can accomplish concrete results and personally contribute to their electors' well-being is through resolving the problems brought to them by constituents. The significance of casework to the members' sense of purpose and self-esteem can be great. Finally, attention to constituency casework can be related to larger policy concerns. In the Ontario legislature New Democratic MPPS have become adept at generalizing the problems of their constituents into comprehensive attacks on government policy and administration coupled with prescriptions for reform. One technique is to raise, in question period or in estimates, the particulars of one person's difficulties, ask that they be remedied, and then contrast the underlying policy that gave rise to the problem with one's own party position. NDP members have used this approach effectively in fields such as workers' compensation, nursing home standards, and health care policy.

A survey of provincial legislators carried out in 1972 demonstrated that Ontario MPPS were exceeded only by British Columbia MLAS in the amount of time they devoted to constituency service.[20] The greater resources made available to members of the Ontario legislature in the interim have not reduced their interest in constituency casework, but are of uncertain effect in freeing the members from the burden of dealing personally with the problems of individual constituents.

195 Services to members

TELEVISION IN THE HOUSE

The proceedings of the Ontario legislature were first televised in March 1969 during the budget speech,[21] but it was not until late in 1975 that television entered the House on a continuing basis as a result of an experiment proposed by the Morrow Committee. The 'experiment' continued for nearly ten years as the opposition repeatedly attempted to introduce a full 'electronic Hansard.'

During this time space was provided in the Speaker's gallery for up to nine separate film and video cameras owned and operated by individual stations and networks. Subject to space limitations, television reporters were given the same unfettered access to the House as the print journalists, and few significant costs were incurred by the assembly. If this was an inexpensive solution to the demand for television, it only proved the truth of the old bromide, 'You get what you pay for': the quality of the coverage was very poor. Lighting in the Chamber was jury-rigged, and managed to be at once harsh yet inadequate. The cameras were low-quality portables that probably had been used to cover fires or Kiwanis luncheons earlier in the day, and the camera angles were bad. (Many MPPS' coverage was restricted to the tops or backs of their heads. One minister excused himself while answering a question to turn his back on the Speaker and speak to the cameras because he said his mother was complaining of seeing only his bald spot when he spoke.) In consequence, much of the coverage tended to be relegated to background for voice-over commentary, with generous use of wide-angle shots with all the intimacy and coherence of a change from the offensive to the defensive teams at a football game. Finally, the coverage was highly selective, and turned on what was deemed newsworthy by the reporters. In practice this usually meant only the leaders' questions, unless the cameras could catch members dozing off or screaming insults, or unless there were demonstrations in the public galleries. Very rarely was anything other than question period covered, and few back-benchers' questions were deemed of sufficient interest to get the cameras rolling; indeed, sometimes the cameras had been removed and set up on the landing outside the Chamber, awaiting the scrum of ministers and leaders after question period, before the back-benchers' questions were asked.

Opinion within the press gallery for years ranged between ambivalence and hostility to the prospect of publicly funded and administered television coverage of the House. Television reporters jealously defended their 'right' to film whatever they wanted in the same fashion that print reporters could write about anything that happened in the House. They were concerned that the implementation of an electronic Hansard on the Ottawa model would restrict them to a communal feed under the control of the Speaker, who would place rigid restrictions against, for example, reaction shots of MPPs who did not legitimately have the floor and disturbances in the galleries. Some were also worried that when public coverage was freely available, their news organizations would reassign them elsewhere.

The hostility of the gallery to the control implied in a House-operated system was an impediment to the establishment of good-quality, publicly funded television coverage of the legislature, but far more fundamental was the Conservative government's steadfast refusal to countenance change. There were three reasons for the government's reluctance. First, depending on the nature of the system chosen and the structural modifications it would entail, the capital costs were expected to run into the millions of dollars; in addition, operating costs would be substantial. Second, some on the government side genuinely believed that public interest in such a costly service would be limited in the extreme. Third, and most important, the government felt that it had the most to lose politically if the House was to be fully covered by television. The profile of the opposition would be substantially raised, and the widespread public indifference to provincial issues, on which a good deal of the Conservatives' success rested, might be threatened.

Accordingly, the numerous feasibility studies, committee trips to visit other television installations, and members' complaints and urgings were to no avail so long as the Tories remained in power. One of the last items of private members' business prior to the 1985 election was a debate on a resolution by Liberal James Bradley that would have authorized a full video Hansard for the Ontario legislature; it was defeated on a straight party vote, 42 to 28.[22]

The introduction of an electronic Hansard service was promised in the Liberal-NDP accord that brought the Liberals to power in June 1985. Within days of the new government's taking office, the Board of Internal Economy had approved in principle an in-house television system, and the Procedural Affairs Committee had been instructed to develop the guidelines for its operation. The committee reported in September 1985; among its key recommendations was a mild disavowal of the type of coverage in operation in Ottawa and in the Saskatchewan legislature. An electronic Hansard attempts to avoid the vexing question of editorializing by permitting coverage only of the member recognized by the Speaker, and thus ignores interjections, reactions, and any other activity going on in the House. As the committee put it, such coverage 'tends to give a distorted view of what is going on and where it is occurring. It is difficult for the viewing public to understand the setting in which a member is speaking and the Speaker presiding.'[23] The committee did not say so, but such practices also make for boring television. A set of guidelines was developed to give the director some flexibility in selecting his shots, which in turn would make for livelier and more realistic coverage, though constraints were still imposed (if vaguely defined); for example, 'applause shots may be taken; however, care should be taken to ensure that the decorum of the Chamber is maintained.'[24]

By the fall of 1986 the television service was in full operation. In addition to $3 million in equipment costs, some $1.7 million in structural work had been incurred, principally in improving lighting in the Chamber, constructing a sophisticated control room nearby, and installing five cameras in unobtrusive recesses above doorways. (Extensive renovations were also made to one of the committee rooms to provide coverage of committee meetings.) A staff of eleven operates the system; operating costs for the first year of full operation were projected to be slightly in excess of $2 million.

The result was a high-quality picture and the use of significantly more interesting angles and techniques (such as split screen when two members are involved in an extended exchange) than would have been possible under a strict electronic Hansard regimen.

The effects of full television coverage on members' behaviour have been minor. Concerns about MPPS' grandstanding for the cameras have generally not been borne out, and the overall decorum of the House has not changed noticeably, though the time-honoured custom of desk-banging to signify approval is giving way to more conventional applause. All parties have consultants on hand to coach members on their television manner, but their advice usually runs to speaking techniques rather than the content or style of speeches. Flamboyant attire is somewhat less in evidence, as is the reading of newspapers. Members generally do not engage in seat-shuffling – filling in behind a colleague who has the floor to give the appearance of high attendance. Television has had one noticeable effect on seating patterns: in all three parties women now sit directly behind or beside their leaders and appear prominently when the leaders are on camera; similarly, the only non-white Liberal member in the Thirty-third Parliament sat directly behind the premier.

As the Procedural Affairs Committee recommended, television reporters continue to be permitted to set up their own cameras in the Speaker's gallery and may cover the House as they did before. Predictably, though, most television news services are content to take the feed from the House system and have removed their cameras from the Speaker's gallery. So far, the practice has not developed at Queen's Park (as it has in Ottawa and in Quebec City) of most reporters' covering the House by watching television rather than by observing proceedings firsthand.

Each day's proceedings are broadcast live and are repeated in the evening; question period is repeated a second time on TVOntario, the province's educational television network. On the mornings that the House does not sit, and during the summer and winter recesses full, coverage is given to the committee meeting in the Amethyst Room, which in a scaled-down fashion has been modified for television on the same principles as the Chamber. The broadcast signal is relayed to a satellite and beamed back across the province for distribution by cable television companies. Generous grants are available for small cable firms to purchase the satellite dishes necessary to receive the signal, or to acquire the equipment to add an additional channel to their offerings. Within a few months of the first broadcast, virtually all major cable operators were carrying the signal.

Partly as a corollary of full television coverage, the House has taken to providing simultaneous translations of its proceedings. French-to-English and English-to-French service is available to members, to spectators in the galleries, and to the television audience. Closed-captioning for hearing-impaired viewers is available on the evening rebroadcast of question period. Largely because of the restrictions imposed by the Canadian Radio-Television and Telecommunications Commission, no voice-over commentary or discussion accompanies the pictures, other than a non-partisan overview of procedure by the clerk of the House prior to the opening of the House each day. Subtitles indicating the business before the House are run periodically, and MPPS are identified when they begin to speak.

Members' offices, caucus offices, and senior legislative staff are provided with monitors that offer coverage of the House and whichever committee is meeting in the Amethyst Room (both are available in English and in French), message services, distillations of the previous day's television news, and coverage of press conferences held in the media studio. The Legislative Assembly Committee oversees the broadcast service closely; though they sometimes find it troublesome, on the whole the staff of the broadcast service welcome the direct line of communication with the members.

By and large, members have been pleased with the televising of House proceedings, though none has the slightest idea of the size of the viewing audience or its reaction to the coverage. A national survey conducted in the fall of 1986 found that 13 per cent of Canadians watched the televised proceedings of the House of Commons or their provincial assembly once a week or more; another 37 per cent tuned in less frequently. The study concluded that televised coverage of Parliament and the provincial assemblies was linked to a heightened interest in politics and to a decrease in respect for elected politicians.[25] It is commonly presumed that the opposition gains more than the government when a parliament is televised.[26] Attention is primarily focused on question period, during which the opposition appears lively, full of innovative ideas, and responsive to public concerns, while the government appears ponderous, bureaucratic, unresponsive, and constantly on the defensive against accusations of incompetence and mismanagement. This need not be so, of course; a good deal depends on the performances given by government and opposition. Moreover, any natural advantage accruing to the opposition through the televising of the House may be offset by a peculiarity of the Ontario legislature: the dominance of party leaders during question period. As was documented in Chapter 4, most of the time and attention in question period goes to the party leaders, so that their skill in fostering a favourable image may be far more significant than other factors in reaping political rewards. Premier David Peterson, for example, is far more effective on television than William Davis and Frank Miller were; his performance in question period may be an important asset to his party.

BOARD OF INTERNAL ECONOMY

A 1974 amendment to the Legislative Assembly Act created the Board of Internal Economy, the first in a Canadian legislature. A number of Canadian legislatures subsequently established similar boards. The Board of Internal Economy is important for two reasons: first, it exercises virtually complete financial and managerial control over the legislature and its administrative arm, the Office of the Assembly;

second, its membership includes representatives from the opposition parties and the government back-benches. One Australian observer has called the Ontario arrangement 'the best model available' for the financial management of Westminster-style parliaments.[27]

Under the act the Speaker chairs the board, and three ministers are appointed to it; usually these are the government House leader, the chief government whip (who was a minister without portfolio under the Conservatives), and a minister who also serves on the Management Board of Cabinet. The government caucus representative has been, in recent times, either the chairman of caucus or the chief whip; from the outset the opposition positions have usually been held by the House leaders. This concentration of financial, administrative, and procedural responsibilities is unfortunate in two respects. First, it promotes the tendency to trade off services for concessions on procedure; on several occasions 'packages' of potential procedural reforms have implicitly or explicitly included the provision of additional services on the understanding that the opposition would back off on their demands for certain extra services. Second, it emphasizes the House leaders' pre-eminent role in the running of all facets of the legislature, and thus contributes to the pervasive 'leave it to the House leaders' attitude.

The board is not a legislative committee in the conventional sense. It does not report to the House, and its meetings are held in camera, though minutes are published shortly after meetings (and, given its tripartisan composition, it has few secrets). Most significantly, it has real power to establish and vary the estimates of those offices which require its authorization: the ombudsman, the provincial auditor, the Election Office, the Commission on Election Finances, the Information and Privacy Commission, and the Office of the Assembly. Except for the Office of the Assembly, the board's scrutiny of the budgets submitted to it is perfunctory; the board is not usually provided with any independent analysis of the financial submissions to it and is not inclined to inquire closely into the details and rationale for budgetary estimates in the way, for example, that Management Board reviews ministry budgets. The budget of the assembly does receive a much more searching analysis, and requests for additional staff or for the funding of particular projects are occasionally reduced or denied entirely. The annual budgets of the legislative committees must be approved by the board; as a rule, the board passes all committee expenses and only looks carefully at (and rejects regularly) requests for travel and for outside staff. Once the board has approved the budgets submitted to it, they are passed along to the treasurer for inclusion in the budget and in the printed estimates books. All estimates reviewed by the board must be publicly considered by the legislature in the same fashion as other estimates; they must, according to the standing orders, be referred to standing or select committee rather than to the Committee of Supply. The Speaker and, sometimes, other board members attend the meeting of the committee that considers the assembly estimates; although the Speaker answers questions, he cannot be said to 'defend' them as ministers defend their estimates.

In addition to its budgetary review function, the board is involved in all types of administrative matters, many relating to services or benefits for members. Opposition MPPS complain that, with the government's clear majority, the board is not as independent as it might appear, or as might be desired. This criticism has some merit, though relatively few issues occasion a clear government-opposition split (and the mere presence of opposition members in the actual decision-making body has a substantial effect). Moreover, the government recognizes that all spending on legislative services is publicly perceived as its doing, and the media love nothing better than stories about MPPS' providing themselves with new perks or facilities.

The board has no secretariat per se, but is served by the administrative arm of the Office of the Assembly. The controller serves as secretary to the board. In addition to the clerk of the House and the controller, senior assembly staff such as the director of assembly services and the director of human resources regularly attend board meetings. Through them the board has call on the eighty-two full-time administrative staff of the assembly, who oversee payroll, personnel, purchasing, and allied functions.

Table 7.1 summarizes the budget of the assembly for 1986–87 according to the 'item' breakdown in the printed estimates books, and shows the allocation of full-time permanent staff.[28] Compared with the other provinces, Ontario ranks low in its legislative spending per capita or per general government expense, though its average spending per legislator, which is probably a more useful indicator, was more than twice as much as in any other province except Quebec.[29]

The spending figures do not include general overhead; maintenance, heating, and the like are paid by the Ministry of Government Services. Identifiable overhead expenses, such as the assembly's internal telephone system, the costs incurred in relocating members' offices, and the rental of commercial office space for the library and the administrative office, are included in 'sessional requirements.' That category is

TABLE 7.1
Assembly expenses and staff 1986–87

	$(000)	Full-time staff
Speaker's Office	1,226	7
Clerk's Office	1,280	24
Hansard	2,688	50
Sessional requirements	10,797	–
Members' indemnities	8,639	–
Caucus support services	7,783	402
Members' support services	14,484	*
Administration	3,369	127
Constituency offices	2,830	*
Legislative Library	4,157	95
Information services	15,281	17
Payment into MPPS' pension plan	1,303	–
Total	73,837	722

SOURCE: Management Board of Cabinet, *Expenditure Estimates 1986–87*, vol 5, part II, 8; *Supplementary Estimates 1986–87*, 21; Board of Internal Economy, 'Office of the Assembly Estimates,' passim
*Included in caucus support services

something of a residual grab-bag of odds and ends; in addition to the expenses just noted, it includes the printing of bills, committee expenses, members' office supplies and postal expenses, the printing of the members' householders, services to the press gallery, and the legislative internship program. The 'members' indemnity' category includes not only MPPS' salaries and their annual tax-free allowances, but also their travel and accommodation expenses and severance payments. The 'members' support services' category represents the salaries and benefits paid to MPPS' secretaries and legislative assistants, both at Queen's Park and in the constituency offices. All party staff, whether they work directly for MPPS, for the leader, or for the caucus, are included under 'caucus support services.' The 127 staff in the administrative category include not only those working in payroll, personnel, and allied pursuits, but tour guides, dining-room staff and others not listed in other groupings.

The basic message of the table is clear: the Ontario legislature is a large institution with very considerable staff resources, and it expends very considerable amounts of money. What does not emerge from these bald statistics is arguably of equal importance with the number and costliness of the staff: their quality. No organization is ever completely free of 'deadwood,' but in virtually every facet of its operation the Ontario legislature has employees who are better qualified, more energetic, and more committed to the concept of an independent, effective legislature than was the case in the 1960s and early 1970s. In all respects the legislature is a far more professional organization than it was at the time of the Camp Commission. On balance this is a welcome development, though its unfortunate corollary is a growing bureaucratization of the legislature and the over-specialization of legislative staff. Most of the new personnel lack the wide-ranging understanding of the institution that was common among legislative staff until recently.

The complexities and scale of modern governance make extensive and competent staff assistance, together with related resources, essential for a legislature to develop a transformative capacity. That great strides have indeed been made along these lines is evident throughout this chapter. Individual MPPs, party caucuses, and legislative committees will never be completely satisfied with the services available to them, but all are vastly better served than they were fifteen or twenty years ago. Moreover, in the crucial matter of staff assistance, improvements have been registered not only in absolute levels of service but in quality: the staff of the Ontario legislature has been thoroughly professionalized. Certainly, a lack of resources no longer stands as a serious impediment to the legislature's becoming more transformative; the question now is whether the members can make use of those resources in ways that will enhance the legislature's role as a transformative institution.

Inevitably, the answer is equivocal. Effective committee work, the influence of private members' business, the possibility of thoroughly researched policy proposals, the release of the member from the demands of his social-worker function – all of which are indicators of an increased transformative capacity – are contingent on the provision of adequate resources, particularly staff. Yet, because of the structural constraints of the parliamentary system and the instinct of elected members to give priority to their re-election, a good part of the improved services is employed in dealing with local constituency problems and in preparing the members for activities, such as question period, that are more arena-like than transformative.

8

The legislature and accountability

Accountability is something of a parliamentary Holy Grail: endlessly discussed, much sought after, yet ultimately of uncertain existence. The record of the Ontario legislature in fostering accountability is mixed, though it has certainly improved in recent years. This chapter focuses on the successes and shortcomings of the legislature's accountability mechanisms. Particular attention is devoted to the work of the Public Accounts, Government Agencies, and Ombudsman committees, and to the legislative scrutiny of regulations. Other accountability processes, chiefly estimates and question period, have been dealt with in earlier chapters.

In order to judge the assembly's ability to hold the government accountable, a clear notion of the concept is essential. Discussions of accountability within the parliamentary setting are often couched in terms of responsible government and ministerial responsibility. This is, of course, entirely appropriate but not always helpful, since there is some confusion as to which aspects of the doctrine of responsible government are myth and which are reality.

The government has its own internal accountability mechanisms, which are quite separate from any parliamentary system of accountability. These internal processes rarely become public, and are based essentially on principles that have more in common with private-sector management techniques than with the fundamentally political precepts of responsible government. C.E.S. Franks has written that 'there cannot be effective accountability to parliament without effective internal accountability.'[1] This may be true, in the sense that in order to answer to Parliament the politicians and senior officials must themselves know the answers, but internal processes are otherwise not particularly germane to the analysis of parliamentary accountability. Parenthetically, the common presumption that they are more effective, especially in holding bureaucrats accountable, is of uncertain validity.[2]

In coming to grips with the notion of accountability to Parliament, several dichotomies need to be distinguished. First, as Franks has shown, accountability to Parliament is only one side of the coin; other channels of accountability are also of fundamental import.[3] Second, in a number of practical ways, issues of financial accountability are treated differently from accountability in non-financial matters. Money is the readily quantifiable, omnipresent life-blood of virtually all government activities, and its significance is understood by and of interest to all. Owing to the widespread and long-standing expectation that details of the government's financial transactions should be public, considerable information is available to members of the legislature. Thus, the processes relating to financial accountability have become more formal and more institutionalized, notably through the work of the provincial auditor and the Public Accounts Committee. Moreover, for the reasons already enumerated, and also in part because of concern with overall levels of government spending (and deficits), more attention has been devoted to improving accountability mechanisms in financial matters than to issues relating to non-financial policy and administration.

A third key distinction is that between the accountability of bureaucrats and the accountability of ministers. Unlike the financial–non-financial distinction, which reflects mainly practical differences, this dichotomy raises fundamental questions about the very nature of accountability. The doctrine of ministerial responsibility as established in Britain during the mid-nineteenth century holds that ministers and ministers alone are responsible to Parliament for all successes and failures; civil servants are to remain anonymous and are responsible to parliament only indirectly through their minister.[4] Even before the dramatic explosion in the scale of the civil service it was becoming apparent that the reality often deviated from the doctrine. In particular, the doctrine that ministers would be expected to resign when major administrative errors in their departments came to light, regardless of their personal involvement, was changing. It is now all but universally accepted that government has grown so large that it is unrealistic and inappropriate to expect a minister to be aware of and responsible for more than a tiny fraction of the steps taken in his name by his civil servants. The McGrath Committee observed that 'the doctrine of ministerial responsibility undermines the potential for genuine accountability on the part of the person [who] ought to be accountable – the senior officer of the department.'[5] The Lambert Commission argued that assigning responsibility to deputy ministers 'does not impair the principle of ministerial responsibility, but reinforces it by replacing myth with reality.'[6]

If increasing attention has been devoted to methods for holding bureaucrats, especially senior bureaucrats such as deputy ministers, directly and publicly responsible to Parliament, the basic principles under which such a schema is to operate, let alone its specific details, are subject to substantial disagreement. The distinction between policy, for which the minister must remain accountable, and administration, responsibility for which adheres to the deputy minister, is exceedingly difficult to define in either the abstract or the specific. Moreover, governments have been unwilling to concede a personal responsibility to parliament on the part of civil servants, a critical component of genuine accountability. Modern styles of government management involve frequent shuffles of senior bureaucrats, so that deputies and other key officials may have changed positions by the time the legislature wants to call them to account for particular actions. The 1980 report of the Ontario Public Accounts Committee echoed the Lambert Report in calling for the personal responsibility of deputy ministers to the parliament,[7] but the government rejected the idea. The chairman of Management Board observed that although 'all public servants wish to fulfill their responsibilities to the legislature ... it is simply beyond the capability of any person to recall and recount explicitly events which may have transpired many years ago.'[8] The dilemma is clear: a deputy cannot be held to account for a predecessor's actions; yet, if the person who took the action is not be made to account, then, as J.S. Mill put it, 'responsibility is null when no one knows who is responsible.'[9]

Another distinction crucial to an appreciation of parliamentary accountability is that between scrutiny and control. 'Control' implies the power to deny, approve, or alter; except in formal, legalistic senses, parliaments lack such power over government policy or spending. Scrutiny, however, is a realistic goal, a goal generally accepted as legitimate by governments that would be loath to submit to parliamentary control. In the words of a 1979 federal government position paper entitled 'The Reform of Parliament,' 'the House of Commons should not govern, but it should poke and pry without hindrance into the activities of those who do.'[10] Parliamentary scrutiny of the executive is intimately tied up with accountability; one of the most effective ways of scrutinizing government is to call the policy-makers and administrators before parliamentary committees to explain and account for their activities.

Perhaps the most important distinction is the least appreciated, and thereby gives rise to much of the lack of clarity in writings about accountability. The Lambert Commission spoke of accountability in the following eloquent yet ultimately unsatisfactory way:

Accountability, like electricity, is difficult to define, but possesses qualities that make its presence in a system immediately detectable ... we see accountability as the activating, but fragile, element permeating a complex network connecting the Government upward to Parliament and downward and outward to a geographically dispersed bureaucracy grouped in a bewildering array of departments, corporations, boards and commissions ... in simple terms, accountability is that quality of a system that obliges its participants *to pay attention* to their respective and assigned responsibilities, to understand that it does matter.[11]

Many other analyses and prescriptions go to some lengths to extol the importance of accountability – or responsibility, or answerability – without addressing the critical question of sanctions. Depending on the potential for sanctions, two very different forms of accountability may be discerned. First, accountability may mean *answerability*: a requirement to report fully and honestly in a public parliamentary forum on one's actions and to accept responsibility for them. Second, accountability may refer to a *liability*, which entails not only a full reporting and admission of responsibility but also the prospect of sanctions or punishments for errors. Accountability, in this schema, should mean more than simply saying that one is sorry. Without the threat of sanctions, the willingness to take 'responsibility' for one's actions can ring hollow indeed. Yet parliaments have no method for imposing formal sanctions on civil servants, and, many would argue, little prospect of punishing ministers for errors. Motions of censure calling for a ministerial resignation inevitably trigger the full weight of party discipline, since they are viewed as matters of confidence in the government and are of little practical value. Thus, 'parliament is practically incapable of punishing improper or inadequate departmental performance by forcing the minister to resign.'[12]

Ministers and bureaucrats will say that calls for the legislature and its committees to assume formal disciplinary powers are unnecessary,[13] since the power of parliamentary committees to publicly embarrass them is sanction enough. Civil servants and ministers alike set great store by their reputations and images, which can be severely damaged either in public meetings when they are called to account for their performance or in reports issued by committees. The prospect of negative media attention and unfavourable public opinion is an extremely powerful weapon available to the legislature and its committees. Whether that weapon is truly effective in fostering accountability is uncertain. Michael Pitfield has suggested that it may do more harm than good: 'a system based almost entirely on scoring political points provides very imperfect mechanisms for bureaucratic accountability, mechanisms that carry great costs for democracy ... when they work, they rarely get at the facts or lead to the best solutions. To the contrary, they often encourage exactly the wrong solution: scapegoating, more red tape and more bureaucracy. More often than not they do not work.'[14] This may be too harsh an interpretation, but it does draw attention to a fundamental feature of accountability: it is an often unintended by-product of the political struggle that characterizes the legislature. Few MPPs are genuinely concerned with accountability for its own sake. Opposition members are interested in embarrassing the government, in bringing to light its errors and extravagances, and in portraying it as incompetent, wrong-headed, or corrupt. In turn, the government is forced to defend its policies and administrative practices in the same public forums in which it is attacked. The net result is a degree of accountability, that depends on the skill and tenacity of the opposition, the resources and procedures available to members, the openness and self-confidence of the government, and the interest of the public and the press. It is worth noting that even those few members who do pursue the accountability of ministers and bureaucrats because they believe it to be important usually lack the technical expertise and the time required to do anything like a thorough job.

Question period, one of the most effective accountability mechanisms available to legislators, was analysed in Chapter 4; estimates, which make only a minimal contribution to accountability, were examined in Chapter 5. The balance of this chapter looks at more specialized accountability processes, such as the Public Accounts Committee, the Ombudsman Committee, and the review of delegated legislation.

THE PUBLIC ACCOUNTS COMMITTEE

The legislature's principal mechanism for promoting financial accountability is the Public Accounts Committee.[15] Although the assembly has

209 The legislature and accountability

had a Public Accounts Committee since 1869, until the 1960s 'the opposition and the Government tended to look upon this Committee as an organized witch hunt; hence it was ignored unless specific charges or allegations were brought up and referred to the Committee.'[16] The best illustration of the committee's efficacy is that it did not meet once during the 1950s.[17] During the next two decades its competence and its influence slowly matured. Key developments in this process included the establishment in 1968 of the practice of selecting the chairman from the ranks of the official opposition, as had long been the case at Westminster and Ottawa; the shift in the orientation of the provincial auditor in the early 1970s from pre-audit to post-audit, with the acompanying provision of detailed critical reports on government spending;[18] and the efforts of Patrick Reid, who chaired the committee for nearly a decade in the 1970s and 1980s, to professionalize it and focus its attention on financial management and accountability for public funds. The most important changes occurred during the minority government era; as one account has noted, 'as late as the early 1970s, the Committee did not have any agenda for meetings; meetings often consisted of members just flipping through the Auditor's Report and the Public Accounts lighting on matters of interest with no preparation, minimal information and no follow-up.'[19]

The mandate of the Public Accounts Committee as set out in standing order 90(i) is to review and report to the House on the *Public Accounts* and on the provincial auditor's reports. The auditor's annual report comments on perhaps two or three dozen questionable instances of governmental spending or management. The annual *Public Accounts*, published in three volumes, contains the province's financial statements, the statements of most major Crown agencies, breakdowns of each ministry's spending according to the estimates format, and a detailed listing of civil service salaries, transfers to grant recipients, and payments to suppliers, consultants, and others who do business with the government. With these documents referred permanently to the committee, it enjoys free rein to delve into virtually any matter of past government spending.[20] In addition, on rare occasions the House will refer matters to the committee. This offers the committee an embarrassment of riches in topics for it to pursue. Typically, half or more of the committee's time is taken up by examinations of items raised in the auditor's report; the balance is given over to the investigation of concerns raised by committee members. Much of this time is devoted almost exclusively to attempting to embarrass the government by bringing to light corruption, political favouritism, and conflict of interest; in short, they are exercises in scandal-mongering.

Of course, individual MPPs cannot set the committee's agenda; they must secure the committee's agreement to inquire into a particular subject. Overall, governments in recent years have been surprisingly amenable to permitting such investigations to take place. Minority governments, of course, have little choice but to accept the agenda proposed by the opposition, but even majority governments have usually chosen to let the committee have its head rather than be accused of covering up or stonewalling. Majority governments sometimes use their numerical advantage to relegate unpalatable subjects, such as government advertising, to positions of low priority on the committee's agenda, but most are dealt with eventually.

In 1986–87 the Public Accounts Committee spent an unusually high proportion of its time looking into matters other than those raised in the auditor's reports. In addition to several weeks of hearings into allegations of conflict of interest against a former minister (which the House had directed the committee to investigate), the committee spent substantial amounts of time on six issues not raised in the auditor's reports: the financing for Toronto's domed stadium; the sale of the Urban Transportation Development Corporation (a controversial Crown corporation); cost overruns at the Ontario pavilion at Expo '86; the effectiveness and propriety of spending by provincially funded safety associations; the investment policies of the IDEA Corporation, a provincial lending agency; and the severance package given the retiring clerk of the House. Even aside from the conflict of interest inquiry, less than one-third of the committee's time in 1986 was devoted to looking into problems identified in the provincial auditor's report.

Especially with respect to the more routine items raised in the auditor's report, a steering subcommittee has a crucial role in setting the committee's agenda. Even if the committee were to forswear its 'special inquiries' it would not have time to hold hearings on every matter commented upon in the auditor's report; therefore the sub-committee chooses the items to be reviewed or passed over. If individual members indicate an interest in particular items in the auditor's report, their wishes are usually accommodated. The selection of items from the auditor's report reflects the seriousness of the criticism and the likelihood that members can get political mileage out of them. The subcommittee does more than save the time of the full committee in determining the agenda; it may, for example, meet in camera with witnesses.

As was noted above, the committee has a virtually unrestricted mandate to inquire into past government spending. Sometimes, however, the opposition would prefer to pursue aspects of current or projected spending on which it senses that the government is vulnerable. Since it is not always possible to finesse the committee's order of reference in order to embark on such endeavours, MPPS have on occasion been frustrated when motions to place controversial current or projected spending on the agenda were ruled out of order. From this frustration was born a provision of the Liberal-NDP accord that promised a widening of the committee's mandate to permit such investigations. (The desire to expand the Public Accounts Committee's ambit when the estimates process offers a perfectly legitimate means of addressing current and future spending speaks volumes about the perceived effectiveness of estimates; as well, it reflects the Public Accounts Committee's capacity to call upon the provincial auditor and his staff for quick and impartial expert assistance.) The House has not formally authorized the expansion of the committee's order of reference to implement this commitment, but the committee's report for 1985 and 1986 observed that 'this expansion seems to have taken place in practice.'[21] Several of the matters reviewed by the committee in 1986 and 1987 were, by any reasonable standard, beyond the legitimate scope of the committee, and the propriety of violating its traditional limitation became the subject of considerable debate within the committee. Other than an elliptical reference in its 1985–86 report to the need for official sanction of its enlarged terms of reference, the committee has not formally sought House approval for the new role it has set itself.

The Public Accounts Committee is unique in having the services of the provincial auditor and his large professional staff. The auditor personally attends all committee meetings, including in camera sessions (and sits beside the chairman), along with two or three of his senior staff. For the most part the auditor will not (unlike his federal counterpart) speak on his own initiative during the committee meetings, but will wait to respond to questions. The auditor is not so passive as might appear, however, for he will often be on close terms with the chairman and other important committee members, and will make his points to them privately. Like any other public servant, the auditor will make available to the committee whatever information it requires, subject to legal restrictions.[22] Unlike other public servants, or indeed any other legislative auditor in Canada, the auditor is required to carry out any audit or other study authorized by a resolution of the Public

Accounts Committee.[23] This is a formidable weapon in the committee's arsenal, and has been used with increasing frequency in recent years, particularly with reference to matters the committee is investigating which did not come before it through the auditor's report.

No set format applies to the committee's 'special studies,' but the procedure for the routine inquiry into items from the auditor's report varies little. Although they are free to attend in their capacity as members of the legislature, ministers very rarely come to meetings of the Public Accounts Committee. Invitations to attend are directed to deputy ministers or, in the case of agencies, boards, and commissions, to chairmen or presidents. The committee calls before it the civil servants rather than the politicians in part to emphasize the bureaucrats' responsibility for administration and in part to avoid the partisanship that inevitably accompanies the appearance of a minister before a committee. Almost invariably, the deputies or chairmen attend personally and bring with them several key staff members who are knowledgeable about the matter in question. Following an opening statement, the deputy and his staff respond to questions from the committee members. The auditor does not usually make an opening statement, as the auditor-general of Canada frequently does at meetings of the federal Public Accounts Committee. This reflects the far less confrontational atmosphere that prevails between the auditor and the bureaucracy in Ontario. With some exceptions, senior officials tend to be conciliatory and co-operative with the committee; they are usually prepared to agree with the auditor's criticism if they believe it is warranted. If they disagree, they tend to do so in a non-confrontational way.

Members of the committee are generally not much interested in management systems or internal operational procedures per se, though when they are presented with clear evidence of waste or incompetence they can be counted on to pursue it doggedly. Though they are concerned with the effective delivery of government policy and the efficient deployment of resources, committee members evince little enthusiasm for the details of administration. The committee research officer prepares briefing notes for the members, including suggested questions highlighting the principal administrative and accountability issues, but these are frequently dealt with in a perfunctory manner; the members tend to concentrate on policy rather than on administration. Routine, auditor-generated matters are usually dealt with in a relatively non-partisan fashion. Many (though not all) government members of the committee recognize that criticism of the bureaucracy need not have a partisan political bent to it. Indeed, during the Conservative era some of the most effective members of the committee were former Tory ministers. The mild distrust shared by most MPPs for senior bureaucrats is never far below the surface at the Public Accounts Committee, and can contribute significantly to the sense of corporate purpose felt by committee members. Such non-partisan dedication to the pursuit of better government is, to be sure, fragile and easily shattered by the highly partisan scandal-mongering side of the committee's activities.

For some years the committee made a single omnibus report near the end of the session, setting out its observations and recommendations on all the matters it reviewed. If the committee was satisfied that a ministry or agency was making a serious effort at rectifying the problems identified by the auditor, it would not make a recommendation, but would simply note the matter in its report. During the 1987–88 session the committee took to issuing a series of interim reports on specific topics. In part this change was designed to draw more attention to the committee's work, which was often lost in the chaotic end-of-session shuffle. As well, it was an attempt to address the committee's lack of attention to follow-up. Unlike the Ombudsman Committee, the Public Accounts Committee made little effort to call officials before it to check on the progress promised by the ministry or recommended by the committee in earlier reports.[24] The committee's expectation now is that ministry responses to interim reports will be monitored, commented upon in later reports, and further followed up if necessary. Once tabled, committee reports often languish on the order paper for long periods, and even when they are called for debate, few members take more than a slight interest in them.

How effective is the Public Accounts Committee in fostering accountability and in improving financial management? Happily, the record is stronger than might be surmised from the foregoing account. Indeed, the Management Board of Cabinet, the central agency primarily concerned with financial control and management, looks upon the Public Accounts Committee as a valuable ally in its constant effort to improve the performance of ministries and agencies. A senior Management Board official monitors all committee meetings and keeps close watch, on Management Board's behalf, of the responses made to the committee by deputies and agency heads.

As with so many other aspects of accountability, the strength of the Public Accounts Committee lies more in the threat of what it might do

214 The Ontario legislature

than in what it actually does. Not all committee members possess the expertise or the inclination to pursue the often dry details of management that seem to be necessary for effective scrutiny. None the less, the bureaucrats are well aware that even if most of the time they can 'get by' the committee with at worst a mild reprimand, they can never be certain that they will not be badly embarrassed, subjected to unpleasant grilling in a public forum, and severely criticized in committee reports and in the media. Reputation and respect are currencies highly valued among senior public officials, and the Public Accounts Committee can damage both, either through naming the bureaucrats whose actions particularly displeased it (as it did in its 1980 report), or by relentlessly harassing of a deputy minister for a series of transgressions until he resigns (as was the case in the fall of 1984).

Not all of the Public Accounts Committee's success is rooted in fear, confrontation, and uncertainty. A good deal of its work consists of low-key, reasonable exchanges of criticism, rebuttal, and discussion of administrative issues. An appearance before the Public Accounts Committee need not be ulcer-inducing for senior public servants, and many of its sessions can be amicable and even productive for the bureaucrats called to account for their stewardship of the public purse. Ultimately, however, underlying the committee's effectiveness is its potential to cause grievous public embarrassment to the government and especially to its bureaucrats.

THE GOVERNMENT AGENCIES COMMITTEE

As early as 1951 the legislature established a Standing Committee on Government Commissions, but it seems to have been a toothless tiger.[25] Other than intermittent inquiries into specific management deficiencies by the Public Accounts Committee and occasional major studies of larger agencies such as the Ontario Municipal Board and the Workmen's Compensation Board, the legislature conducted few serious reviews of agencies, boards, or commissions until 1977. In that year the Procedural Affairs Committee was authorized to review semi-independent agencies 'with a view to reducing possible overlapping and redundancy.'[26] This peculiar mandate must be understood in the context of the then-current enthusiasm for 'sunsetting' (that is, terminating) agencies; in any event, the committee did not hesitate to widen its ken to more interesting concerns. By the time the agency review function was hived off from the Procedural Affairs Committee in 1986 and lodged with the

215 The legislature and accountability

Government Agencies Committee, the terms of reference had been expanded to include 'the operation of all agencies, boards and commissions to which the Lieutenant Governor makes some or all of the appointments, and all corporations to which the Crown in right of Ontario is a majority shareholder, such reviews to be made with a view to reducing possible redundancy and overlapping, improving the accountability of agencies, rationalizing the functions of agencies, identifying those agencies or parts of agencies which could be subject to sunset provisions, and revising the mandates and roles of agencies.'[27] Ostensibly, then, the task of the Government Agencies Committee is to review mandates, administrative structures, reporting relationships, and the like. To be sure, such topics are of concern to the committee,[28] but the primary focus of members' interest lies in the policies carried out by the agencies under review.

Each year the committee reviews as many as a dozen agencies, ranging from the small (the Wolf Damage Assessment Board, the Fire Code Commission, and the Old Fort William Advisory Committee) to the large (the Ontario Lottery Corporation, the Liquor Control Board of Ontario, and the Ontario Human Rights Commission). It has not taken on the very largest agencies, Ontario Hydro and the Workers' Compensation Board, for these are subject to repeated scrutiny by other committees. In the committee's first decade eighty-seven of Ontario's several hundred agencies were reviewed, a handful of them more than once. The reviews typically consist of several hours of formal meetings with the board and its top executives (often with a tour of board facilities) during which the agency makes an opening statement and then responds to MPPS' questions. Committee staff prepare detailed reports on the agency's organization and activities and suggest possible lines of inquiry. Usually, however, most of the discussion with the agency concerns the advisability and the effectiveness of its policies. The committee has experimented with calling for briefs and comment from agencies' client groups or other interest groups, but as a rule this procedure is not followed. Press attention to the committee's work is minimal, and its proceedings tend to be low-key and non-partisan (two facts that are not independent of one another); almost never do ministers or even parliamentary assistants turn up at committee meetings to provide political protection.

Particularly for the smaller agencies, which are rarely mentioned, let alone reviewed, during estimates debates, scrutiny by the Government Agencies Committee is an unusual experience, and may well be their only personal contact with members of the legislature. Agency reviews are rather less focused than Public Accounts Committee inquiries, which are invariably premised on a specific problem or criticism, and they tend to be less probing and less adversarial. They can be valuable exercises, not only in informing MPPs about the work of various low-profile agencies, but also in drawing to the agencies' attention their responsibility to the Assembly. The uncertainty principle is at work here: agencies can never be sure what will happen when they are called for review, especially since many agency heads and board members, unlike deputy ministers, have only the vaguest sense of the powers and practices of legislative committees.

During each session of the legislature the committee produces a report on the agencies it has reviewed. The report includes recommendations on policy as well as on matters structural and administrative. On occasion, committee reports have called for the termination of an agency, the reduction of its role, or its amalgamation with another government organization, but such proposals have little influence on the government's thinking. This is not to say, however, that agencies can afford to ignore the work or the recommendations of the committee. As one former MPP wrote, the value of the mechanisms available to the legislature for the scrutiny of agencies is 'limited but real ... for a Crown Corporation to know that it could be called to explain and that on occasion one of these committees could get tough is probably better than no accountability at all.'[29]

THE OMBUDSMAN COMMITTEE

The ombudsman's duty to seek the redress of administrative injustices through the investigation and, if necessary, the public reporting of alleged cases of maladministration or arbitrary bureaucratic action entails a strong element of accountability.[30] As an officer of the legislature, the ombudsman clearly plays a role in fostering government accountability to the legislature. In Ontario this accountability is greatly enhanced through a committee of the House which deals exclusively with the ombudsman and his recommendations.

Most of the basic features of the Ontario committee system are essentially variations on parliamentary committees in Canada and elsewhere. This is not true of the Standing Committee on the Ombudsman, which is unique in Canada and perhaps in British parliamentary systems.[31] Established in 1976 as a means of resolving a serious

217 The legislature and accountability

disagreement between the ombudsman and the government over the expropriation of land in North Pickering in the early 1970s, the committee has evolved a distinctive relationship with the ombudsman and plays a key role in what has come to be called 'the ombudsman process.'

The committee's order of reference directs it to 'review and consider from time to time the Reports of the Ombudsman as they become available.'[32] The committee spends some time each year analysing and discussing with the ombudsman his (usually annual) report to the legislature; invariably, the committee concentrates on questions of backlog and delay in resolving complaints. Far more significant and time consuming are the committee's detailed reviews of all 'recommendation denied' cases summarized in the ombudsman's report – that is, cases in which a governmental organization has refused to accept the recommendation of the ombudsman.[33]

The committee receives from the ombudsman all relevant documentation, with the names of complainants and ministry staff as well as any identifying references removed. Public hearings are then held, and the government and the ombudsman are called upon to put forward the facts of the case, their interpretation of those facts, and their reaction to one another's positions. Questioning of the ombudsman's staff and government officials (which is usually led by the committee counsel) is rigorous and pointed, so that both 'sides' must be prepared to convince the committee that the actions they have taken are well documented, fair, and reasonable.[34] The process is somewhat akin to a quasi-judicial tribunal or royal commission in which evidence is brought out by staff counsel. An indication of importance of the committee process is the unresolved case that is settled just before the review, when the government suddenly sees the wisdom of the ombudsman's position; the prospect of appearing before the committee with a shaky case seems, like the prospect of hanging, to concentrate the mind wonderfully.

During its hearings the committee is no more accepting of the opinions or interpretations of the ombudsman than it is of the views or conclusions of the government. It takes great pains to be, and to be seen to be, entirely fair and unbiased. Once the evidence is in, the committee adopts a stance described by one former chairman as 'weighted neutrality'; although the committee evaluates the evidence objectively, it leans towards the ombudsman's position in a dispute.[35] The committee set out the rationale for this approach in one of its early reports, arguing that if it 'choose not to support a recommendation of the Ombudsman after it had satisfied itself [that the Ombudsman had complied with his legislation and that the governmental response was inadequate or unreasonable] ... it would seriously undermine the effectiveness and credibility of the Ombudsman in the eyes of the people of the Province of Ontario and the members of the public service.'[36]

Most of the time the committee supports the conclusions reached by the ombudsman, but it has been known to reject them. In the normal fashion, the committee's recommendations are adopted or rejected (but rarely amended) by the House. Divisions are unusual; when the question is put, the government frequently though not uniformly supports the committee recommendations even when they favour the ombudsman over a ministry or an agency. Such recommendations, even when concurred in by the assembly, have no binding legal force,[37] but are generally implemented by the government. A key element underlying the committee's success is its extensive follow-up on earlier recommendations. The ombudsman's annual report contains a 'scorecard' of past recommendations indicating those to which the government to have responded inadequately; ministries that do not implement committee recommendations to the satisfaction of the ombudsman know that they will be called back before the committee to explain publicly why they have not fulfilled the express wishes of the legislature.

The effectiveness of the Ombudsman Committee stems in part from its members' willingness to put in long, unrewarding hours reviewing anonymous cases; but far more crucial is the markedly non-partisan atmosphere that surrounds its activities. Clearly, given the committee's mandate, the opportunities for direct political confrontation are not as numerous as they are in other committees or in the House, yet issues have surfaced in the committee which, in a different setting, might well have resulted in bitter, protracted partisan conflict. The almost Pavlovian government back-benchers' response of defence and counterattack against any criticism of the government is rarely triggered in the Ombudsman Committee. This may reflect their appreciation that complaints to the ombudsman are directed not at politicians and their policies but at the judgment and fairness of the bureaucrats, who are often disliked and distrusted by the members. Similarly, opposition MPPS usually manage to curb their desire to make partisan attacks on the government. In addition, their constant exposure to constituents' problems inclines MPPS to sympathize with those who have genuine grievances against government; in turn, this disposes the

219 The legislature and accountability

committee members to concentrate on rectifying injustices rather than on scoring political points, particularly since the complainants are anonymous. One important benefit of this apolitical approach is that the civil service takes the committee and its recommendations seriously.

The committee has been a mixed blessing for the ombudsman. The first ombudsman called the committee 'the final arrow in the ombudsman's quiver,' and it is true that the realization in the bureaucracy that rejection of an ombudsman's recommendation will entail a public hearing before a committee of the legislature strengthens the ombudsman's position. By the same token, however, the ombudsman's staff know that each case they investigate may eventually come before the committee. This has been a factor in the extensive documentation – critics would say the needless red tape – that has come to characterize the Ontario ombudsman's approach and that has contributed to the length of time required to complete investigations. More significant, though, have been the occasional confrontations between the ombudsman and the committee, all of which have been generated by the ombudsman's objections to the committee's typically wide interpretation of its mandate. These few clashes have soured the ombudsman's relations with the legislature and have hurt his public image. The impression should not be left that the ombudsman and the committee are constantly at odds or that their relationship is one of mistrust and dislike, for their dealings are mostly amiable and respectful; none the less a potential for conflict exists which is scarcely imaginable between, for example, the Public Accounts Committee and the provincial auditor.

One recent brouhaha illustrates that potential. For several years the committee unsuccessfully sought the authority to review the estimates of the ombudsman, arguing that this was a natural extension of its mandate. In 1982, as part of its routine review of the ombudsman's operations, the committee requested that the ombudsman provide it with certain financial information. The ombudsman refused, contending that no part of the committee's order of reference justified the request and that compliance with the request would compromise the ombudsman's independence. The confrontation, which badly damaged the incumbent ombudsman's relations with the legislature (and probably destroyed any chance of his reappointment), was resolved by the formal reference by the House of the ombudsman's estimates to the committee. The fears of the ombudsman and his advisers that, once given this power, the committee would be inclined to meddle in internal administrative matters have proved groundless. This estimates review is every bit as pointless a ritual as other committees' treatment of estimates.[38]

The final noteworthy aspect of the Ombudsman Committee is its unique power to make regulations. Section 16(1) of the Ombudsman Act empowers the legislature to establish 'general rules for the guidance of the Ombudsman in the exercise of his functions.' This power to formulate 'rules,' which are deemed to have the force of regulations under the Regulations Act, has been delegated to the Ombudsman Committee. To date the committee has proposed only one set of rules to the House, which adopted them without amendment.[39] Significantly, the committee felt confident in proposing these rules only after a lengthy process of discussing them with the ombudsman, canvassing members' opinions, and setting out the areas of concern and possible recommendations in earlier reports. In short, the committee does not take lightly its power to propose rules to the assembly.

Though its weapons are different from those in the usual parliamentary arsenal. the Ombudsman Committee clearly assists the legislature in carrying out its responsibility of holding the government – in this case principally the bureaucracy – accountable.

DELEGATED LEGISLATION

The activities of the Ontario government carried out through regulations and other statutory instruments are almost entirely immune from legislative scrutiny and thus from any real accountability. Every year thousands of pages of regulations are passed;[40] they cover a tremendously wide range of subjects, from minor 'administrivia' to welfare benefit levels, designation of toxic substances, pollution control orders, and rules for municipal planning. The legislature has virtually no role in this process. The legal power to make regulations has been delegated by the House to the government (rare indeed is the statute that fails to empower the cabinet to make regulations pertaining to its subject-matter), with no requirement that they come before the legislature for approval or even debate.

All regulations are referred to the Standing Committee on Regulations and Private Bills, in accordance with section 12 of the Regulations Act, which calls for a committee to review the legality of regulations. The committee's prime responsibility is to ensure that regulations do not exceed the ambit of the enabling statute, do not have a retroactive

221 The legislature and accountability

effect, and do not impose taxes (as opposed to setting licence fees);[41] it is specifically prohibited from considering the merits of the decisions and policies imposed by the regulations. Not surprisingly, MPPS show virtually no interest in this highly legalistic task. They are content to have the committee lawyer vet the regulations as they are promulgated and draw to their attention any that appear to transgress the guidelines for the proper form of regulations; only in the most exceptional circumstances does this process rise above a pro forma ritual. It is certainly useful for someone to cast an expert eye over the form and legality of regulations on the assembly's behalf, but the real concern with regulations has to do with their content and substance. MPPS are free to question and criticize the substance of regulations in question period, estimates, and elsewhere, but this is very much a hit-and-miss process, and usually is limited to high-profile issues. In Ontario neither individual members nor committees have shown much interest in endowing the legislature with greater scope for reviewing the merits of regulations. A partial exception is the June 1988 report from the Regulations and Private Bills Committee, which puts forward a series of recommedations designed to expand considerably the legislature's involvement in the regulation-making process.[42] The report suggests, inter alia, that Ontario adopt procedures similar to those that have been in place in Ottawa since 1986. Under this proposal the Regulations Committee would be empowered to recommend to the House the repeal of specific regulations; its report would be automatically adopted (and the regulation repealed) unless the House voted to reject the report within twenty sitting days.

The effect of such a reform is rather less than might be expected, however, since in order to maintain its non-partisanship the Regulations Committee would not examine regulations on their merits. Instead, the other standing committees would review the policies entailed in the regulations, but they would lack the power to force a binding House decision on their passage. Thus, members could overturn regulations only on narrow technical grounds. Amending the standing orders and the Regulations Act to allow standing committees to review the merits of regulations would not be a major advance. The difficulty is not with the procedure for getting regulations before these committees, since a committee that was really interested in a specific regulation would probably employ the annual-report ruse to do so. (Moreover, if committees were granted completely open terms of reference, as is discussed in the following chapter, they could examine regulations at will). Rather, the problem is finding enough time and interest among the committee members to pursue regulations. It is for this reason that delegated legislation constitutes a black hole for accountability in the Ontario legislature.

CONCLUSION

In this profoundly imperfect world, the Ontario legislature's record in holding the government accountable rates a bare pass, though it is only fair to add that its performance has improved markedly in recent years. In evaluating the legislature's success a distinction should be made between the mechanisms available to the members and the extent of the members' use of those mechanisms. A variety of potentially exacting avenues of accountability are open to members: question period offers the prospect of raising issues and criticisms with daunting immediacy in the most public forum possible, in a manner over which the government has no control; committees create an opportunity for detailed and continuing review; and specific procedures are in place that enable the assembly to scrutinize in some detail the government's past and future spending.

The growth in the scope and complexity of government has undercut the effectiveness of these mechanisms. Without information, the formal accountability procedures are blunted. Members' requirements are twofold: they need access to the detailed information that only government can provide, and they need assistance, in the main staff assistance, to collect, process, and evaluate that information. As was demonstrated in Chapter 7, members of the Ontario legislature are now fairly well served by personal, caucus, and non-partisan staff, so that the principal issue is the government's attitude towards providing information to the public and to the legislature. Recent Ontario governments have shared the reticence of governments everywhere about revealing information, but by Canadian standards they have been reasonably forthcoming (though both the press and the opposition continually dwell on what they see as the excesses of government secrecy). The passage of freedom of information legislation in 1987 (which came into force in 1988) holds the potential for significantly improving members' ability to gain access to material the government might prefer not to release. Whether the members will actually make good use of the legislation, and whether it represents the critical ingredient for improved governmental accountability that some have claimed,[43] will remain, for some time, an open question.

223 The legislature and accountability

Analyses of accountability tend to focus on members' capacity to get to the bottom of alleged improprieties and errors, and to ferret out damaging revelations about administrative incompetence and policy intentions – in short, to probe for weaknesses. Yet an important if less newsworthy element of accountability operates on quite a different level: the role of the legislature in forcing the government to specify its priorities, its policies, and its plans. Governments tend to be vague in setting out what they are doing so that it is difficult to measure their success or failure, so that they can avoid making specific commitments, and so that conflicts and trade-offs with other policies do not become evident. Through question period, estimates, and committee inquiries the opposition can force the government to clarify its policies and explain their operation. This may well lead the opposition to focus on problems and errors; but even when it does not, the public confirmation and explanation of governmental plans and policies – or of the government's inability or unwillingness to be specific about its actions – is important.

The accountability process depends heavily on the press. Without press coverage, or at least the threat of press coverage, parliamentary accountability mechanisms lose a good deal of their force. If few MPPs are interested in accountability for its own sake, in management processes, or in the detailed routine of administration, fewer still are the members of the press gallery who have any concern whatsoever for such matters. They instantly dismiss discussion of details of policy or administration as boring and rush off in search of horses on the payroll. This naturally discourages MPPs from pursuing with much vigour many of the more mundane accountability questions that might, for example, characterize a meaningful consideration of estimates. And yet the press is sufficiently unpredictable that the apprehension of what *might* come out and what *might* be reported in an unfavourable way is always present in the mind of government. Former Premier William Davis was said to have insisted that his ministers not do anything they would not want to see reported on the front page of the *Globe and Mail*. Now, the *Globe* does not rely exclusively on legislative sources for stories critical of government, but question period and committee inquiries can generate substantial journalistic interest. Paradoxically, the press are fundamentally important in making accountability processes work, though their inattention to particular facets of the process is to a large degree responsible for their ineffectiveness.

If the level of accountability in the Ontario legislature is one of bare adequacy, what are the links between accountability and transformative capacity? In Ontario, legislative accountability is only rarely about formal sanctions or concrete actions; mostly it is about requiring the government to put its record on the line and to accept the political consequences of criticism. Accordingly, it would be difficult to interpret the advances in accountability detailed in this chapter as anything other than improvements in the performance of arena functions. That this is so underlines an important point about the arena – transformative distinction. Even if one is strongly of the view that our legislatures should, in and of themselves, make policy and take decisions – in short, be transformative – much valuable work can occur in arena legislatures or in legislatures engaged in arena-type activities.

9
The process of reform

Among the possible ways of categorizing parliamentary reform, two are especially germane to an inquiry into the reform of the Ontario legislature. First, changes may occur incrementally and develop gradually out of existing conditions, or they may represent significant departures from the past and be qualitative rather than quantitative. In Ontario, improvements to services have been largely incremental; significant exceptions include the provision of publicly funded constituency offices in 1976 and the establishment of an electronic Hansard a decade later. The Ontario experience with services for members illustrates that even if changes are made in piecemeal fashion their total effect can be great. The second method of categorizing reform turns on the question whether changes are generated in response to a widespread consensus on the direction of reform or whether they reflect the enthusiasms of a few active reformers. Although in Ontario there is general agreement that change is necessary, there is no consensus about the form that change should take; and few reform issues are pursued actively by more than a handful of members and staff.

THE CAMP COMMISSION

As Schindeler has documented, the legislature's procedures and facilities scarcely changed from Confederation until the 1960s.[1] John Robarts, who served as premier during the 1960s, was said to have 'brought the Ontario legislature into the twentieth century':[2] sessions were lengthened from a few weeks to an average of over 100 days a year, public funding was provided for opposition research and caucus support, and question period was allowed to emerge as a significant component of the legislative day despite the absence of any standing order to legitimize its existence. In 1970, following a committee report,[3] the rules underwent their first major revision since 1939 (rules committees in the 1940s and early 1960s had proposed important changes, but their recommendations were not acted upon). In addition to formally establishing question period and placing global time limits on supply debates, these amendments to the standing orders streamlined antiquated procedures – for example, by doing away with the cumbersome ways and means provisions and by eliminating the need for two days' notice of the introduction of bills.

Such changes, however welcome they may have been, only made up for decades of neglect and gave members on both sides of the House a sense of how far they still had to go. They did not fundamentally alter the essential subservience of the legislature to the cabinet. At the same time, a technocratic reorganization of the executive was undertaken as a result of the work of the Committee on Government Productivity (COGP); the legislature, which was explicitly excluded from COGP's terms of reference, was threatened with further eclipse.[4] Thus, partly in response to pressure from its own back-benchers, in June 1972 the government established a commission to review all facets of the Ontario legislature, 'with particular reference to the role of the Private Members and how their participation in the process of Government may be enlarged.'[5] The commissioners were chosen to represent the three political parties: the chairman was Dalton Camp, the Tory éminence grise; he was assisted by the journalist Douglas Fisher, a former CCF-NDP member of Parliament, and Farquhar Oliver, who had served as leader of the Ontario Liberal party on three separate occasions and as MPP for Grey South from 1926 to 1967. Although these selections drew widespread praise, not all MPPs accepted the underlying premise that the legislature was not to be trusted with its own affairs.

The main task of the Commission on the Legislature lay not so much in divining the legislature's problems, for those were never obscure, as in proposing workable remedies acceptable to the government. This it did with consummate skill. Taken individually, none of the commission's recommendations was so outlandish as to invite out-of-hand government dismissal; collectively, they amounted to a blueprint for far-reaching reform. The commission's work was almost entirely free of partisan wrangles, and its reports were executed with thoroughgoing pragmatism; for example, after a report was issued, publication of the next report was delayed until the government had acted upon the earlier report's recommendations. Between May 1973 and October 1975 the commission produced a total of five reports (though one report dealt only with party finance, a topic appended to the commission's terms of reference when it became apparent that the commission was a convenient and respected vehicle for dealing with this suddenly troublesome issue).[6]

Detailed recommendations were made to improve members' working conditions, their financial rewards, their ability to participate effectively in lawmaking, and their resources and opportunities to criticize the government. The commission recognized that extensive tinkering was not the answer; fundamental reform of the legislature's position in the structure of government was the only satisfactory solution. The overarching theme of the commission's work was the need for a legislature independent of the political executive and its bureaucratic apparatus. Much of the responsibility for the legislature's subservience was laid at the members' door: 'They have been neither jealous enough of their rights nor zealous enough in standing up for them ... the Commission senses that the executive has not so often seized such authority as it has simply occupied ground which the members have abandoned.'[7] In contrast, the executive was largely absolved of blame: 'The Commission does not want to suggest, even vaguely, that the Ministers in Ontario and their senior officials have any contempt for the legislature or view it as merely an inconvenience to be suffered or ignored.'[8] This may have been an adroit strategy for maximizing influence, but as an analysis of political developments it was too charitable by far to the government.

The first report from the commission, published in early 1973, concentrated on members' compensation and pensions, and contained some preliminary comments on possible mechanisms for extracting the assembly from the benevolent but uncomprehending tutelage of the Ministry of Government Services. Most of its key recommendations were implemented through an amendment to the Legislative Assembly Act in December 1973. Just as the bill was being passed into law, the second report was released. That report expanded on the theme of an independent legislature and suggested the means for achieving this goal: an independent Speakership supported by a professional administrative apparatus not responsible to the ministry. It also proposed a range of improvements in services for members, including the provision of a personal secretary or assistant for each MPP and better funding for caucus research. This report was not greeted as enthusiastically by the government as its predecessor had been. Although the government did bring forward legislation to implement most of its principal recommendations through amendments to the Legislative Assembly Act in December 1974, one participant was of the view that 'the basic problem remains because the government has really not accepted the idea of an independent legislature.'[9] Still, the amendments did guarantee each member a personal assistant, grant the Speaker the authority to prepare the assembly's spending estimates (as well as jurisdiction over certain portions of the Legislative Building), and establish the Board of Internal Economy and the Office of the Assembly. Powerful backroom pressure was exerted on the government after the bill was introduced, with the result that a number of significant changes were made to the bill in committee. Among these were provisions granting the clerk of the House tenure for life during good behaviour and the representation of opposition members on the Board of Internal Economy (initially, the government had accepted the commission's proposal that the board be composed of the Speaker and three ministers).

The commission's two final reports appeared in September and October 1975, in the midst of an election campaign. Procedure, rule changes, and committee structure were the subjects of the fourth report; the fifth report was a hodge-podge of leftovers and loose ends. The fourth report analysed the procedures of the House and offered a host of suggestions for improving them; less haphazard scheduling of House business, a reduction in party leaders' dominance of question period, enhanced opportunities for members to call for papers and information, a mechanism for the House (and perhaps as few as fifteen MPPS) rather than the government to decide whether to examine legislation in the House or in committee, a moderate form of 'closure by agreement,' the sharp curtailment of throne and budget debates, a more formal time-allocation procedure for estimates, and the genuine consideration of private members' business, including study in committee. A radically revamped committee system, premised on three key notions, was proposed: first, select committees would be phased out; second, 'largish' (twenty- or twenty-five member) committees would be struck on an ad hoc basis to consider individual pieces of legislation in the fashion of British 'standing' committees; third, small permanent committees (of seven or eight members) would scrutinize estimates and carry out special inquiries. On petition of one-third of the House, reports presented to the House would be referred to committee. Finally, without specifying its preference, the commission advocated an end to the standing orders' virtual silence on committee procedure and the status of committee witnesses.

The fifth and final report dealt with matters not touched on or resolved in earlier reports. It called for a wholesale renovation of the Legislative Building, unrestricted radio and television access to House proceedings, publicly financed constituency offices, and a province-wide information reference service. The last two recommendations grew out of the commissioners' insistence that 'there must be a halt to the growing emphasis on the MPP as a constituency case-worker and information officer.'[10] On the premise that 'a more effective legislature requires substantially more Members,'[11] the report suggested an expansion of the House to 180 members.

MINORITY GOVERNMENT AND REFORM 1975-81

The October 1975 election returned the Conservatives to office, but for the first time in more than three decades they found themselves in a minority position. Though important reforms had come to fruition during the previous few years of majority government, the minority situation lubricated the wheels of change. Their numerical superiority gave the opposition parties an unparalleled opportunity to force the government to defer to their wishes, and they were determined to make the best use of it. Less obvious but of great importance was the shift in attitude occasioned by minority government. The government, when faced with an impasse, could no longer resort to bulldozer tactics; the opposition found itself with unaccustomed influence not only over House business, but over the very fate of the government. Both sides recognized the need for forthright and effective communication, and a sophisticated consultation process quickly developed among the House leaders, who heretofore had been of little consequence. The resulting orderly management of the House proved to be in everyone's interest. Other important departures from past practice not reflected in formal rule changes included the appointment of opposition MPPS as committee chairmen, and the appointment of a member of the opposition as deputy Speaker and later as Speaker. In these and other ways minority government encouraged MPPS of all parties to take the legislature more seriously.

Early in the new legislature a small select committee was struck to review and report upon the fourth and fifth Camp Commission reports.

Such a committee (quickly styled the Morrow Committee after its chairman, the longtime Tory back-bencher and former Speaker Don Morrow) was thought necessary not only because it would give members a direct involvement in prospective rule changes but also because many of the Camp Commission's suggestions were cast in imprecise language. In short order the committee presented a report advocating constituency offices for all MPPs and the experimental presence of radio and television in the House.[12] The 'experimental' nature of television in the House was something of a fraud, for members of the committee knew that once the cameras were admitted it would be virtually impossible to remove them. The attainment of publicly funded constituency offices required more than sleight-of-hand: the opposition had to threaten to precipitate a full-scale confrontation before the premier would agree to them.

The procedural issues raised in the final two Camp Commission reports were subject to rather more protracted negotiations. Despite a primal government–opposition division within the committee, its work was marked by genuine compromise and conciliation. Both sides gave ground substantially, though the end product reflected the opposition's control of the committee and the persistence with which they set forth their arguments. After several months of intense deliberations, the Morrow Committee produced a second interim report in June 1976.[13] For the most part the report consisted of relatively moderate recommendations for implementing the Camp proposals. It concurred with most of Camp's ideas, though it modified a good number of them; it rejected more effective closure provisions, fixed dates for terminating the estimates debates, and, perhaps most significantly, rejected key elements of the commission's proposed committee structure. Instead, the Morrow Committee recommended twenty-member policy committees to consider estimates and legislation, with small subcommittees to mount the special investigations previously undertaken by select committees.

At the committee's direction the chairman took the then unusual step of moving the report's adoption in order to enhance the likelihood of its recommendations being considered seriously by the House. Several months passed before the parties turned their attention to formal negotiations on the report. The disposition of the report was thrashed out in an enlarged version of the House leaders' committee, which included the whips and several members of the Morrow Committee who were unwilling to abandon their work to the private deal-making of the House leaders. Each party set out its lists of demands and concessions;

tough but amicable negotiations ensued, and compromise prevailed, though all parties held firm to certain stands. Illustrative of the horse-trading was the opposition's agreement not to sit on Wednesdays (which the government wanted to retain as cabinet day) in exchange for the lengthening of question period from forty minutes to an hour. Three long days of intense bargaining culminated in a marathon session lasting well into the night before the Christmas prorogation. The end product was a government motion encompassing a broad range of changes to the standing orders, to be undertaken on a trial basis, which passed after a short debate.[14]

The government turned down the committee's proposals for individual research assistants for MPPS, and postponed most of the recommendations on committees pending further review. Other Morrow proposals fell by the wayside (for example, the opposition's right of reply to ministerial statements), but a great many significant changes did find their way into the legislature's rules. Among the more important were the revamped procedure on private members' business, which ensured that they would come to a vote (though the government had insisted on a provision whereby twenty members could block a vote); the lengthening of question period; the requirement for compendia of background information to be tabled with government bills and policy statements; an effective end to sitting past 10:30 PM without the consent of the opposition; a provision for twenty members – in effect, either of the opposition parties – to refer legislation to a standing committee rather than Committee of the Whole after second reading; and a provision for twenty members to send a report of an agency or ministry to committee for study. Virtually all of the changes favoured the opposition over the government.

A final report from the Morrow Committee was published in February 1977; it dealt primarily with the physical facilities of the legislature. In addition to detailing the urgent need for a fullscale refurbishing of the Legislative Building, the report offered suggestions for improved radio and television coverage of the House, dealt with a handful of minor procedural matters left over from the second report, and reiterated the need for personal research assistants and the MPPS' apparent widespread support for the idea.[15] It was acknowledged that the costs would run into the millions of dollars, and little came of this report save a rancorous House debate late in 1977, which was most notable for the chief government whip's pointed criticism of the cabinet for its lack of interest in the report.[16]

The provisional standing orders were just beginning their initial shakedown when the government called an election in the spring of 1977. With the return of another minority government, a fair trial for the new rules was ensured. In the fall of 1978 the Procedural Affairs Committee brought in a new set of standing orders which refined and consolidated the provisional and the regular standing orders. In this exercise, no new ground was broken; but by the same token no ground was lost, since none of the 1976 advances were altered in any significant way.

The committee system, which had largely been left out of the 1976-78 round of reforms, was the subject of a major report by the Procedural Affairs Committees in June 1980. Entitled 'Proposals for a New Committee System,' the report was essentially a discussion paper, prepared for the committee's consideration, that was rushed into print during an election scare. The radical revisions to the committee system it recommended did not enjoy strong support from any of the parties. Together with the general unwillingness to embark on major reforms during the run-up to an election, this lack of support was fatal to any prospect of the ideas set out in the report being acted upon.

The report was premised on the recognition that the scope for expanding committee work was limited, and that the pressing need was to improve and reorganize the committee system. It proposed that committees be small (with a maximum of ten members) and that in most cases substitutions not be permitted. A rationalization of committee work was proposed that would see legislation reviewed in ad hoc committees in the mould of British 'standing' committees; all estimates, budget papers, tax legislation, and matters of fiscal policy would be referred to a Finance and Economic Affairs Committee; the policy field committees would concentrate on policy reviews and other special studies.[17] Though the changes it recommended, and particularly the suggestion that estimates be effectively abandoned, seemed too unsettling for many Ontario members, the report became an object of considerable interest in Canadian parliamentary circles;[18] several of its ideas prefigured reforms made to the committee system in the House of Commons in the 1980s.

In the course of its review of committees, the Procedural Affairs Committee tried without success to come to grips with the thorny problem of the legal position of committee witnesses. Recognizing that it was getting into deep water, the committee reported that the many uncertainties relating to the protection and liability of committee witnesses needed to be resolved.[19] Though it set out some principles for dealing with witnesses, the committee wisely called for expert assistance from the Ontario Law Reform Commission. The attorney-general acceded to the committee's request that the matter – and the eleven specific questions posed in the committee report – be studied by the commission. In September 1981 the Law Reform Commission released an exhaustive, authoritative review of the difficult legal and constitutional issues, and its recommendations for legislative reform.[20] Although the Procedural Affairs Committee attempted more than once to stimulate action on the Law Reform Commission's recommendations, most of them are yet to be implemented.

MAJORITY GOVERNMENT AND STAGNATION 1981–85

The return to majority government following the March 1981 election brought an abrupt halt to the progress of reform. Though the Conservatives were not shy about using their regained majority – what Premier William Davis called 'the realities of March 19' – to override opposition objections or proposals on a wide range of policy fronts, majority government was not the calamity for legislative processes that some have portrayed. The drive towards reform had lost its momentum; in the natural ebb and flow of legislative developments, enthusiasm for change had waned significantly. Most of the key Camp Commission recommendations had been implemented, save those relating to committees, and few members thought parliamentary reform deserved a high priority. Moreover, if it was true that (except in some minor improvements to services) the majority years 1981 to 1985 marked a hiatus in reform, far more significant was the absence of attempts to roll back earlier reforms and return to the excesses of the pre-1975 era. No amendments were made to the standing orders during these years, so that all of the significant rule changes made in 1976 were retained. In addition, the extensive interparty consultations among House leaders continued as before, as did most of the intangible advances registered during the minority period – for example, the postponement of estimates when a critic was absent. This enlightened attitude was not born entirely of altruism, of course, for the government well recognized that it stood to gain the most from a smoothly orchestrated House, and that few of the reforms represented serious threats to a majority government. Not all government members appreciated this approach; 'We've gotten our majority back – why don't we use it?' was a complaint often heard from Conservative back-benchers.

The Procedural Affairs Committee continued to review the practices and rules of the House, and produced five reports on standing orders and procedure. Just before Christmas 1981 the committee tabled a report on private bills that proposed a series of uncontroversial reforms.[21] The proposed reforms were also uninteresting to members, and the report languished on the order paper for the balance of the parliament. The next major report, released late in 1982,[22] reprised the earlier recommendations on streamlining the private bills procedure and responded to the Ontario Law Reform Commission's *Report on Witnesses before Legislative Committees*. With the exception of a recommendation that a brochure be prepared to explain to witnesses how committees worked and what the witnesses' rights and obligations were, the principal proposals entailed amendments to the Legislative Assembly Act. The most important of these would have enabled committees routinely to go directly to the Speaker for a warrant without requiring authorization from the House; prevented evidence given before a committee from being used in a civil proceeding; and provided for the possibility of fines for breaches of privilege or contempts of the House on the grounds that the only existing punishment, imprisonment, was too inflexible. The report also contained a handful of procedural recommendations, the most important of which were for full Hansard service for all committees, for mandatory government responses to committee reports, and for points of privilege to be prohibited until after question period, as is the Ottawa practice.

In exploring reform possibilities for Ontario, the committee was much influenced by the work of the House of Commons reform committee, struck in the wake of the infamous bells episode.[23] It adopted several of the Ottawa innovations, and it also attempted to emulate the approach developed by the federal committee as explained by an all-party panel of MPS that appeared before the Procedural Affairs Committee. The federal committee members advised their Ontario counterparts to strive for unanimity or at least consensus among the parties, and also that it was futile and indeed inadvisable constantly to be looking over one's shoulder at the House leaders, trying to anticipate their views.[24]

The ensuing report, published in March 1984, copied the Lefebvre Committee's ideas about imposing time limits on members' speeches (forty-five minutes), incorporating up to ten minutes of questions and comments after most speeches, and introducing a ten-minute period for members' statements at the beginning of the day. Also in this report were proposals to limit ministerial statements to twenty minutes and to increase back-bench participation in question period by limiting party leaders to two supplementaries and other members to one. If the number of supplementaries was reduced, the loser would not be the member posing the original question, but question period generally. The current practice of the opposition parties' having a supplementary on one another's questions, made for a lively counterpoint in which each opposition member had to be alert and ready to give his party's perspective on the issues raised by the other opposition party. Repeated Liberal complaints about the inequity of the question period rotation, which granted equal priority to the twenty-one-member NDP caucus and the thirty-four-member Liberal caucus, came to naught. The committee also proposed incorporating into the standing orders a codification of existing committee practice.

The most contentious issue, and the issue of most concern to the government, involved the ringing of the division bells. As elsewhere in Canada, for most types of votes there were no limits on the length of time the bells summoning MPPs could ring, and the custom had developed that the Speaker would not order the voting to begin until the party whips signalled that they were ready. Both the House of Commons and the Manitoba legislature had been paralysed for extended periods, and a similar situation had been averted in Ontario in May 1982 only when the Liberal opposition decided that three days of bell-ringing had adequately expressed its distaste for a sales tax bill. The problem was the subject of hurried discussion in the Procedural Affairs Committee, which in late May 1982 tabled, for discussion only, a one-item report recommending that division bells be limited to eight hours.[25] It soon became evident that this proposal would not do. The government wanted a procedure for preventing such episodes, and the opposition was hesitant about giving up a potentially valuable weapon. The suggested compromise was cumbersome and convoluted: a series of time limits on bell-ringing, and a provision for a notice of motion to proceed to a vote on the disputed matter after several days, interspersed with cooling-off periods during which normal business would take place. The government had wanted a faster way of overcoming a potential deadlock, and the proposal quickly disappeared from view.

A final, short, punchless report on the leaking of committee reports was tabled in June 1984.[26] Significantly, this was the only one of the committee's procedural reports to be debated during the Thirty-second Parliament.[27] The government did allow an inconclusive debate on the proposals for a new committee system, though it was evident to all that the recommendations in the report had no prospect of acceptance.[28] Throughout this period intermittent discussions were held among the House leaders about possible agreements on reform, but nothing concrete ever emerged. The government had little incentive for reform, and only a few members on the opposition side had much interest in what was evidently a futile proposition. There was more enthusiasm for the itinerary of the much-travelled Procedural Affairs Committee than for serious reform of the House.

THE LIBERAL-NDP ACCORD

Reform of the legislature did not rank among the leading issues of the 1985 election, though it was clearly a component of the new, more 'open' approach to government espoused by the Liberals. When the Liberals and the New Democrats were negotiating the accord that led to the establishment of a Liberal government in the summer of 1985, agreement was reached easily on basic principles for legislative reform. Indeed, the first of the accord's three documents spelling out common objectives dealt exclusively with reforming the legislature.[29] Included under this rubric were several matters that were only tangentially related to the assembly, and owed more to the open-government theme: a freedom of information bill (long advocated by both parties); election finance reform; and the broadening of civil servants' political rights. More directly legislative in nature were commitments to televise the proceedings of the House; to revive the committee to oversee Ontario Hydro; to 'reform ... the House by strengthening and broadening the role of committees and individual members and increasing public involvement in the legislative process'; to expand the mandates of the provincial auditor and the Public Accounts Committee to permit an examination of current and proposed expenditures; and to establish a committee to inquire into ways of reforming public sector appointments.[30]

Canadian experience has shown that the most favourable time for genuine parliamentary reform is early in the first term of a new government. Though the record of reform during the first year of the Liberal government at first blush seems impressive, on closer inspection the accomplishments are less significant than the missed opportunities.

The principal vehicle for the promotion of reform was the Procedural Affairs Committee. Significantly, the core membership of the committee did not change appreciably from what it had been during the

237 The process of reform

Conservative majority. This meant that the committee was able to build on the bonds of trust established in preceding years (not least between Michael Breaugh, the NDP chairman, and the leading Tories, Richard Treleaven and Norman Sterling); but by the same token, it meant that the committee lacked major infusions of new ideas and approaches.

The committee quickly set to work. First on its agenda was the question of television in the House. Since the basic decision to proceed with assembly-controlled coverage had already been taken, the committee was largely limited to commenting on the details of implementation and on the issue of how rigidly the coverage should conform to the 'electronic Hansard' model. As was discussed in Chapter 7, the committee reported early in September; its report was adopted by the House just two days into the fall sitting. By mid-November the committee had produced a major report containing a wide range of recommendations on the larger topic of procedural reform. With the exception of a subsequent report on the public appointments process, this proved to be the committee's principal contribution to the reform debate. This was unfortunate, since the document, which set the parameters for possible reform, consisted primarily of proposals recycled from earlier reports or taken from the report of the Special Committee on Reform of the House of Commons (the McGrath Committee), which had been published in Ottawa in June 1985.[31] Indeed, the report produced in November 1985 was in all essentials the same report the previous Procedural Affairs Committee had prepared prior to the 1985 election. The point is not that the earlier recommendations were ill-advised or made in haste, but that they were developed in a political context in which the prospect for reform was much narrower than that opened by the new government. The committee therefore confined itself to putting its previous ideas into a workable form, and did not seek to raise more fundamental reform issues.

Of the recommendations that went beyond the committee's earlier reports, a number were clearly inspired by the reports of the Lefebvre or McGrath committees: the election of the Speaker by secret ballot, the abolition of evening sittings, the establishment of a parliamentary calendar, the inclusion of a more precise definition of 'confidence' in the rules, and the creation of an intendant of parliament with authority over the parliamentary precincts. Other ideas, though new to Ontario, were established practice in other Canadian jurisdictions, such as the removal of appeals against Speaker's decisions and the right of opposition reply to ministerial statements, which would follow rather than precede question period. The only departures in the report were recommendations that the ringing of division bells be limited to fifteen minutes unless the whips advised the Speaker that absent members required more time to return to the House to vote, in which case up to twenty-four hours' delay might be permitted; and that the Board of Internal Economy meet in public, with three days' public notice of its agenda. (Along with this went a recommendation that cabinet representatives on the board be reduced from three to two, and that members other than whips and House leaders be selected to serve on the board.)

In addition to the more straightforward limits on bell-ringing, the only significant departures from the committee's 1980, 1982, and 1984 reports were the scotching of the forty-five minute limit on speeches that was proposed in 1984; the recommendation that, like other members, party leaders be allowed only a single supplementary during question period, and some revisions to the design of the committee system. The broad principles underlying the 1980 proposals for a new committee system were retained, though the suggested maximum committee size of ten was reduced to eight, its limits on substitution and its referral of petitions to the Ombudsman Committee were dropped, Ottawa-style 'opposition days' were added to the estimates process, and a formal mechanism for allocating chairmen among parties was suggested.

The November 1985 Procedural Affairs Committee report was unusual in that it contained two dissenting opinions, both from Conservatives. Norman Sterling's dissent focused on the inequities of equating, for both the question period rotation and the allocation of chairmanships, the fifty-one member Conservative caucus with the NDP caucus of twenty-five. Richard Treleaven expressed reservations about many recommendations; some were clearly his personal views (for example, his objection to replacing the term 'previous question' with 'a motion for closure'), but others – on committees, time limits for divisions, members' statements, question period, and so on – were widely interpreted as a reflection of uncertainty within the Tory ranks as to the advisability of the committee recommendations.

Shortly before the Procedural Affairs report was tabled, the treasurer had published a paper, entitled 'Reforming the Budget Process.'[32] Among its suggestions was a proposal for a legislative committee on economic and fiscal affairs, similar to the finance committee mooted in the 1980 'Proposals' report. This document appeared too late to have a significant impact on the thinking of the Procedural Affairs Committee, though it did signify that the government was willing to consider a radical revision of the estimates process and of the procedure relating to financial management and economic policy.

The Procedural Affairs report was the subject of an evening's debate, which was adjourned without a vote. This debate had a distinctly perfunctory air to it, for everyone recognized that the decision on which aspects of the report would be accepted and implemented would be made by the House leaders and the whips. The whips took the lead in the negotiations because of the government House leader's heavy ministerial load, and because of uncertainty over the Conservative House leadership (Dennis Timbrell, the House leader, was preparing to leave public life).

The whips did not begin to negotiate in earnest until March 1986. Prior to that date the committee's proposals had been put to each party caucus for discussion. The Tories formed a special caucus committee to review the report and held several full caucus meetings on it; inevitably, most members were interested only in a few specific recommendations, particularly those relating to times of sitting, members' statements, and question period. The NDP and the Liberals also 'caucused' on the pending reforms; though the turnout was good, only a handful of MPPS showed much interest in more than a few high-profile reforms. From these sessions, from discussions with the party leadership, and from their own appreciation of the recommendations, the whips each brought to the negotiations lists of preferred, acceptable, and unacceptable proposals. From the outset the agreement was that the only reforms that would be implemented were those on which consensus was reached. This ensured general support for whatever changes were adopted, but at the cost of each party's having an effective veto over all recommendations. (The interparty dealing that led to the 1976 reforms had been conducted on a different basis: if a party vehemently objected to a specific proposal, it had to offer a substantial concession in return.) Together with the understanding that only the recommendations of the Procedural Affairs Committee were on the table – that is, that no new issues could be raised – this severely limited the scope for agreement. For example, the Conservatives refused to accept the proposal to refer all estimates to a finance committee that would intensively review only a few sets of estimates, since they believed that no minister should be able to escape an annual scrutiny of his estimates. The idea of a parliamentary calendar was rejected by the Liberal government, since the premier had already scheduled a trip to Asia for the early fall of 1986, when, under the proposed calendar, the House would be sitting. Ad hoc bills committees were thought to be unworkable by both the Liberals and the Conservatives.

A good deal of genuine give and take did transpire at the whips' meetings. The recommendation for members' statements was, for example, subject to extensive negotiations. The cabinet was hesitant, fearing that members' statements would be used by the opposition to attack the government, which would have no chance for rebuttal. Sensing correctly that members' statements would primarily be an extension of question period, the Liberals sought unsuccessfully to shorten question period by ten minutes. They were adamant, however, that the opposition party leaders should not be given a 'prime time' platform for government-bashing; in return for the exclusion of the opposition leaders from members' statements they agreed also to exclude not only the premier but the ministers.

The overall atmosphere of the interparty negotiations was amicable, perhaps because the stakes were not particularly high and there was not much sense of urgency about reform, at least by comparison with the 1976 round of reforms. In turn, this reflected a realization that attitudes were more important than rules in contributing to an effective legislature. As well, the unfamiliar circumstances in which the Liberals and the Conservatives found themselves contributed to their conservative approach to change. The Liberals, though more sympathetic to the plight of the opposition than most governments, had certainly lost the keen enthusiasm for reform that had characterized them not long before. Moreover, the Liberal whip, Joan Smith, had been elected only a few months earlier, and was understandably cautious about agreeing to potentially troublesome changes. Many Conservative MPPS, so recently and rudely deposed from power, had not fully come to terms with their new lot on the opposition benches. Some, therefore, approached possible reforms with the presumption that they would be back in office shortly and should be wary about strengthening the opposition. This was not a universal view; the Tory whip, Ernie Eves, explicitly denied that it coloured his thinking,[33] but it certainly affected that of some of his caucus. Perhaps more significant was the Tories' lack of experience in opposition. As their House leader put it, 'My attitude about certain proposals which a year ago were an anathema to me all of a sudden became rather enlightened.'[34] None the less, by the time the whips sat down to negotiate the reform package, the Conservatives had

had only thirteen weeks' sitting time in opposition. Moreover, many senior caucus members were shell-shocked at their being turned out of office, and made only feeble attempts to adapt to an opposition mentality. Others devoted their attention to the bitter leadership fight within the party. In short, for a variety of reasons, the Tories did not bring to the bargaining table a tough, seasoned opposition perspective.

Topics of discussion among the whips included not only the changes to the standing orders envisioned by the Procedural Affairs Committee, but also amendments to the Legislative Assembly Act arising from the committee report and from other sources. Although general agreement was reached about the substance of changes to the act, only the new standing orders were brought forward for House approval. A brief and essentially pro forma debate took place, and the new rules were adopted on 28 April 1986; they were to come into force the next day. These were provisional standing orders that would lapse on 18 December 1986, though the general expectation was that, subject to fine-tuning, the changes were of much more than experimental status. In fact, they were extended for the rest of the parliament, and subsequently into 1989. The amending of the act remained on the agenda, but by the end of 1988 no legislation had been introduced.

Not surprisingly, in view of the ground rules for the negotiating process, the deal struck by the whips differed from the committee's proposals in many important particulars. Even excepting those that would require amendments to the Legislative Assembly Act, or would be implemented by means other than through the standing orders, more important recommendations were rebuffed by the whips' committee than were accepted, even in modified form. The following committee proposals were not incorporated into the provisional standing orders of April 1986: the election of the Speaker by secret ballot; the elimination of appeals from Speaker's rulings; the adoption of a parliamentary calendar; the prohibition against the raising of points of privilege until after question period; the provision for ministers' statements to follow rather than precede question period; the fifteen-minute limit on division bells; the provision of full Hansard service to all committees; a striking committee to propose committee membership; the establishment of ad hoc bills committees; the reference of all estimates to a finance committee; the provision for 'opposition days'; the appointment of a maximum of eight members to committees; and a definition of 'confidence' in the standing orders. Ranged against this litany of rejection was a less impressive list of reforms sanctioned by the whips:

Monday-to-Thursday House sittings and the elimination of evening sittings (the committee had proposed sitting from 1:00 PM to 6:00 PM; the whips settled on the period from 2:00 PM to 6:30 PM, plus a sitting from 10:00 AM to noon on Thursdays for private members' business); a twenty-minute limit on ministerial statements with opposition responses (the committee had recommended five minutes per party per statement, but the whips allowed five minutes in total per party); a ten-minute period for members' ninety-second statements (the committee proposal had been for all members to be eligible to participate, but the whips excluded ministers and party leaders); a requirement that the government respond to committee reports within 120 days; a simplified emergency debate procedure that would lift most of the burden of decision from the Speaker; a ten-minute 'mini-question period' after speeches (the whips added the proviso that no one member could speak for more than two minutes, with two minutes reserved at the end for rebuttal); the automatic referral of statutory annual reports to committee; the apportionment of committee chairmanships by party (the whips included an addendum that the Finance Committee would be chaired by a government MPP and the Public Accounts Committee by a member of the official opposition); and the establishment of the Finance and Government Agencies committees. The whips agreed to a few other recommendations from the Procedural Affairs Committee, such as the inclusion in the standing orders of committee terms of reference and substitution procedure; these represented only a codification of existing practices, and were not significant advances.

Even before it received the accord's imprimatur, the Procedural Affairs Committee was intrigued by the possibility of legislative committees' reviewing senior government appointments, as advocated by the McGrath Committee. After it was formally given the mandate to 'examine and report on the methods by which it believes appointments should be made to Agencies, Boards and Commissions,'[35] the committee travelled to American legislatures to gain firsthand evidence of how the practice worked in a congressional setting. In early 1986 hearings were held at Queen's Park. The committee had to deal not only with the highly controversial question of committees passing judgment on order-in-council appointments, but also with the larger issue of the government's overall appointment policy. Although the discussion was generally couched in terms of affirmative action, quotas for certain disadvantaged social groups, fairness in hiring, and the like, the subtext was clearly the government's patronage prerogative. In June 1986, after receiving discreet assurances that the Premier's Office was favourably disposed to its ideas, the committee released its report.[36]

Recognizing that the right to make appointments was undoubtedly the government's, the committee argued that the legislature should have a role to play in the process. Other than espousing the rather vague notions that the appointment process should be open, the positions publicly advertised, and the appointments made 'on the principles of democratic pluralism,'[37] the committee made few concrete pronouncements about the substance of government appointments. Perhaps its most interesting proposal was that no new appointments be made to agencies, boards, and commissions during an election campaign; instead, expiring appointments should be extended by three months. The official government response to the report called this recommendation a 'significant improvement in the appointments process' and accepted it without qualification.[38] The government agreed with the overall thrust of the report's other recommendations on making appointments, though it contended that several of them were already in operation.

Following the lead of the House of Commons, which had accepted the notion of review of order-in-council appointments (but not the prospect of their rejection as envisioned by the McGrath Committee),[39] the report proposed that committees be empowered to review appointments, hold hearings, call witnesses, and report their views to the House. A committee would indicate only that it did or did not concur in a proposed appointment, in the expectation that the government would consider an adverse report 'a sound reason to reconsider its appointment.'[40] Although the government allowed that this proposal might have merit, it refused to commit itself since to do so 'would entail a significant departure from parliamentary tradition.'[41]

The final section of the report dealt with the appointment of senior House officers and officials, such as the ombudsman, the provincial auditor, and the chief election officer, who are responsible to the assembly rather than to the government. Senior House officers would be selected by a legislative committee, subject to a vote in the House (except for the director of administration, who would be picked by the Board of Internal Economy). This procedure was followed for the appointment of the new clerk, and the government response indicated that it considered it to be in force for other similar positions. The government also accepted the recommendations concerning the director of administration and the assembly officials who reported to the Speaker. Because the committee's recommendations entailed the rejection of the government nominee if the review committee failed to reach an undefined 'consensus,' the government's acquiescence marked a very substantial extension of the House's authority over its servants.

THE PHOENIX OF REFORM 1987-88

Clearly, the major legislative concern facing the new Liberal majority government after the 1987 election was what to do with its eager, ambitious back-benchers. The apparent disintegration of the massive Mulroney majority in Ottawa offered a dire warning of the fate awaiting a government with large numbers of restive back-benchers. Accordingly, much effort was expended in improving the operation and effectiveness of the government caucus. Reform of the legislature was a lower priority, but it did remain on the agenda, partly because it was recognized that some of the 1985 Procedural Affairs Committee's recommendations had merit, but chiefly because of a growing distaste for the hollow ritual of the estimates. The opposition parties, with smaller caucuses, faced a heavier burden in preparing for estimates, and Liberal ministers, like their Tory predecessors, had come to regard estimates as a colossal waste of time and energy.

Accordingly, it was agreed that another attempt would be made to 'do something about the estimates,' and that certain loose ends from the 1985-86 revisions to the standing orders would be addressed. The House leaders turned the matter over to the Legislative Assembly Committee; the task eventually fell to an informal all-party group composed of Doug Reycraft, the new chief government whip (who was not a member of the Legislative Assembly Committee), and two committee members who had been leading figures in the reform process since 1977, Michael Breaugh of the NDP and Norman Sterling of the Conservatives. Legislative Assembly Committee Chairman Herb Epp also participated, but Reycraft was the principal government negotiator. This ad hoc committee met intermittently from November 1987 until the following spring. By mid-April 1988 they had concluded negotiations, not just on a package of reforms relating to the estimates, but on a wide range of rule changes, mostly but not entirely inspired by the 1985 Procedural Affairs report. Their recommendations ran to nearly fifty single-spaced pages, although a large part of the document they produced consisted of the technical amendments to the standing orders necessary to implement their proposals.[42]

Some of the suggestions put forward by the ad hoc reform committee were routine housekeeping matters, such as standardizing the usage of the term 'sessional day' and removing minor anomalies and inconsistencies in the standing orders. Many of their recommendations were of substantial import, but none carried the potential significance of the estimates reforms, which consisted of three proposals. First, a new estimates committee, chaired by a member of the opposition, would examine six sets of estimates a year, with some expectation that reductions or deletions would be recommended; all other estimates would be automatically passed. Each party would select two sets of estimates, which would be reviewed for up to fifteen hours apiece in the committee. A three-hour concurrence debate in the House on the committee's report and its recommendations would conclude the process.[43] Second, twelve opposition days a year would be apportioned between the two opposition parties according to their numbers. On these days the opposition would set the topic for debate, which could take place either in the House or in the Committee of the Whole, but non-confidence motions would not be permitted. As a trade-off for raising the yearly number of opposition days from six, as recommended by the Procedural Affairs Committee, to twelve, emergency debates would be done away with, though unanimous consent could be granted for a debate on a genuine emergency. Third, in five policy committees, each party would be permitted up to fifteen hours to review the policy and administration of one or more ministries as designated by the parties.[44] The hope was that these exercises would be more focused than the estimates reviews had been, and that they would not require the same degree of time-consuming, all-encompassing preparation.

Additional recommendations from the ad hoc committee included ideas revived from the 1985 Procedural Affairs report as well as some new reforms. Among the former were the parliamentary calendar, the abolition of appeals against Speaker's rulings, and the election of the Speaker by secret ballot. Among the latter were proposals that the terms of reference for committees be completely open, that private members be given the power to designate whether their bills were to be sent to a standing committee or the Committee of the Whole after second reading, that a fourth presiding officer be appointed, and that the number of members required to refer bills or other matters to committee, to block late sittings, or to block votes on private members' business be lowered from twenty to twelve. This last change was justified by the argument that the Legislative Assembly Act specified twelve members as the basis for recognizing parties in certain circumstances, and that this was a more appropriate benchmark than the quorum, twenty members.[45] The true explanation, of course, was that in the wake of the 1987 Liberal landslide neither opposition party could muster twenty members. Of the major Procedural Affairs recommendations not implemented in 1986, only two were not revived: the proposals for an intendant of parliament and for ad hoc bills committees.

The House adjourned at the end of June 1988 with the fate of the reform package very much in doubt. The NDP and Conservative caucuses were prepared to trust the judgment of their representatives on the ad hoc committee and, as seasoned veterans, were reasonably knowledgeable about and comfortable with the proposed rule changes. The Liberal caucus, however, which was mainly composed of newly elected members who were uncertain about the proposals' implications, was suspicious of what seemed needless concessions to the opposition, and annoyed at its not having been consulted during the negotiations. An even more serious stumbling-block was the cabinet, where the reform package encountered serious resistance. Although it was evident that some minor components of the deal reached by the ad hoc committee were subject to further change, the opposition made it clear that the essentials of the estimates package were not negotiable. The NDP in particular warned in private and in public that if the package was not accepted, it would insist on using every last minute of the time scheduled for estimates debates, thereby clogging the government's fall agenda (unusually, estimates consideration had not even begun by the summer recess). Despite all this, when the session ended in March 1989 the reform package seemed no closer to implementation.

CONCLUSION

Since the end of 1976, when the changes generated by the Camp Commission were largely in place, most of the reform efforts in the Ontario legislature have reflected what Paul Thomas has called in a similar context 'a naïve faith in institutional tinkering.'[46] Only a very few reforms can be called truly significant advances, among them the introduction of electronic Hansard and major improvements in members' staff resources and support services. Most of the changes, and especially those having to do with House procedure and committee structure, have been essentially incremental and have not fundamentally altered the operation of the legislature or the capabilities of its members. Reports recommending reforms have been available in great numbers, but none possesses the vision and eloquence of the McGrath Committee report. Indeed, it is no coincidence that the report advocating the most thoroughgoing changes, the 1980 proposals for a new committee system (and the report's descendant, the 1985 omnibus Procedural Affairs Committee report), has thus far proved almost entirely unacceptable. There are several explanations for this generally unimpressive record.

First, there is a pervasive view among members that procedural matters are technical and boring, and that when they need to use the procedures someone will be there to tell them what to do. This results in a general lack of interest in the possibilities of reform, so that the pool of members willing and able to contribute new ideas is limited. Most members willingly defer to the whips and House leaders on matters relating to the House, and thus come to see their role in reform processes as one of reacting to proposals brought down by the House leaders rather than one of actively participating in developing new ideas. In addition, no recent Speaker has played an active role in fomenting procedural reform; Speakers' efforts at improving the legislature have been almost entirely confined to matters of administration and provision of services. There may be sound reasons for this reticence, but in other provinces strong leadership from Speakers has contributed significantly to reform.

Another explanation is the widespread 'zero-sum' thinking about reform – the view that any change that assists the opposition necessarily harms the government, and vice versa. This attitude encourages members to view the process of parliamentary reform as an exercise in horse-trading: if the opposition gains something, then the government must receive something in return. Members rarely think in terms of reforms aimed at improving the institution as a whole. Some changes, such as the abolition of night sittings, are advantageous both to government and to opposition, but even in such apparently neutral reforms members are hypersensitive to possible partisan advantage. The quid-pro-quo approach to reform has generally been restricted to matters procedural; issues of improvements in services and facilities, in which the opposition has little to offer, usually are treated differently. Even here, though, a government-versus-opposition attitude is evident, since the implicit presumption on the government side is usually that enhancements to services favour the opposition. Moreover, it is not unknown for deals to be struck whereby better services are exchanged for concessions on procedural issues. In short, reform is hampered by an inability to look beyond partisan advantage to the improvement of the legislature as a whole.

Third, members, particularly those charged with taking the lead in reform – the Procedural Affairs and Legislative Assembly Committees – have suffered from a failure of imagination. In their reviews of standing orders and procedures they have confined themselves largely to discussions with the House leaders and to the study of developments in the Canadian and British Houses of Commons (and, to a much lesser degree, in other provincial legislatures, primarily Quebec). They have travelled repeatedly to the United States, but their recommendations reveal no congressional influences. Turning first to Ottawa and Westminster for inspiration is natural and laudable, but should be only a beginning; many interesting ideas can be gleaned from legislatures outside the British tradition. West Germany and the Scandinavian countries, which combine cabinet-parliamentary systems with strong committee systems and substantial parliamentary influence on policy,[47] offer more innovative examples than the United States, where legislatures are fundamentally different from ours in operation and approach. Yet, no attempts have been made to explore the lessons of European parliaments. Instead, members have been mostly content to recycle recommendations developed in earlier legislatures or in the McGrath Committee report.

Altogether too many members, even those who are interested in change, fail to reflect seriously on the purpose of a legislature, and are thus content to tinker with the rules rather than pursue more far-reaching changes. Consider, for example, the ten minutes of House time given over to ninety-second statements by private members. This procedure has become very popular among MPPS and is widely regarded as a tremendous success, but it has enhanced the effectiveness and influence of the House and its members not a whit.

It may well be that the pragmatism that permeates the legislature inclines members away from thinking about ideal parliaments. In turn, this hinders their coming to grips with the fundamentally important question of the constraints to reform imposed by the framework of the British parliamentary model. They may recognize that the structure and behaviour of the parliamentary system restrict the possibilities open to them, but they have generally not addressed the possibility of the Ontario legislature's becoming transformative.

And yet the underlying, if not always explicitly articulated, objective of reformers in Ontario, at least since the time of the Camp Commission, has been to render the legislature more transformative: to give it and its members a greater influence over policy, to enhance its power vis-à-vis the government. At the same time, it is fair to categorize much of the reform efforts as aimed at improving procedures so that the legislature can more effectively act as an arena. Perhaps the mixed record of success for would-be reformers reflects an uncertainty about the appropriate mix of arena and transformative elements within the legislature. In fairness it must be admitted that at least some of the key participants have thought at length about such questions, but they have not spoken openly of their vision of what the legislature might become for fear of needlessly antagonizing the traditionalists or the government.

A question of some importance both for analysts and for would-be reformers is whether the cause of reform is helped or hindered when only a few members, principally whips, House leaders, members of the Legislative Assembly Committee, and the Speaker, take an active interest in reform. Given the delicate balancing act that is often necessary to achieve any results, it might be argued that the fewer involved the better; too many participants may make it impossible to reach consensus. Conversely, if greater numbers of members were active in the process, the pressure for meaningful reform might be more difficult to withstand. In addition, an intellectual leavening might occur as members other than the usual close-knit group brought their ideas and experiences to bear on questions of parliamentary reform.

The legislative bureaucracy has a key role in the processes of reform, though its net impact is uncertain. The senior officials of the assembly are highly competent and genuinely committed to parliamentary reform. Yet they may be a mixed blessing. As bureaucrats they have a vested interest, if not an inherent tendency, to promote change in such a way as to maximize their influence and authority. This may mean that members receive contradictory advice and pressure from different sectors of the legislative bureaucracy. Similarly, senior officials tend to be wary and critical of one another's proposals lest they enlarge empires or threaten bureaucratic power bases. For the same reasons, once they are entrenched in powerful positions and comfortable with the status quo, legislative bureaucrats – like bureaucrats everywhere – can easily develop strongly conservative attitudes to reform.

More generally, significant reform may be markedly more difficult to achieve as the legislature becomes more institutionalized. Not just the legislative bureaucrats, but the whips, the House leaders, and the leading members of the Legislative Assembly Committee, may all be less open to reform because they approach it with one eye fixed on its possible effect on their positions. It is not accidental that of the two great opportunities for reform of the Ontario legislature, in 1975–77 and 1985-87, the achievements of the earlier period – that is, prior to the far-reaching institutionalization that now characterizes the assembly – were far more substantial.

10

The Ontario legislature: An assessment

In examining the details that are the trees of legislative operations, it is easy to lose sight of the parliamentary forest. The most important question to be asked about the Ontario legislature – as about any parliamentary institution – is how effective it is. 'Effectiveness' cannot be measured without a knowledge of the functions legislatures are meant to perform. This chapter attempts to evaluate the Ontario legislature in terms of the functions commonly attributed to legislatures: lawmaking, representation, leadership recruitment, scrutiny of government activity, nation-building, conflict management, debating the issues of the day, legitimizing the political system, linking the governed with the governors, and maintaining the government in office.[1] Many of these functions overlap or are variations on a theme.

As a subnational body, the Ontario legislature has historically played relatively little role in nation-building. For reasons rooted in the nature of Ontario society, neither has it been an important instrument of province-building, as have the assemblies of, for example, Saskatchewan and Quebec.[2] Similarly, since the legitimacy of the Ontario political system has never been seriously questioned, the legislature is not called upon to foster legitimacy in the face of serious strains. To be sure, legislatures are inherently legitimizing institutions, since '[they] symbolize – by their existence, by their procedures, or through the processes by which their members are elected – popular participation in the political arena.'[3] Moreover, as Ronald Butt has noted, the roots of Parliament in Britain lie not so much in lawmaking as in the processes by which the king 'could obtain the consent, or at least the acquiescence, of influential sections of the people for his acts of government.'[4] Unlike the federal House of Commons, though, the Ontario legislature enjoys the luxury of being able to pursue other tasks without the need to confront major issues of legitimacy. This is tied in with the significant differences in the extent to which the House of Commons and the Ontario legislature are called upon to mobilize support for specific government policies; this topic is discussed below.

The recruitment of political leaders can be looked at in two ways. First, in a broad sense, a parliament possesses the undoubted authority to select and dismiss teams of political leaders. For the most part, the public selects the government through the electoral process, and the legislature simply confirms the choice; but in times of minority government the legislature can play a decisive role.

Cabinet ministers are drawn from the membership of the House, and parliamentary experience and performance are key elements in the recruitment and promotion of leaders. As Loewenberg and Patterson have suggested, 'legislatures produce leaders; they are not merely passive environments in which those with previously established qualities make their mark.'[5] The Liberal cabinets appointed after the 1985 and 1987 elections were anomalies in that many ministers were brought into cabinet with no legislative experience; but they can be explained by the peculiar political circumstances of the day, not the least of which was the limited amount of talent available among the rather small pool of experienced MPPs. In general, it has been very unusual for newly-elected members to be appointed directly to the cabinet. The legislature is a testing-ground for prospective ministers; in addition, ministers' promotions or demotions depend not only on their competence in running their ministries but on their parliamentary abilities. Of course many powerful political decision-makers, be they senior civil servants or political advisers in the premier's office, are recruited and promoted entirely outside of parliamentary channels. Indeed, the power and influence wielded by such non-parliamentary figures may be part of a serious failing in the legislature's fulfilment of its recruitment function. As with the House of Commons in Ottawa, membership turnover in the Ontario legislature is high and career duration low; this undoubtedly detracts from the capacity of members – individually and collectively – to participate effectively in governance.[6]

The representative function may also be subdivided.[7] The more traditional notion of representation has been one of members' responsibility for bringing forward the views of their constituents on matters of public policy – Walter Bagehot's 'expressive function.' Members' willingness and ability to represent public concerns and opinions are related to, though by no means solely dependent on, the degree to which they themselves are representative of the population. Data presented in Chapter 2 demonstrated that in important respects MPPs do not reflect the composition of Ontario society. This is less significant today than in the past, because the public's views are expressed not only through members' actions and speeches in the House but by the groups and organizations that take part in public hearings before legislative committees. This direct expression of diverse viewpoints in a public parliamentary forum is in some ways a notable advance, but the problem identified by C.E.S. Franks with respect to Ottawa is also evident at Queen's Park: parliamentary committees 'are inevitably going to hear more from the organized, advantaged segments of society than from the disorganized and poor.'[8]

The second aspect of representation is an increasingly important one: members' provision of assistance to individual constituents in dealings with government. This may simply mean offering advice and information, or it may entail active intervention with government agencies on behalf of constituents. The Ontario legislature scores high in its performance of this 'ombudsman function,' no doubt because it combines tangible political benefits with psychological satisfaction for members. As was discussed in Chapter 7, the preoccupation with constituency service has been widely criticized for diverting members' attention from their other duties. In view of the substantial support services now available to members to relieve them of the burdens of constituency work, it seems reasonable to conclude that members who devote undue amounts of time to constituency work do so willingly, and that the failing – if failing it is – lies with the individual MPPs rather than with the institution.

The legislature's performance of the accountability function was explored in some detail in Chapter 8. The legislature's scrutiny of the government's activities is very much hit-and-miss, though its effectiveness has grown by leaps and bounds over the past two decades.

It has long been recognized that parliaments are places for talking rather than doing. Indeed, in John Stuart Mill's phrase, they serve as arenas for the clash of ideas and opinions. This is closely related to Bagehot's notion of parliament's role in educating the public on the great issues of the day. The Ontario legislature's record as a forum wherein issues are debated and the public enlightened is mixed. The staggering complexity of many crucial issues and the sheer scope of government activity make it impossible for any legislative body to mount comprehensive debates on more than a few important matters of public policy. Although it is understandable that the legislature has only a limited capacity to debate thoroughly a wide range of issues, this is a matter of some consequence in a parliament which is, after all, primarily arena rather than transformative in nature.

The legislature is handicapped by the low salience of provincial politics in Ontario, for which it must shoulder part of the blame. It is preoccupied with issues of limited scope or only local import; larger concerns, such as the role of technology in Ontario's society and economy, the wise use of natural resources, and the implications of the province's ethnic diversity, are almost never subject to debate. And, in common with most other parliaments in this country, the Ontario legislature warrants very low marks for its abject failure to devote proper attention to federal–provincial concerns.

Conversely, the legislature deserves credit for bringing key social and political problems to public attention, for keeping them in the forefront of political discourse, and ultimately for contributing to substantial policy changes. Among such issues are extra-billing by Ontario doctors and the larger question of the nature of the province's health care system; the action and performance of Ontario Hydro, especially with respect to nuclear power; and the effectivness and fairness of Ontario's workers' compensation policies. To be sure, many policy areas can be cited where legislative attention has resulted in no notable policy shifts. But these should not be construed as failures, for the parties have been forced to clarify and defend their policies and to mobilize public opinion in support of their positions. In this way crucial issues are presented to the public, as are the parties' stances. Together with the ability to hold the government accountable for its actions and policies, this ranks as perhaps the greatest strength of the arena legislature.

The parliamentary function that most commonly comes to mind, and is embodied in the very word 'legislature,' is that of lawmaking. The easy presumption that lawmaking is equivalent to policy-making is misleading in at least two respects. First, a good deal of governmental policy does not entail legislation, and requires no or only token authorization from the legislature. More significantly, the latent functions of the lawmaking process are more closely related to conflict management than to policy development:

Contrary to expectations, the function of legislatures in lawmaking is to identify the political conflicts in a society and to subject them to a process which reduces them to a minimum. By viewing lawmaking in this way, one can make sense of some apparently ritualistic, wasteful and baffling ways in which legislatures spend their time, of the elaborate customs of courtesy with which legislators treat each other, of the enactment of ceremonial resolutions, and of the diversion of substantive disputes into procedural wrangles. These activities may well serve to reduce conflict among members of a legislature, to emphasize matters on which agreement is easy, and to regulate the really controversial matters by the use of complicated rules of procedure.[9]

Any inquiry that seeks to determine the legislature's effectiveness as a lawmaking body is predestined to reach a dismal conclusion. Since the rise of disciplined political parties, Westminster-style parliaments have been better understood as law-passing rather than lawmaking bodies. Cabinet and the bureaucracy are the true lawmakers; typically, all the important policy questions are settled before legislation reaches first reading. Even in Britain, where MPs have shown substantial independence in recent years (to the point of government back-benchers' amending government bills in ways unpalatable to the cabinet, or defeating them outright), Parliament finds itself reacting to government initiatives, and in general lacks both the clout and the mechanisms for much genuine lawmaking.

A more fruitful line of inquiry begins by asking a broader and more important question: what influence does the legislature have in the policy-making process? Or, as the term has been used throughout this book, what is its transformative capacity? Here the conclusions are not quite so negative. One indication that the legislature is far more significant in policy-making than it was two or three decades ago is the active interest that professional lobbyists take in it. Although Queen's Park sees nothing like the tumult of lobbyists who pervade the larger American legislatures, their presence around the Legislative Building and their participation in committee activities stems from more than an appreciation of the House's policy-making impact. For example, their courting of back-bench members may have less to do with the members' current influence than with their prospect of being elevated to cabinet. Furthermore, interest group leaders often make public presentations to legislative committees not so much because they believe that they can affect policy, but because they wish to justify themselves to their membership. Nevertheless, lobbyists do take the legislature and its members seriously as contributors to the policy process. This is true not only of the inexperienced interest groups that concentrate on legislative committees because they overestimate their power, but also of the sophisticated professional lobbyists who understand precisely the committees' role. The notable success of the chiropractic lobby in Ontario, in the face of opposition from powerful bureaucratic and professional interests, was due in large part to well-orchestrated campaigns directed at members of the legislature,[10] as was the passage of the 'gay rights' amendment to the Human Rights Code.[11]

Policy ideas can be initiated and promoted in the legislature. Clearly, this is easier if the issues are essentially non-partisan, such as family violence or human rights, or if the government has yet to adopt a firm policy. Even if the broad outlines of policy have been settled, matters of detail may be susceptible to legislative influence. As Franks has noted, 'Parliament tends to be most effective in handling specific questions to identifiable interests.'[12]

Legislative influence on policy need not be confined to non-partisan issues or to details. By pointing up flaws in government policy, by generating interest in policies, and by mobilizing public opinion and interest group activity, the opposition can put pressure on the government to alter policies on which the parties are sharply divided. Moreover, as with other functions, such as accountability, assessments of the legislature's policy influence that examine only what it does can lose sight of the importance of what it prevents. As Michael Mezey has put it, 'Legislatures which do not possess the power to initiate or even to compel changes in policy proposals may have a more subtle power of informally setting the parameters within which those with policy-making power actually operate. All government proposals may pass the legislature unopposed and unamended simply because the government refrains from introducing legislation that will provoke substantial legislative opposition.'[13]

In short, legislatures have the potential to affect policy whether they are operating in adversarial or consensual modes.[14] The most effective means by which individual members and opposition parties can influence policy are committees and private members' business, though question period can also be useful if the opposition adopts a confrontational approach.

Affecting policy by blocking government initiatives or by casting them in a bad political light combines elements of the transformative and the arena legislatures. In this way, as in any number of other ways detailed in this book, the Ontario legislature has become decidedly more transformative over the past two decades. It is now a far more active and important player in the policy process than it has been. All the same, its influence remains confined primarily to details; to a few important and highly public controversies; and to uncontentious issues. By and large, the structures and, more important, the conventions of the British parliamentary model limit the policy roles of the opposition and of government back-benchers. So long as the Ontario legislature is unwilling to alter fundamentally the tenets of Westminster-style parliamentary democracy, it will necessarily remain an arena legislature that focuses on debate, accountability, and the ventilation of public grievances and party positions.

Franks has convincingly argued that a good deal of the malaise in the Parliament of Canada stems from the intolerable burden of mobilizing consent for major government policies after the decisions are made. The increasingly centralized and secretive nature of policy development has meant that major reformist policies such as the national energy programme, the tax reforms in the 1981 budget, and the changes in the Crow's Nest freight rates have emerged 'from the private womb of bureaucracy and cabinet, not from the dialectic of party or public discussion. Consent and understanding had not been developed for them before they became fixed government policy.' The opposition found that it could gain political mileage by aligning itself with the interests that stood to lose under the new policies, and that its most potent weapons were stridency and delay: 'Under these conditions the parliamentary legislative process became warfare ... [and in consequence] the government, where possible, does everything in its power to avoid parliament.'[15] This insightful analysis has profound implications for parliament's role in the policy-making process, and for parliamentary reform generally. Happily, Franks's argument has little validity for the Ontario legislature. Despite obvious similarities, fundamental differences mark the House of Commons and the Ontario legislature. Comparisons between the two ought to be made with care, especially the implicit comparisons which presume that reform measures appropriate for Ottawa will be equally applicable to Queen's Park.

Ontario is arguably the most socially, economically, and geographically diverse province, yet its diversity is of a much lower order of magnitude than that of the nation as a whole. There are no tensions comparable to those between central Canada and the west or between French and English Canada. The fundamental political divisions that structure national politics – and on which the question of consent is centred – are less pronounced in Ontario. The Ontario legislature has not been asked to deal with the number or range of major, bitterly divisive policies that have confronted the House of Commons. In part this is because of the continuous record of gradual reform in recent decades; in part it reflects the province's characteristic moderation; and in part it is because the great issues of state tend to be national rather than provincial.

Perhaps by virtue of the inherent nature of Ontario politics, or perhaps by happenstance, in recent times no unexpected government announcements of major controversial policies have required extensive post-decision consent-building by the legislature. The Conservative government's reversal of decades of dogma in its stunning 1984 decision to proceed with full public funding of separate schools undoubtedly would have generated epic battles in the House had not all three parties supported the measure. The issue of extra-billing, which had been extensively debated in the legislature for years, was an important campaign issue during the 1985 election; when the government brought in legislation to ban the practice, the public already understood the issue and was broadly supportive. The 1986 sexual-orientation amendment to the Human Rights Code, which lacked broad consent and elicited venomous opposition both in the House and among the public, originated not with the government but with the NDP. Other recent controversies that transfixed the legislature (occasionally to the point of immobility), such as the government purchase of an oil company in 1981 and the sudden imposition of a public sector restraint program in 1982, have been largely ignored by the public.

The data presented in Chapter 5 showed clearly that delays in the government's legislative program have not been a problem in Ontario. Most of the delays that do occur are attributable to the crowded government agenda and the length of time consumed by the public hearing process rather than to opposition intransigence. The 1986–87 session was marked by the widest range of major legislative initiatives in decades; if Ottawa-style wars of parliamentary attrition centring on the securing of consent were going to occur, they would have occurred then. The Ontario legislature has by and large been free of the principal symptoms of the Commons' malaise – 'the prolonged, brutal, degrading and generally unproductive parliamentary processes.'[16]

Important changes to the policy process in Ottawa over the past two decades have inadvertently contributed to parliamentary influence. Such is the thesis of Paul Pross, who argues, contrary to Franks's view, that bureaucratic pluralism is to Parliament's advantage.[17] Unlike

259 The Ontario legislature: An assessment

Franks (and many other observers), Pross contends that central dominance of the policy process is a myth; instead, Ottawa has come to be characterized by a 'diffusion of power.' Bureaucratic pluralism has spawned a fundamental shift in the nature of interest group politics: 'A system of pressure group politics in which access sprang from the ability to provide specialized information has been changed into one in which legitimation is equally important ... a system of pressure groups in which specialized communication obtains access shuns parliament, whereas one in which legitimation is the wherewithal for participation cultivates parliament.'[18] This in turn enhances Parliament's policy influence, albeit to a moderate degree.

Pross's analysis is germane to the Ontario legislature, but not, as might be surmised, because similar arguments apply. Although there is an element of bureaucratic pluralism in the government of Ontario, by and large the Ontario cabinet and its central agencies have not lost control over the policy process to nearly the same extent as has occurred in Ottawa. Nevertheless, the Ontario legislature has been the beneficiary of developments in Ottawa through a 'demonstration' effect. Interest groups in Ontario, particularly those of greater size and influence, are increasingly seeking to legitimize their positions and their relationship with government by appearing before legislative committees in the same manner as their Ottawa counterparts. If the similar developments in interest group behaviour in Ontario and in Ottawa are not attributable to common changes in policy processes, they may reflect the widespread expectation, both in the public at large and within the interest group community, that parliamentary institutions are appropriate and worthwhile venues in which groups can present their demands and their arguments. By doing so they enhance both the legislature's influence over policy and its performance of the representation function.

The record of the Ontario legislature in recent years gives rise to optimism and to pessimism about its prospects for improvement. On the positive side, as has been documented throughout this book, notable advances have been recorded in the opportunities for private members to scrutinize government, to serve their constituents, and to contribute to policy formulation. Committees have developed impressively in their independence, the quality and scope of their work, and their significance in the policy process. The level of services available to members has greatly improved. The Speakership and the administrative apparatus of the assembly have gained all but complete independence from the government. In short, the Ontario legislature has matured and developed greatly.

Moreover, the legislature has initiated a number of important reforms and advances, and has been a leading force in parliamentary reform in this country. It was the first jurisdiction in Canada to institute a Board of Internal Economy with opposition representation. Effective and meaningful procedures for private members' business were established in Ontario in 1976 nearly a decade before Ottawa significantly reformed its rules; in most other Canadian legislatures, private members' business is a charade. No other Canadian legislature has a committee comparable to Ontario's Standing Committee on the Ombudsman; the Ontario Public Accounts Committee remains unique in its ability to direct the provincial auditor to carry out inquiries; and the Liberal-NDP accord of 1985–87 has substantially widened the range of possible responses to minority government situations anywhere in Canada.

Still, the Ontario legislature has some distance to go before achieving full maturity. Missed opportunities and unfulfilled potential characterize the recent history of the legislature almost as much as do achievements and successes. The legislature is like a person in late adolescence: it possesses the physical attributes of adulthood, but remains emotionally and psychologically immature. Though it is certainly capable of sophisticated, responsible behaviour, and of powerfully influencing the world around it, its range of experience is limited and it lacks confidence in its own abilities. Like a typical teenager, the legislature is uncertain of its role and looks to others for guidance. It will have to consider carefully the course of its development and analyse its inherent strengths and weaknesses; ultimately, it must decide what it wants to become.

The legislature's collective failure to reflect on its reason for being and on its potential is well illustrated in the narrow range of sources it turns to for inspiration in its future direction, a topic discussed in Chapter 9. Similarly, it seems at times slavishly committed to outmoded precepts derived from British practice; it fails to recognize that one of the hallmarks of the Westminster model has been its capacity to adapt to changing circumstances. A recent privilege case illustrates this point. An MPP who took part in a trade union demonstration against a large bank had his accounts cancelled and a major business loan suddenly called in. A reasonable argument could have been made that the bank's punitive action was designed to intimidate the member and his colleagues and prevent them from performing their duty as MPPS, and thus fell under the broad rubric of privilege; however, the committee to which the case was referred decided the issue on the narrow legalistic ground that the bank's action was not related to any 'proceeding in parliament' – the traditional criterion for a breach of privilege.[19] Whether MPPS' privileges should be extended to cover their activities outside of the House and committee sittings is less important than the loss of an opportunity to rethink the whole notion of parliamentary privilege as it applies in Ontario in the late twentieth century.

Members unwilling to question existing concepts of parliamentary privilege are unlikely to bring about more fundamental alterations in the nature of the legislature. Thus, although the legislature may become somewhat more transformative, it will remain in essence an arena. Accordingly, we must be reasonable and realistic in our expectations.[20] MPPS will never mirror precisely the social characteristics of their constituents; parliamentary accountability will always be a hit-and-miss affair; major political decisions will continue to be the preserve of cabinet; many important issues will receive at best a cursory review in the legislature. None the less, the record of the past two decades reveals remarkable improvements in the Ontario legislature, its members, its staff and services, its procedures, its committee system, and its accountability mechanisms. The Ontario legislature has developed into a sophisticated, active, and in many ways effective parliament. Its accomplishments and strengths should be trumpeted, not belittled; but it is neither unfair nor unrealistic to expect further maturation and enhanced effectiveness.

Notes

CHAPTER 1 The setting

1 A few denizens speak of working at 'the park,' but this term has not caught on generally in the fashion of 'the hill' in Ottawa.
2 This account is heavily dependent on the details provided in Eric Arthur, *From Front Street to Queen's Park: The Story of Ontario's Parliament Buildings* (Toronto: McClelland and Stewart, 1979), ch. 5.
3 Ibid., 71
4 Eric Arthur has described the quantity and quality of these carvings as unequalled in any building erected in North America over the past century: ibid., 86.
5 As many as twenty additional members could be added without requiring major structural renovations to the building.
6 That the physical setting of legislatures is of more than aesthetic interest is demonstrated in Charles T. Goodsell, 'The Architecture of Parliaments: Legislative Houses and Political Culture,' *British Journal of Political Science* (July 1988).
7 F.F. Schindeler, *Responsible Government in Ontario* (Toronto: University of Toronto Press, 1969)
8 Quoted in W. Stewart Wallace, 'Political History, 1867–1912,' in Adam Shortt and Arthur G. Doughty, eds., *Canada and Its Provinces* XVII (Ontario) (Edinburgh: University of Edinburgh Press, 1914), 103
9 A glimpse into the volatility of members' voting tendencies may be had from J.D. Livermore, 'The Ontario Election of 1871: A Case Study of the Transfer of Political Power,' *Ontario History* LXXI (March 1979), 39–52.
10 Schindeler, *Responsible Government*, 81–4

11 Sandfield Macdonald's administration (1867–71) was nominally a coalition, but is better understood as the outcome of a major political realignment. On paper, Mowat faced a minority House after the 1894 election, but the Patrons were so readily swayed to the Liberal cause that the government was never really in a minority situation.
12 Donald C. MacDonald, 'Modernizing the Legislature,' in Donald C. MacDonald, ed., *The Government and Politics of Ontario*, 3d ed. (Toronto: Nelson, 1985), 50
13 On the working and impact of minority government see Vaughan Lyon, 'Minority Government in Ontario, 1975–1981: An Assessment,' *Canadian Journal of Political Science* XVII (December 1984), 685–706.
14 On the various concepts of responsible government, see A.H. Birch, *Representative and Responsible Government* (London: Allen and Unwin, 1964), ch. 1.
15 Nelson Polsby, 'Legislatures,' in Fred Greenstein and Nelson Polsby, eds., *Handbook of Political Science* 5 (Reading, Mass.: Addison-Wesley, 1975), 277
16 This account of the background to the accord draws upon Graham White, 'Ontario,' in Roderick Byers, ed., *Canadian Annual Review of Politics and Public Affairs, 1985* (Toronto: University of Toronto Press, 1989), 259–304, and Rosemary Speirs, *Out of the Blue: The Fall of the Tory Dynasty in Ontario* (Toronto: Macmillan, 1986), ch. 6.
17 For the full text of the accord, see Rand Dyck, *Provincial Politics in Canada* (Toronto: Prentice-Hall, 1986), 325–7.
18 In a formal statement announcing his intention to call on Liberal leader David Peterson to form a government, Lieutenant-Governor John Black Aird noted that the accord was 'a joint political statement ... [of] no legal force or effect.' Office of the Lieutenant Governor, Statement, 19 June 1985.
19 Bob Rae, 'Changing the Confidence Convention in Ontario,' *Canadian Parliamentary Review* VIII (Winter 1985–86), 12–14
20 Michael Atkinson and Graham White, 'The Development of Provincial Legislatures,' in Harold D. Clarke, Colin Campbell, F.Q. Quo, and Arthur Goddard, eds., *Parliament, Policy and Representation* (Toronto: Methuen, 1980), 272
21 For an analysis that disputes the 'rightward drift' interpretation of NDP ideology, see J.T. Morley, *Secular Socialists: The CCF/NDP in Ontario – A Biography* (Montreal: McGill-Queen's University Press), ch. 5.
22 David Denver, 'Britain: Centralized Parties with Decentralized Selection,' in Michael Gallagher and Michael Marsh, eds., *Candidate Selection in*

Notes to pages 15–17

Comparative Perspective: The Secret Garden of Politics (London: Sage, 1988), 47–71; for Canadian practices, see Robert J. Williams, 'Candidate Selection,' in Howard Penniman, ed., *Canada at the Polls 1979 and 1980* (Washington: American Enterprise Institute, 1981), 90–120.
23 Edward Crowe, 'The Web of Authority: Party Loyalty and Social Control in the British House of Commons,' *Legislative Studies Quarterly* XI (May 1986), 163, 167
24 Alan Cairns, 'The Electoral System and the Party System in Canada, 1921–1965,' *Canadian Journal of Political Science* I (March 1968), 55–80
25 The Family Coalition Party ran 36 candidates in the 1987 provincial election and attracted nearly 50,000 votes on a platform characterized by religious fundamentalism, a strong emphasis on traditional family values, and vehement objection to abortion and gay rights.
26 See, inter alia, John Wilson, 'The Red Tory Province: Reflections on the Character of the Ontario Political Culture,' in Donald C. MacDonald, ed., *The Government and Politics of Ontario*, 2d ed. (Toronto: Van Nostrand Reinhold, 1980), 208–26; S.F. Wise, 'Ontario's Political Culture,' in MacDonald, *Government and Politics of Ontario*, 3d ed. 159–73; Peter Oliver, 'On Being an Ontarian,' in Peter Oliver, *Public and Private Persons: The Ontario Political Culture 1914–1934* (Toronto: Clarke Irwin, 1975), 2–14; and Morley, *Secular Socialists*, ch. 2.
27 See, in particular, Wilson, 'The Red Tory Province.'
28 Gad Horowitz, *Canadian Labour in Politics* (Toronto: University of Toronto Press, 1968), ch. 1
29 Reg Whittaker, 'Images of the State in Canada,' in Leo Panitch, ed., *The Canadian State: Political Economy and Political Power* (Toronto: University of Toronto Press, 1977), 28–68
30 See, for example, the data presented in David Elkins, 'The Sense of Place,' in David Elkins and Richard Simeon, *Small Worlds: Provinces and Parties in Canadian Political Life* (Toronto: Methuen, 1980), 16–21 and in Jon H. Pammett, 'Public Orientation to Regions and Provinces,' in David J. Bellamy, Jon H. Pammett, and Donald C. Rowat, eds., *The Provincial Political Systems: Comparative Essays* (Toronto: Methuen, 1976), 94–8.
31 Richard Simeon and David Elkins, 'Provincial Political Cultures in Canada,' in Elkins and Simeon, *Small Worlds*, 31–76. This conclusion, based on extensive survey data, might initially be thought not to square with the fact that the turnout at Ontario provincial elections is the lowest in Canada. That this reflects trust, complacency, and the primacy of national politics more than alienation and lack of efficacy is suggested by the fact that turnout in Ontario at federal elections has historically been 10 to 15

266 Notes to pages 17–25

per cent higher than in provincial elections. See Graham White, 'Social Change and Political Stability in Ontario: Electoral Forces 1867–1977,' PhD thesis, McMaster University, 1979, tables III-2 and III-3.
32 Polsby, 'Legislatures,' 291

CHAPTER 2   The participants

1 Data on members' social characteristics were gleaned from the *Parliamentary Guide*, from the clipping service of the legislative library, from personal knowledge, and, in the case of MPPs for whom these sources proved incomplete, from questionnaires. The assistance of the party House leaders, Robert Nixon, Mike Harris, and Ross McClellan, is gratefully acknowledged.
2 In this and succeeding tables the following points should be noted: two Liberal cabinet ministers who resigned owing to conflict of interest allegations during 1986 are included in the cabinet; the two members who left the NDP in the fall of 1986 to join the Liberals are considered Liberals; and the Speaker is included with the Liberal back-benchers.
3 Donald R. Matthews, *U.S. Senators and Their World* (New York: Vintage, 1960)
4 See, for example, the discussion of formal and informal 'buddy' systems for newly elected members in Julia Wilson, 'The ABC's of Being an MPP: The Role Socialization of New Legislators at Queen's Park,' Ontario legislative internship paper, June 1986.
5 In the eight provincial elections held in 1985 and 1986 excepting Ontario and British Columbia, where 33 per cent of the MLAs had previous municipal experience), the range of members who were former municipal politicians was 11 per cent to 23 per cent: Robert J. Fleming and Michael Wiebe, eds., *Canadian Legislatures: The 1985 Comparative Study* (Toronto: Office of the Assembly, 1985), 15–19, and Robert J. Fleming and Patrick Fafard, eds., *Canadian Legislatures: The 1986 Comparative Study* (Toronto: Office of the Assembly, 1986), 70–81.
6 Michael M. Atkinson and Graham White, 'The Development of Provincial Legislatures,' in Harold D. Clarke, Colin Campbell, F.Q. Quo, and Arthur Goddard, eds., *Parliament, Policy and Representation* (Toronto: Methuen, 1980), 261
7 Census of Canada, 1981, catalogue 92-912 (volume 1), Table 1-1
8 Sylvia Bashevkin, *Toeing the Lines: Women and Party Politics in English Canada* (Toronto: University of Toronto Press, 1985), 70–6; and 'Women's Participation in the Ontario Political Parties, 1971–1981,' *Journal of Canadian Studies* XVII (Summer 1982), 44–54

Notes to pages 25–9

9 Janine Brodie, *Women and Politics in Canada* (Toronto: McGraw-Hill Ryerson, 1985), ch. 6
10 Twenty women were elected in the 1987 election, representing 15.4 per cent of the House (the highest proportion of any Canadian legislature outside the Yukon Territory). All but three held seats in Ottawa, London, Hamilton, Toronto, and the suburban fringe of Toronto.
11 Members who did not indicate a religious affiliation in public documents were asked to indicate in the questionnaire the religion in which they were raised. Several MPPs labelled themselves 'Protestant'; they are included in the category 'Other Protestants' (chiefly Baptists and Lutherans), which is not precisely comparable to the percentage of the population described as 'other Protestant.'
12 Calculated from data in J.T. Morley, *Secular Socialists: The CCF/NDP in Ontario: A Biography* (Montreal: McGill-Queen's University Press, 1984), tables 5 and 6 (for 1943 and 1967) and in F.F. Schindeler, *Responsible Government in Ontario* (Toronto: University of Toronto Press, 1969), 37–8 (for 1963). See also Robert James Williams, 'Political Recruitment in Ontario: A Study of the Twentieth-eighth Parliament,' PhD thesis, University of Toronto, 1973, 111.
13 The 1981 census permitted respondents to indicate more than one ethnic origin. The figure of 53 per cent reflects those who claimed purely British origin; another 6.3 per cent showed 'British' as one of their origins. Since MPPs with partly British origins were classified according to their other origin, the fairest census comparison is with the single-origin British.
14 These overall similarities mask certain discrepancies within the broadly defined European groups. The 1986 legislature, for example, contained no Greeks, Hungarians, or Czechs (all groups of some numerical importance in the general population).
15 All those indicating an Asian, African, Caribbean, or native Canadian origin were included in this group; only a small proportion of these cited multiple origins, such as British and Asian.
16 In 1987 three MPPs of non-European ancestry were elected, including the first members of Chinese and South Asian descent; still, they constituted only 2.3 per cent of the House.
17 Census of Canada, 1981, catalogue 93-942 (E-576), table 1
18 Williams, 'Political Recruitment,' 103
19 Data on occupational composition of the labour force taken from Census of Canada, 1981, catalogue 92-917, table 1. The definition of farmer is a generous one, and includes a wide range of farm workers (classification 718/9).

20 Graham White, 'Lawyers in Government: A Preliminary Study,' in Roy J. Matas and Deborah J. McCawley, eds., *Legal Education in Canada* (Montreal: Federation of Law Societies of Canada, 1987), 766–9
21 See, for example, socio-economic data on provincial MLAS and federal MPS in Harold D. Clarke, Richard G. Price, and Robert Krause, 'Backbenchers,' in David J. Bellamy, Jon H. Pammett, and Donald C. Rowat, eds., *The Provincial Political Systems: Comparative Essays* (Toronto: Methuen, 1976), table 1; see also Neil Guppy, Sabrina Freeman, and Shari Buchan, 'Representing Canadians: Changes in the Economic Backgrounds of Federal Politicians 1965–1984,' *Canadian Review of Sociology and Anthropology* XXIV (August 1987), 417–30.
22 Schindeler, *Responsible Government*, 38–42; Morley, *Secular Socialists*, 170–1
23 The 1987 election returned fewer farmers, more lawyers and business types, and about the same proportion of teachers as the 1985 contingent: Robert J. Fleming, ed., *Canadian Legislatures 1987–88* (Ottawa: Ampersand Communications Services, 1988), 74.
24 Williams, 'Political Recruitment,' 123
25 Data in *Canadian Legislatures 1987–88* indicate a substantial rise in the formal education of the 1987 MPPS in comparison with those elected in 1985 (p. 74).
26 The average age of newly elected provincial members in 1985 and 1986 ranged from 43.6 to 49.4 (in Ontario, the average age was 47.3): Fleming and Wiebe, eds., *Canadian Legislatures 1985* 15–19; Fleming and Fafard, eds., *Canadian Legislatures 1986*, 70–81.
27 Williams, 'Political Recruitment,' 119
28 Allan Kornberg, Harold D. Clarke, and Arthur Goddard, 'Parliament and the Representational Process in Contemporary Canada,' in Clarke et al., eds., *Parliament, Policy and Representation*, 5
29 A.K. McDougall, 'Some Tentative Hypotheses Leading to a Generational Analysis of Legislatures,' paper presented at the University of Waterloo, 25 November 1980
30 Walter White and Lawrence Leduc Jr, 'The Role of Opposition in One-Party Dominant Systems: The Case of Ontario,' *Canadian Journal of Political Science* VII (March 1974), 94
31 Frederick J. Fletcher and Arthur Goddard, 'Government and Opposition: Structural Influences on Provincial Legislators,' *Legislative Studies Quarterly* III (November 1978), 658
32 Conrad Winn and James Twiss, 'The Spatial Analysis of Political Cleavages and the Case of the Ontario Legislature,' *Canadian Journal of Political Science* X (June 1977), 306–9

Notes to pages 33–8

33 One journalist wrote of the Liberal party program of that era, 'It is hard to base a party philosophy on the merits of a few subordinate clauses': Jonathan Manthorpe, *The Power and the Tories: Ontario Politics 1943 to the Present* (Toronto: Macmillan, 1974), 172.
34 Harold D. Clarke, 'The Ideological Self-Perceptions of Provincial Legislators,' *Canadian Journal of Political Science* XI (September 1978), 623
35 Harold D. Clarke, Richard G. Price, and Robert Krause, 'Constituency Service among Canadian Provincial Legislators,' *Canadian Journal of Political Science* VIII (December 1975), 530–1
36 Clarke, Price, and Krause, 'Backbenchers,' 277
37 Ibid., 227
38 Michael M. Atkinson, 'Policy Interests of Provincial Backbenchers and the Effects of Political Ambition,' *Legislative Studies Quarterly* III (November 1978), 640
39 Michael M. Atkinson, 'Comparing Legislatures: The Policy Role of Backbenchers in Ontario and Nova Scotia,' *Canadian Journal of Political Science* XIII (March 1980), 73
40 Ibid., 71
41 This is not a matter on which hard data are readily available; however, I am aware that over the past decade, when controversial though nonpartisan changes have been proposed to provincial adoption law, more than a half dozen MPPs have mentioned in public debate or in private discussions that they are adoptive parents.
42 Paul Thomas, 'The Role of House Leaders in the Canadian House of Commons,' *Canadian Journal of Political Science* XV (March 1982), 125
43 The very fact that he wrote a book about his time in the legislature marks him as unusual; see Morton Shulman, *Member of the Legislature* (Toronto: Fitzhenry and Whiteside, 1979).
44 For an overview of Ontario's political parties, see Joseph Wearing, 'Political Parties: Fish or Fowl?' in Donald C. MacDonald, ed., *The Government and Politics of Ontario*, 3d ed. (Toronto: Thomas Nelson, 1985), 238–61.
45 If the opposition leader's party is in power nationally, he may have substantial indirect influence on federal patronage. The relationship between the Ontario and the federal wings of both the Liberal and the Conservative parties has been, at times, distant, and indeed frosty, with an attendant reduction in the Ontario leader's role in the dispensing of patronage.
46 The functions and operations of whips and House leaders in Ontario are essentially similar to those of their Ottawa counterparts; see Thomas, 'Role of House Leaders,' and Martin Westmacott, 'Whips and Cohesion,' *Canadian Parliamentary Review* VI (Autumn 1983), 14–19.

47 See Charles Clarke, *Sixty Years in Upper Canada* (Toronto: William Briggs, 1908), 232.
48 The current chief government whip has stated that, in his capacity as whip, a seat on the Board of Internal Economy would be more useful than a seat at the cabinet table: interview, 21 June 1988.
49 Thomas, 'Role of House Leaders,' 133
50 This 'Government House Leader's Group' is smaller and has a less extensive mandate than the 'Legislative Planning Group' of the Conservative government. Meetings of the latter group were often attended by the most senior officials in the Premier's Office and by the secretary of Cabinet; it played an important role in strategy and in policy development.
51 Thomas, 'Role of House Leaders,' 135
52 Philip Norton, *The Commons in Perspective* (Oxford: Martin Robertson, 1981), 28
53 The government whip's office insists that all members clear out-of-town trips with it while the House is in session, so as to ensure that no more than half a dozen Liberal MPPs are available for votes, unless opposition members are away on the same trip. The 'pairing' of members, whereby members on opposite sides of the House agree to refrain from voting if the members they are paired with are absent, is almost unknown in the Ontario legislature.
54 In the fall of 1988 staff changes were made to the Government House Leader's Office to make it much more overtly partisan.
55 Committee on Government Productivity, *Interim Report No. 1* (Toronto, 1970), 7
56 Shortly after the 1987 election Premier David Peterson decided to limit postings as parliamentary assistants to one year: Duncan McMonagle, 'Premier Planning to Keep His Army in Fighting Form,' *Globe and Mail*, 29 October 1987. In October 1988 the premier dropped half of the parliamentary assistants, appointed an equal number of new parliamentary assistants, and shuffled others; twenty-nine of sixty-three back-benchers held parliamentary assistantships.
57 Catherine Thompson, 'The Parliamentary Assistant in Ontario,' Ontario legislative internship paper, June 1984
58 Paul Thomas, 'The Role of National Party Caucuses,' in Peter Aucoin, ed., *Party Government and Regional Representation in Canada* (Toronto: University of Toronto Press, 1985), 93
59 In the fall of 1988 the chairmanship of the government caucus was made an elective office.
60 Morley, *Secular Socialists*, ch. 6

Notes to pages 50–8

61 Thomas, 'Role of National Party Caucuses,' 91–120
62 Peter McCormick, 'Politics after the Landslide: The Progressive Conservative Caucus in Alberta,' *Parliamentary Government* IV (1983), 8–10
63 The activities and political significance of two recent task forces are analysed in Bill Acres, 'Opposition Party Caucus Task Forces in Ontario, A Case Study: The NDP "Work, People and Technological Change Task Force," October 12, 1983 to February 22, 1984,' Ontario legislative internship paper, August 1984; and Marya Duckworth, 'The NDP Task Force on Health and Safety, 1986,' Ontario legislative internship paper, July 1986.
64 No women have ever held the position of Speaker (or of deputy Speaker, for that matter). In 1987 Marietta Roberts was appointed deputy chairman.
65 Roderick G. Lewis, *The House Was My Home: An Informal Guide for Members of the Legislative Assembly of Ontario* (Toronto: Queen's Printer, 1987), 57–9
66 Ontario Commission on the Legislature, *Second Report* (December 1973), 1
67 Phillip Laundy, *The Office of Speaker in Commonwealth Parliaments* (London: Quiller Press, 1984), 136
68 Legislative Assembly of Ontario, *Journals*, 3 April 1980, 45
69 *Debates*, 21 April 1981, 3–5
70 Legislative Assembly of Ontario, Standing Committee on Procedural Affairs and Agencies, Boards and Commissions, *Report on Standing Orders and Procedure (No. 4)*, November 1985, 1–5
71 Philip Norton, 'Behavioural Changes: Backbench Independence in the 1980s,' in Philip Norton, ed., *Parliament in the 1980s* (Oxford: Basil Blackwell, 1984), 36
72 The tremendous success of Ottawa's first election of a speaker by secret ballot offers some reason to believe that this is an overly pessimistic interpretation, but only time will tell. On Ottawa's experience, see Gary Levy, 'A Night to Remember: The First Election of a Speaker by Secret Ballot,' in Paul W. Fox and Graham White, eds., *Politics: Canada*, 6th ed. (Toronto: McGraw-Hill Ryerson, 1987), 519–24.
73 The ad hoc committee on reforming the standing orders has again proposed abolishing all appeals to speakers' rulings.
74 David Callfas and Smirle Forsyth, 'Motion of Censure against the Speaker,' paper presented to the annual conference of Canadian Clerks-at-the-Table, 1982
75 The 1904 casting vote of Speaker William Charlton provides a good illustration of how early Speakers viewed their role: he voted to defeat an opposition amendment on the ground that it would 'interfere with' a government bill; *Journals*, 22 April 1904, 297–9.

76 *Debates*, 2 June 1980, 5038
77 The ad hoc rules committee has proposed the addition of a second deputy chairman, with an informal agreement that two of the four presiding officers be drawn from the opposition.
78 Ruling by Speaker Stokes, 15 April 1980; *Debates*, 786–7. The ad hoc rules committee has recommended that decisions of the chairman of the Committee of the Whole be appealable to the Speaker.
79 When the deputy Speaker and the deputy chairman have come from opposite sides of the House, they have sometimes paired their votes.
80 The Legislative Assembly Act, RSO 1980, c. 235, s. 33
81 Some of these administrative duties are outlined in Hon. John E. Stokes, 'The Role of Speaker,' *Municipal World*, November 1980, 289–91.
82 This unusual provision in the Legislative Assembly Act gave rise to a brouhaha in the fall of 1986 when Roderick Lewis, having announced his retirement, effectively refused to leave office until he was granted an enormous severance package; he claimed that the 1974 amendment to the act had given him the job for life.
83 The government believed that the first clerk assistant, John Holtby, was too helpful to the opposition. Moreover, his relationship with the clerk had soured, and the government found it easier and more to its liking to remove Holtby and retain the clerk.
84 Lewis's traditionalism is evident in his book of reminiscences and procedural commentary, *The House Was My Home*.
85 Board of Internal Economy, *Minutes*, meeting 13/87, 14 December 1987
86 Standing Committee on the Legislative Assembly, *Report on Appointments in the Public Sector* (1986), 30–3
87 Cabinet Office, 'Government Response to the Report of the Standing Committee on the Legislative Assembly on Appointments in the Public Sector,' 27 October 1986
88 *Minutes*, meeting 13/87
89 For a history, see Office of the Provincial Auditor of Ontario, *The First One Hundred Years* (Toronto, 1986).
90 See chapter 8.
91 The Audit Act, RSO 1980, c. 35, s. 3. The Legislative Assembly Committee's *Report on Appointments in the Public Sector* recommended that government nominees for provincial auditor and ombudsman be reviewed by the Public Accounts Committee or the Ombudsman Committee, and that unless 'consensus' (undefined) was reached, the government should withdraw its nomination. The government has signified its acceptance of this

recommendation, though amendments to the relevant statutes seem to be required to give it binding force.
92 For an account of the Ontario ombudsman, see Donald Morand, 'Ontario,' in Gerald A. Caiden, ed., *International Handbook of the Ombudsman: Country Surveys* (London: Greenwood Press, 1983), 63–70.
93 Frederick J. Fletcher, 'The Crucial and the Trivial: News Coverage of Provincial Politics,' in Donald C. MacDonald, ed., *The Government and Politics of Ontario*, 3d ed. (Toronto: Nelson Canada, 1985), 194
94 Ibid., 205

CHAPTER 3 The legislature at work I: An overview

1 David Truman, *The Governmental Process* (New York: Knopf, 1951), 343–4
2 Edward Crowe, 'Consensus and Structure in Legislative Norms: Party Discipline in the House of Commons,' *Journal of Politics* XLV (November 1983), 908
3 Carolyn Thomson, 'This Place: The Culture of Queen's Park,' Ontario legislative internship paper, 1987. This section draws heavily on Thomson's paper.
4 Ibid., 19–20
5 See, for example, the deference that characterized the early legislative career of John Robarts, who was first elected in 1951: A.K. McDougall, *John P. Robarts: His Life and Government* (Toronto: University of Toronto Press, 1986), ch. 3.
6 An example: several times in recent years, a party that wished to present amendments to legislation at Committee of the Whole was asleep at the switch when the Speaker asked whether the bill should be ordered for third reading; invariably, the other parties granted unanimous consent to give them the opportunity to send the bill to Committee of the Whole.
7 RSO 1980, c. 235
8 An earlier Legislative Assembly Act, almost identical with the 1876 version, had been disallowed by the federal government, presumably for attempting to take on too many parliamentary powers.
9 F.F. Schindeler, *Responsible Government in Ontario* (Toronto: University of Toronto Press, 1969), 130
10 The last MPP who did not belong to one of the three principal parties was Joe Salsberg, the Labour Progressive (Communist) member from St Andrew's until 1955.
11 *Journals*, 1986–87, 78, 88–9, 285

12 A. Fraser, G.A. Birch, and W.F. Dawson, *Beauchesne's Rules and Forms of the House of Commons*, 5th ed. (Toronto: Carswell, 1978)
13 Charles Gordon, ed., *Erskine May's Parliamentary Practice*, 20th ed. (London: Butterworths, 1983)
14 By custom, members are not permitted to debate matters before the courts. In Ontario in the 1960s this convention was rigidly enforced by the Speaker. In effect, substantive policy areas were thus removed from legislative debate (for example, the government prosecution of corporations for violations of environmental or labour law). In 1970 a standing order was adopted allowing some latitude in this area.
15 Samuel Beer, *Modern British Politics* (London: Faber, 1969), 350
16 Philip Kaye, 'Party Discipline and Legislative Voting,' paper prepared for the Ontario delegates to the 24th Commonwealth Parliamentary Association Canadian Regional Conference, July 1984. Mr Kaye has kindly provided me with unpublished data covering the final few months of the Thirty-second Parliament, which confirm the earlier pattern.
17 See Crowe, 'Consensus and Structure.'
18 Alex Kostiw, 'Party Discipline in the Ontario Legislature,' Ontario legislative internship paper, June 1984, 11
19 Ibid., 10
20 In the fall of 1986, as a crucial vote approached on the highly controversial issue of including sexual orientation in the Ontario Human Rights Code, Premier Peterson indicated that his MPPs were free to follow the dictates of their consciences, but personally called several members in an attempt to sway their votes or at least persuade them to abstain.
21 Ibid., 13
22 This is an estimate provided by senior Hansard officials.
23 NDP Leader Bob Rae, speaking in the third-reading debate on the French Language Services Act, *Debates*, 18 November 1986, 3405
24 Under the French Languages Services Act, which was passed late in 1986, 'everyone has the right to use English or French in the debates and other proceedings of the Legislative Assembly' (s. 3(1)) and, as of 1991, all public bills are to be introduced in both languages.
25 See the ruling by Speaker Edighoffer, 25 May 1987, *Journals*, 73.
26 Standing order 19(d) 8–11
27 For a complete list of expressions declared to be parliamentary or unparliamentary, see Office of the Clerk, *Precedents of the Legislative Assembly 1867–1987*, 44.2 (appendix 2 of Roderick G. Lewis, *The House Was My Home: An Informal Guide for Members of the Legislative Assembly of Ontario* [Toronto: Queen's Printer, 1987]).

Notes to pages 82–7

28 *Debates*, 24 April 1981, 70–2
29 On the difference between points of order and points of privilege, see Roderick G. Lewis, 'A Note on Privilege and Order in Ontario,' *Canadian Parliamentary Review* V (Winter 1982–83), 11.
30 Quoted in Sam Cureatz, 'Some Thoughts on Parliamentary Debate in Ontario,' *Canadian Parliamentary Review* VI (Summer 1983), 25
31 Standing Committee on Procedural Affairs, *Report on Standing Orders and Procedure (No. 2)* (March 1984), 9
32 Standing Committee on Procedural Affairs and Agencies, Boards and Commissions, *Report on Standing Orders and Procedure (No. 4)* (November 1985), 51
33 Ontario Commission on the Legislature, *First Report* (May 1973), 5
34 Ontario Commission on the Legislature, *Fourth Report* (September 1975), 49–51
35 See Gordon Vala-Webb, 'Wrestling Inflation and the Opposition to the Ground: The NDP Delay of Bill 179,' Ontario legislative internship paper, 1983.
36 *Report on Standing Orders and Procedure (No. 2)*, 2
37 *Report on Standing Orders and Procedure (No. 4)*, 49
38 Following the election of September 1987, the House opened in early November and sat until 23 December. To accommodate an opposition filibuster on the government's response to free trade, the House sat between Christmas and New Year's Day for the first time in memory; the House also met for single weeks in January and February 1988, and the session continued from early April until the end of June, resumed in October and picked up again in January 1989. The 1987–88–89 session was thus the third in a row in which the 'normal' schedule did not obtain, thereby raising the question whether a new pattern of sittings is emerging. If a parliamentary calendar is instituted, as was suggested by the ad hoc reform committee (discussed in Chapter 9), this question would be settled.
39 The report of the ad hoc reform committee proposed to rectify this anomaly.
40 Schindeler, *Responsible Government*, 261
41 This excludes Wednesdays, which for most of this period were counted as official sitting days, even though the House did not meet.
42 A solid argument can be mounted that it is improper for committees to meet between sessions, but the niceties involved have never been of concern in Ontario. Elsewhere the problem is resolved by not formally proroguing one session until just before another is to start. On this question see Gordon Barnhart, 'The Effects of Prorogation on Legislative Committees,' and David Mitchell, 'Another Look at the Effects of Prorogation on Legis-

lative Committees,' papers presented to the annual conference of the Canadian Society of Clerks-at-the-Table, St John's, Newfoundland, July 1983.
43 *Report on Standing Orders and Procedure (No. 4)*, 10
44 Untitled report of the ad hoc committee on reform, dated 12 April 1988, 40–1
45 In the 1870s Saturday sittings were routine, but have been highly unusual since then.
46 Initially, under the 1986 rule changes, the time for sitting was from 2:00 PM until 6:30 PM. With the additional time taken by members' statements and opposition replies to ministerial statements, however, question period was beginning roughly half an hour later than before. This caused the press gallery to complain about difficulties in making deadlines, and at their request the opening was moved forward to 1:30 PM.
47 Since both opposition parties fell below twenty members in the 1987 election, they have lost the power to block a late sitting (the rule requires that twenty members object) unless they act together. The ad hoc reform committee has proposed that only twelve members need object.
48 See Andy Anstett and Paul Thomas, 'Manitoba: The Role of the Legislature in a Polarized Political System,' in Graham White and Gary Levy, eds., *Provincial and Territorial Legislatures in Canada* (Toronto: University of Toronto Press, 1989).
49 Schindeler, *Responsible Government*, 156
50 *Fourth Report*, 8–32
51 In 1976 the undignified custom, still common in other provincial legislatures, of members rising to introduce groups of visiting schoolchildren, seniors, boy scouts, and others was done away with.
52 The unusually large amount of time spent on third reading in 1986–87 resulted entirely from a Conservative filibuster on a bill to ban the practice of extra-billing by physicians.
53 Schindeler reports that, in total, about four and a half hours were devoted to questions in 1964 (*Responsible Government*, 199); since the session totalled roughly 270 hours (calculated from data on pages 155 and 156), an estimate of 1.7 per cent suggests itself.

CHAPTER 4   The legislature at work II: Routine proceedings

1 *Debates*, 29 April 1986, 140
2 House of Commons, Table Research Branch, *Précis of Procedure* (Ottawa: Clerk of the House, 1985), 24
3 *Debates*, 30 April 1986, 184
4 The ad hoc reform committee has proposed that the time for members'

statements be increased so as to accommodate three rather than two members from each party.
5 Sir Charles Gordon, ed., *Erskine May's Parliamentary Practice*, 20th ed. (London: Butterworths, 1983), 355–7; see also the ruling of Speaker Cass, *Journals*, 25 June 1970, 173–5.
6 Ruling by Speaker Stokes, 23 October 1979, *Debates*, 3732–3.
7 Ontario Commission on the Legislature (hereinafter Camp Commission), *Fourth Report* (September 1975), 33
8 F.F. Schindeler, *Responsible Government in Ontario* (Toronto: University of Toronto Press, 1969), 199
9 Camp Commission, *Fourth Report*, 9
10 Ruling of Speaker Stokes, 30 November 1978, *Journals*, 218–19
11 Rulings of Speaker Stokes, 8 December 1978, *Debates*, 5845–6, and Speaker Turner, 9 November 1983, *Debates*, 2933
12 For examples, see Office of the Clerk, *Precedents of the Legislative Assembly of Ontario 1867–1987*, 103.1 (Appendix 2 of Roderick G. Lewis, *The House Was My Home: An Informal Guide for Members of the Legislative Assembly of Ontario* [Toronto: Queen's Printer, 1987]).
13 The Procedural Affairs Committee had recommended that leaders also be limited to one supplementary: *Report on Standing Orders and Procedure (No. 4)* (November 1985), 24.
14 David Doherty, 'The Effectiveness of Question Period in the Legislative Assembly of Ontario,' Ontario legislative internship paper, June 1981, 3
15 Patrick Weller, *First among Equals: Prime Ministers in Westminster Systems* (London: Faber, 1985), 171. The figure would have been even greater than 20 per cent had the premier's occasional absences forced the opposition to direct questions it had planned for him to ministers.
16 Data on questions in 1984 were collected in a similar fashion as those gathered for Table 4.2, but are not presented here.
17 Doherty, 'Effectiveness of Question Period,' 6
18 The distinction between the policy concentration of the NDP and the non-programmatic approach of the other opposition party was more clear-cut in 1986–87, for the first three topics of Liberal questioning in 1984 were education, the environment, and the economy.
19 The figures in the following two sentences are ratios of the percentages of the questions asked by the leaders and back-benchers. For example, the Conservative leader asked 5.1 per cent of his questions on labour/WCB, and his back-benchers asked 1.9 per cent of their questions on this topic; thus, proportionately, the leader asked 2.7 times as many labour/WCB questions as the back-benchers.

20 This analysis excludes topics on which neither leaders nor back-benchers asked more than a handful of questions.
21 Doherty, 'Effectiveness of Question Period,' 15
22 Frederick J. Fletcher, 'The Crucial and the Trivial: News Coverage of Provincial Politics,' in Donald C. MacDonald, ed., *Government and Politics of Ontario*, 3d ed. (Toronto: Nelson, 1985), 200
23 Ibid.
24 Doherty, 'Effectiveness of Question Period,' 18
25 Fletcher, 'Crucial and the Trivial,' 200
26 Thomas A. Hockin, 'The Prime Minister and Political Leadership: An Introduction to Some Restraints and Imperatives,' in Hockin, ed., *Apex of Power: The Prime Minister and Political Leadership in Canada* (Scarborough: Prentice-Hall, 1971), 10
27 See, for example, *Debates*, 23 October 1984, 3513–16.
28 Maurice Champagne, 'Questions for Debate in the Quebec National Assembly,' *Canadian Parliamentary Review* V (Spring 1982), 17–19
29 The following account draws heavily on Cheryl Mitchell, 'The Politics of Written Questions in Ontario,' Ontario legislative internship paper, June 1984.
30 Philip Norton, *The Commons in Perspective* (Oxford: Martin Robertson, 1981), 111–12
31 Schindeler, *Responsible Government*, 194–5
32 Mitchell, 'Written Questions,' 18
33 Quoted ibid., 16
34 *Debates*, 18 April 1984, 881–2
35 *Debates*, 27 October 1986, 2815; 1 December 1986, 3809
36 *Debates*, 13 June 1988, 4318–19
37 Mitchell, 'Written Questions,' 14
38 Schindeler makes no mention whatsoever of petitioning; the Camp Commission found that in the early 1970s, members seldom tabled petitions (*Fourth Report*, 11).
39 The ad hoc reform committee has proposed a loosening of the formal restrictions on petitions, including the prohibition against requests for money.
40 In some ways it was more effective than a normal filibuster. Since petitions come before the orders of the day are reached, the government had no procedural recourse for ending it as long as the opposition still had petitions to read. Indeed, the treasurer was unable to deliver his budget speech in the House because the NDP refused to interrupt their reading of petitions.
41 *Fourth Report*, 71.

42 In fact, the ad hoc reform committee proposes doing away with all possibility for debate.
43 Graham White, 'Committees, Petitions and the Redress of Grievances,' in *Background Papers for the Fifth Canadian Regional Seminar* (Toronto: Commonwealth Parliamentary Association, 1979), 56–63
44 Camp Commission, *Fourth Report*, 61
45 Schindeler, *Responsible Government*, 204–5
46 According to Alex C. Lewis, *Parliamentary Procedure in Ontario* (Toronto: King's Printer, 1940), 40, the requirement that the prospective debate be on 'a matter of urgent public importance' was construed to mean 'a single specific matter of recent occurrence,' thus ruling out general or continuing problems such as unemployment as well as possible future developments.
47 Standing order 34(c)(i) of the 1978–86 rules
48 As part of its package of reforms to the estimates process, the ad hoc committee on reform has proposed that emergency debates be abolished.
49 Lewis A. Froman Jr, *The Congressional Process: Strategies, Rules and Procedures* (Boston: Little Brown, 1967), 63

CHAPTER 5 The legislature at work III: Legislation and finances

1 Nelson Polsby, 'Legislatures,' in Fred I. Greenstein and Nelson Polsby, eds., *Handbook of Political Science* 5 (Reading, Mass.: Addison-Wesley, 1975), 277
2 The process of 'carrying bills over' is discussed below.
3 1986–87 was probably typical in that nearly half the government bills (45 per cent) originated in three ministries: Attorney-General, Municipal Affairs, and Consumer and Commercial Relations (the principal regulatory ministry); seven ministries had from five to nine bills before the House, thirteen had from one to four, and seven ministries brought forward no legislation.
4 F.F. Schindeler, *Responsible Government in Ontario* (Toronto: University of Toronto Press, 1969), 215–18
5 For an account of one such all-out campaign of delay, see Gordon Vala-Webb, 'Wrestling Inflation and the Opposition to the Ground: The NDP Delay of Bill 179,' Ontario legislative internship paper, June 1983.
6 The late James Renwick (an NDP member from 1964 to 1984) would occasionally insist on hearing the introductory statement before the Speaker put the question, on the grounds that he had a right to know what he was being asked to vote upon, but this sensible practice never caught on.

280 Notes to pages 123–5

7 As described below, eight government bills were 'carried over' from the previous session, and were deemed to have second reading on the first day of the new session; these are excluded from the current discussion.
8 In 1984 only 11 of 63 government bills called for second reading had to wait as much as five weeks for this stage. Much of the raw data on which the tabulations of duration and timing of legislative stages were based were kindly supplied by Barbara Hibbard, formerly of the Office of the Government House Leader (to whom no responsibility adheres for my interpretations).
9 Schindeler, *Responsible Government*, 171
10 Ontario Commission on the Legislature (hereinafter Camp Commission), *Fourth Report* (Toronto: Queen's Printer, 1975), 13
11 Schindeler, *Responsible Government*, 169, explains that passage of a hoist motion was more final than simply defeating a bill at second reading in that the question at second reading was whether the bill should *now* be read a second time. Thus, a negative vote would leave open the possibility of the bill's being moved for second reading later in the session. Current practice is simply for the member to say, 'I move second reading of bill x' (the key word 'now' is no longer part of the formula). Bills lost on division at second reading are universally considered defunct for the session, and are removed from the order paper. Thus, the hoist amendment has lost its special character. Lewis maintains that the hoist is still more final than a simple defeat at second reading; See Roderick G. Lewis, *The House Was My Home: An Informal Guide for Members of the Legislative Assembly of Ontario* (Toronto: Queen's Printer, 1987), 92.
12 A division is a formal vote in which all members present are officially recorded as being for or against the motion (abstentions are not permitted in Ontario). All questions must be decided by votes, but in most instances the Speaker's estimation of the balance of oral ayes and nays is allowed to stand; in such cases, the official record shows only whether the motion passed or was defeated, not how specific individuals voted. Any five members can require that a division be held after the Speaker announces his opinion on the results of the voice vote (the ad hoc reform committee has recommended that this number be reduced to three).
13 Although the standing orders provide for bills to be referred to standing or select committee, no government legislation has been referred to a select committee since the mid-1970s.
14 In addition to the time consumed in the Committee of the Whole, delay occurs because standing order 66(c) prohibits consideration of the bill until the second day after the referral.

15 The best illustration occurred in 1978: a major piece of occupational health and safety legislation had been amended in standing committee in ways so unpalatable to the government that it refused to proceed with the bill. After months of wrangling, compromises were reached and effected by reconsidering the offending amendments in Committee of the Whole.
16 This was in fact done with the mammoth and highly controversial rent review bill of 1979–80. It is not a common practice.
17 Formally, budget approval from the Board of Internal Economy (see Chapter 6) is required for committees wishing to travel outside the capital, but no committee's request to hold public hearings anywhere in Ontario would be refused by the board.
18 In 1984 only two of the fifteen government bills that went to standing committee did not also go through Committee of the Whole.
19 Paul G. Thomas, 'The Influence of Standing Committees of Parliament on Government Legislation,' *Legislative Studies Quarterly* III (November 1978), 683–704
20 The rules and practices regarding admissibility of amendments to bills in Committee of the Whole apply with equal force to standing committees.
21 *Debates*, 2 June 1966, 4172–3
22 *Debates*, 5 December 1969, 9399–9400
23 *Debates*, 4 July 1977, 312–13, 325
24 A listing of all unproclaimed acts or sections of acts can be found in the 'Table of Proclamations' in the annual statute book.
25 Terri L. Hilborn, 'Private Members' Bills and Resolutions in the Ontario Legislature,' Ontario legislative internship paper, June 1981
26 Ibid.
27 Schindeler, *Responsible Government*, 176–87
28 Ibid., 144
29 That is, separate lotteries are conducted for each party, so that a rotation of government, official opposition, and third party is maintained in assigning the order for private members' business.
30 Prior to the April 1986 revision of the standing orders, private members' business was debated on Thursday afternoons. This simple change has been salutary not only because the atmosphere is more conducive to real debate than was the case when it followed the politically charged histrionics of question period, but also because afternoons are more susceptible to being displaced by emergency debates, non-confidence motions, and the simple press of business. In 1984 on only 12 of 21 Thursdays did debate on private members' business take place; in 1986–87 on only 3 Thursdays did private members' business not take place.

282 Notes to pages 134–48

31 The ad hoc committee on reform has proposed that more members be able to share the available time by limiting the sponsor of the bill or resolution to 12 minutes and allotting 15 minutes to each party to allocate among its members.
32 The ad hoc committee on reform has recommended that as a matter of course the sponsor of a bill be permitted to designate whether it is to go to Committee of the Whole or to a specific standing or select committee.
33 R.V. Stewart Hyson, 'The Role of the Backbencher – An Analysis of Private Members' Bills in the Canadian House of Commons,' *Parliamentary Affairs* XXVII (summer 1974), 262
34 Hilborn, 'Private Members' Bills'
35 Ibid., 19
36 This section draws heavily on Donald L. Revell, 'Private Legislation in Ontario,' *The Law Society of Upper Canada Gazette* XIX (May 1985), 290–323.
37 Ibid., 293, 294. The British 'hybrid bill,' which combines elements of public and private legislation, is unknown in Ontario.
38 For example, the Ontario Landscape Architects Act prohibited non-members of the Ontario Landscape Architects Association from advertising themselves as landscape architects.
39 Evert A. Lindquist, *Consultation and Budget Secrecy* (Ottawa: The Conference Board in Canada, 1985), 12–13
40 In this section, as at Queen's Park, the term 'estimates' not only refers to the specific dollar values of government spending proposals, but also is used as shorthand for 'the process for legislative review of the estimates documents.'
41 My thanks are due to Alex McFedries of the Clerk's Office for supplying data on estimates time.
42 For a variety of reasons, not least the anticipation of extensive reforms to the estimates process, only slightly more than half the available estimates hours were assigned in 1988; no ministry was allocated more than thirteen hours.
43 Robert L. Stanfield, 'The Present State of the Legislative Process in Canada: Myths and Realities,' in William A.W. Neilson and James A. MacPherson, eds., *The Legislative Process in Canada: The Need for Reform* (Montreal: Institute for Research in Public Policy, 1978), 39–50
44 Standing Committee on Resources Development, *Minutes*, 28 May 1984
45 I once unsuccessfully attempted to convince a veteran opposition member that it wasn't against the rules to move for a reduction in the estimates.

46 Frequently, motions for interim supply are passed within hours of the date by which the government's spending authority is to cease. This creates a far more problematic situation than might first appear, since delaying or halting the sophisticated electronic financial transfers endemic in government requires at least one or two days' lead time.
47 Management Board of Cabinet Act, RSO 1980, c. 254, s. 4
48 Michael J. Gough, 'Legal Aspects of Ontario Finances,' paper presented to the Financial Officers' Council, 31 March 1981, 19
49 *Journals*, 26 June 1981, 115
50 *Annual Report of the Provincial Auditor of Ontario for the Year Ended March 31, 1987* (November 1987), 206-10
51 Gough, 'Legal Aspects,' 16
52 See chapter 6.
53 *Annual Report of the Provincial Auditor*, 10-15; Standing Committee on Public Accounts, *Special Report on the Estimates Process* (June 1988). On the ad hoc committee's proposals, see Chapter 9.

CHAPTER 6 Committees

1 As in the House, although proceedings are electronically recorded and later transcribed, an 'interjectionist' is present to take down interjections, to identify the speaker, and to verify the spelling of names and technical terms.
2 In the fall of 1988 some committees began to experiment with a rectangular table arrangement so that members would not have their backs to other members.
3 To the great consternation of some and the great relief of others, smoking is sometimes, at the discretion of individual committees, been banned in the often poorly ventilated committee rooms.
4 The obvious inference that members are not paying attention to the business before the committee is not always warranted. On several occasions, while working for committees, I was astounded to hear members who had seemed entirely oblivious to witnesses' testimony recount with precision points the speakers had made.
5 It is up to members to draw the chairman's attention to the lack of a quorum; this almost never happens, except occasionally as a stalling tactic.
6 No hard sociometric evidence is offered in support of this less than self-evident proposition. It is based on my involvement in a great many committee meetings.

7 Much could be written of committee travel, only some of it libellous. For present purposes, the most noteworthy fact is that when travelling, members of all parties socialize with one another. In off hours, groups of members organize themselves for meals and other amusements in different ways; the only party-related behaviour is the tendency for all New Democrats to stick together, even when (as they often do) they join other groups.
8 Both select and standing committees are 'select' in the sense that they are composed of only selected members. The technically correct appellation, 'standing select committee,' lapsed some years ago.
9 A.K. McDougall, *John P. Robarts: His Life and Government* (Toronto: University of Toronto Press, 1986), passim
10 Ontario Commission on the Legislature (hereinafter Camp Commission), *Fourth Report* (Toronto: Queen's Printer, 1975), 64–78.
11 Hon. Robert F. Nixon, *Reforming the Budget Process: A Discussion Paper* (Toronto: Ministry of Treasury and Economics, October 1985)
12 *Journals*, 28 April 1986, 55
13 See Chapter 9.
14 The standing orders refer in several places to 'recognized political parties' but nowhere define them. For the purposes of payments to leaders, whips, and House leaders, the Legislative Assembly Act speaks of parties with 'a recognized membership of twelve or more persons in the Assembly,' but does not address the more general question of defining party groups. In the absence of specific guidance, it presumably is up to the Speaker to recognize the existence of a 'party' in the House in the same way Speakers in Saskatchewan and Alberta have decided which of two parties with the same number of members should be recognized as the official opposition. See, for example, Gerald Amerongen, 'Statement Concerning Status of the Leader of the Official Opposition, Alberta Legislative Assembly, March 11, 1983,' *Canadian Parliamentary Review* VI (Spring 1982–83), 44–5, and Vaughan Myers, 'Designating the Official Opposition, Alberta: A Speaker's Nightmare,' *The Table* LII (1984), 59–87.
15 The standard committee configuration in the Liberal majority parliament was six Liberals, two New Democrats, and two Conservatives, plus the chairman.
16 Office of the Government House Leader, 'Government Response to the Second and Third Reports of the Special Committee on Reform of the House of Commons,' 9 October 1985
17 See the ruling by Speaker Turner, *Journals*, 21 January 1983, 292–3.

18 The ad hoc committee on reform has proposed that committees simply be granted open-ended terms of reference to deal with any matter relating to the ministries under their aegis.
19 Since an order of the House would be required to specify that a committee was not to have such power, the provision is redundant.
20 The language of both the act and the empowering order of the House – 'for which the Speaker *may* issue his Warrant' – gives discretion to the Speaker. On two occasions requests for warrants have been refused: in 1980, when a committee wanted to issue a warrant to a senator, and in 1986, when a committee sought a warrant against a person resident in the province of Quebec (both witnesses appeared before the committees of their own volition).
21 The Select Committee on Plant Shutdowns and Economic Adjustment of 1980–81 was given the power to ask directly for a warrant, as was customary for select committees. Unusually for a select committee, it met extensively while the House was still in session and thus occasioned the peculiar situation of having the Speaker issue warrants without direct authorization from the House while the House was sitting.
22 For a thorough discussion of Speaker's warrants and other issues relating to committee witnesses, see Ontario Law Reform Commission, *Report on Witnesses before Legislative Committees* (1981), ch. 2.
23 Charles Gordon, ed., *Erskine May's Treatise on the Law, Privilege, Proceedings and Usages of Parliament,* 20th ed. (London: Butterworths, 1983), 687
24 Interview broadcast on CBC radio, 23 July 1986
25 Some years ago an MPP claimed to have hit upon the crucial distinction between standing and select committees – coffee: select committees had it provided but standing committees did not. Alas for taxonomic precision, this difference is no more.
26 Even if a committee met for only thirty minutes, this was considered a 'sitting.' Most sittings, however, were about two hours, and some lasted two and a half hours or more; two hours is a reasonable average.
27 No Ontario committee has ever begun an enquiry by issuing a discussion paper and inviting response, as did the Parliamentary Task Force on Regulation.
28 Roberta Jessup, 'The Select Committee on Plant Shutdowns and Economic Adjustment,' Ontario legislative internship paper, June 1982
29 Ibid., 23
30 See, for example, Royal Commission on Financial Management and Accountability, *Final Report* (Ottawa: Supply and Services, 1979), 399–400 (the Lambert Report).

31 The Clerk's Office publishes a pamphlet, 'Standing Committee Procedure: A Guide for Committee Chairmen'; but this deals in the main with formal rules and powers, and does not address most of the difficult questions chairmen encounter.
32 Standing Committee on Procedural Affairs and Agencies, Boards and Commissions, Report on Standing Orders and Procedure (No. 4), November 1985, 82
33 The ad hoc committee on reform has recommended that full Hansard service be made the norm for all committees.
34 Sometimes committees pass special motions authorizing the release of their reports before the reports are presented to the House.
35 For a discussion of two fruitless investigations into leaked reports, see Standing Committee on Procedural Affairs and Agencies, Boards and Commissions, *Report on the Premature Disclosure of the Interim Report of the Select Committee on Economic Affairs and Report on the Matter of Privilege relating to the Premature Release of the Confidential Draft Material of the Select Committee on Energy*, January 1986.
36 Standing order 30(c)
37 An inventive perversion of this rule took place in 1980: the Justice Committee made a report requesting a Speaker's warrant for documents relating to the collapse of a trust company which the government did not want to release. The government was most unlikely to bring the adjourned debate back before the House, so the committee chairman dutifully moved the adjournment of the debate and urged the House to defeat his motion, which it did; thus, the debate continued and the report was adopted later the same day. See *Journals*, 20 November 1980, 213–14.
38 C.E.S. Franks, 'The Dilemma of the Standing Committees of the House of Commons,' *Canadian Journal of Political Science* IV (December 1971), 464
39 Nelson Polsby, 'Legislatures,' in Nelson Polsby and Fred Greenstein, eds., *Handbook of Political Science*, vol. 5 (Reading, Mass.: Addison-Wesley, 1975), 278

CHAPTER 7 Services to members

1 Donald C. MacDonald, *The Happy Warrior: Political Memoirs* (Toronto: Fitzhenry and Whiteside, 1988), ch. 5; *Debates*, 15 January 1987, 4581
2 Standing Committee on the Legislative Assembly, transcript, 29 March 1988, M18-M39
3 Order in council 3195/78, made pursuant to section 94(1) of the Legislative Assembly Act, RSO 1980, c. 235

4 F.F. Schindeler, *Responsible Government in Ontario* (Toronto: University of Toronto Press, 1969), 116
5 For complete data on salaries in 1986, see Robert J. Fleming and Patrick Fafard, eds., *Canadian Legislatures: The 1986 Comparative Study* (Toronto: Office of the Assembly, 1986). A hold-over from an earlier era is the fact that members' salaries are officially termed 'indemnities.' The term signified that members were originally paid to compensate them for losses to their regular income while they attended sessions in Toronto. The allowances and the basic indemnity are set out in sections 60–69 of the Legislative Assembly Act.
6 Statistics Canada, bulletin 72-002
7 Fleming and Fafard, *Canadian Legislatures*, 89
8 For details, see the Legislative Assembly Retirement Allowances Act RSO 1980, c. 236. For a comparison of legislative pension plans, see Randall Chan, 'Pension Plans for Canadian Legislators,' *Canadian Parliamentary Review* IV (Winter 1981–82), 29–36.
9 For a summary of the commission's recommendations over the years and the action taken on them, see Commission on Election Finances, *Eleventh Report Containing Recommendations in Respect of the Indemnities and Allowances of Members of the Legislative Assembly*, April 1988.
10 Employees of the NDP caucus are organized as a local of the Ontario Public Service Employees' Union; employees of the Conservative and Liberal caucuses are not unionized.
11 The 'second' staff person in the constituency office is frequently more than one person working on a part-time basis.
12 Office of the Assembly, *Manual of Administration*, section 4-4-6
13 Fleming and Fafard, *Canadian Legislatures*, 106–7
14 Board of Internal Economy, *Minutes*, Meeting 7/81, 25 May 1981
15 For a history of Ontario's Hansard service and details of its operation, see Peter Brannan, 'Reporting the Spoken Word: The Ontario Experience,' *Canadian Parliamentary Review* V (Summer 1982), 11–14.
16 For other minor perks and allowances, see Office of the Assembly, *Allowances and Services: A Guide for Members of the Ontario Legislature*, 1986
17 Although more than half the Tory incumbents lost, no non-incumbent Tory won; moreover, owing to redistribution, three ridings saw two 'incumbents' in the running.
18 Michael Krashinsky and William J. Milne, 'Some Evidence on the Effect of Incumbency in Ontario Provincial Elections,' *Canadian Journal of Political Science* XVI (September 1983), 489–500, and 'The Effect of Incumbency in the 1984 Federal and the 1985 Ontario Elections,' ibid., 337–44

19 This is of course the ombudsman's job description. Ontario has a large Ombudsman's Office, which by Canadian standards enjoys a fairly high profile. That profile, however, remains much lower than that of an MPP; moreover, the impression exists, justified or otherwise, that although it is thorough, the Ombudsman's Office is slow, legalistic, and highly bureaucratic.
20 Harold D. Clarke, Richard E. Price, and Robert Krause, 'Constituency Service among Canadian Provincial Legislators: Basic Findings and a Test of Three Hypotheses,' *Canadian Journal of Political Science* VIII (December 1975), Table 1, 530
21 A.K. McDougall, *John P. Robarts: His Life and Government* (Toronto: University of Toronto Press, 1985), 224
22 For a fuller treatment of the electronic Hansard issue under the Conservatives, see Lorraine Luski, 'Should the Ontario Legislature Televise Its Proceedings?' Ontario legislative internship paper, December 1984.
23 Standing Committee on Procedural Affairs and Agencies, Boards and Commissions, *Television Coverage of the Proceedings of the Legislative Assembly*, September 1985, 6
24 Ibid., A-3
25 Michael Adams, 'Canadian Attitudes towards Legislative Institutions: A New National Survey,' in Fleming and Fafard, *Canadian Legislatures*, 25–32. One American study concluded that the televising of legislatures was of electoral benefit to incumbents provided that their districts were small or homogeneous, but members with large, diverse districts were more likely to be defeated if their Houses were televised. See W. Mark Crain and Brian Goff, 'The Effects of Televised Legislatures on Election Outcomes,' Working Paper 84-41 (Fairfax, Va.: Center for Study of Public Choice, George Mason University, 1984). Though the conclusion is intriguing, the dangers in presuming its applicability to a parliamentary system are legion.
26 See Richard G. Price and Harold D. Clarke, 'Television and the House of Commons,' in Harold D. Clarke, Colin Campbell, F.Q. Quo, and Arthur Goddard, eds., *Parliament, Policy and Representation* (Toronto: Methuen, 1980), 68–9. Certainly, this was the primary reason for the Conservatives' refusal to proceed with full coverage when they were in power.
27 Kenneth Wiltshire, 'Staffing and Appropriations of Parliament,' in J.R. Nethercote, ed., *Parliament and Bureaucracy* (Sydney: Hale and Iremonger, 1982), 309
28 The Office of the Assembly program technically includes the Commission on Election Finances and the Electoral Boundaries Commission, but only

because they don't conveniently fit elsewhere. Since they are not intrinsically legislative in nature, they are excluded from this discussion.
29 Fleming and Fafard, *Canadian Legislatures*, 140–1

CHAPTER 8 The legislature and accountability

1 C.E.S. Franks, *The Parliament of Canada* (Toronto: University of Toronto Press, 1987), 252
2 For a discussion of the Ontario government's system, see Price Waterhouse Associates and the Canada Consulting Group, *A Study of Management and Accountability in the Government of Ontario* (January 1985).
3 Franks, *Parliament of Canada*, ch. 11
4 See A.H. Birch, *Representative and Responsible Government: An Essay on the British Constitution* (London: Allen and Unwin, 1964), ch. 11.
5 Special Committee on Reform of the House of Commons (the McGrath Committee), *Report* (June 1985), 21
6 Royal Commission on Financial Management and Accountability (the Lambert Commission), *Final Report* (March 1979), 57
7 Standing Committee on Public Accounts, *Final Report* (December 1980), 12
8 Letter from the chairman of Management Board to the chairman of the Public Accounts Committee, 11 August 1981, cited in Standing Committee on Public Accounts, 1981 Report (December 1981), 4
9 Quoted in Birch, *Representative and Responsible Government*, 20
10 Hon. Walter Baker, 'Position Paper: The Reform of Parliament' (November 1979), 2
11 Lambert Commission, *Final Report*, 9–10 (emphasis in original)
12 T.M. Denton, 'Ministerial Responsibility: A Contemporary Perspective,' in Richard Schultz, Orest M. Kruhlak, and John C. Terry, eds., *The Canadian Political Process*, 3d ed. (Toronto: Holt, Rinehart and Winston, 1979), 357
13 See T. Patrick Reid, 'Issues of Accountability and Ministerial Responsibility in the Ontario Government, 1983–84,' paper presented to the annual meeting of the Canadian Council of Public Accounts Committees, Charlottetown, Prince Edward Island, July 1984.
14 Quoted in Robert D. Carman, 'Accountability of Senior Public Servants to Parliament and Its Committees,' *Canadian Public Administration* XXVII (Winter 1984), 545
15 For additional accounts of this committee, see T. Patrick Reid, 'Public Accounts Committee: Ontario Legislature,' *The Parliamentarian* LXI (October 1980), 247–53; Mary Gibbons, 'Ontario's Public Accounts Com-

mittee: In Theory and in Practice,' Ontario legislative internship paper, July 1982; and Standing Committee on Public Accounts, 1985 and 1986 Report (February 1987), 93–8.
16 F.F. Schindeler, *Responsible Government in Ontario* (Toronto: University of Toronto Press, 1969), 250.
17 Ibid.
18 See Chapter 2.
19 Gibbons, 'Ontario's Public Accounts Committee,' 5
20 Technically, recent spending which has yet to be reported in the *Public Accounts* should be off limits to the committee, but it is not hard to find an entry in the previous year's *Public Accounts* that can serve as a springboard to the topic the committee wishes to investigate.
21 Standing Committee on Public Accounts, 1985 and 1986 Report, 98
22 Under the Audit Act (RSO 1980, c. 35, s. 19), for example, the auditor may not release to anyone, including the committee, his working papers.
23 Ministers may ask the auditor to carry out various studies, but he can accept or reject the commission at his discretion.
24 The committee has for some time sought written responses to its recommendations from deputy ministers and agency heads. These responses are circulated to the members and are forwarded to the auditor for inclusion in his next report, but they are not actively examined by the committee.
25 Schindeler, *Responsible Government*, 237
26 *Journals*, 28 June 1977, 22
27 Standing order 90(f)
28 Throughout this section, references to 'the committee' treat the Procedural Affairs Committee and the Government Agencies Committee as the same entity.
29 Michael Cassidy, 'Crown Corporations and the Canadian Legislatures – A Vain Search for Accountability,' *The Parliamentarian* LXIII (July 1982), 134
30 This section is an updated summary of Graham White, 'Ontario's Select Committee on the Ombudsman,' *The Table* L (1982), 52–61.
31 See R. Gregory, 'The Select Committee on the Parliamentary Commissioner for Administration,' *Public Law* (1982), 49–66. The Scandinavian parliaments all have committees that deal with ombudsmen, but direct comparisons with the Ontario committee are difficult because the institutional contexts are very different. Alberta and New Brunswick also have legislative ombudsman committees, but these have little in common with the Ontario committee.
32 Standing order 83(g)

291 Notes to pages 217–21

33 Such cases represent only a small proportion of the cases investigated by the ombudsman, and may vary from as few as two or three to as many as two dozen. In most cases the ombudsman does not support complaints against the government; when he does support a complaint, the government usually accepts his recommendation.
34 Since the complaints investigated by the ombudsman are mainly administrative, although they may have policy overtones, almost invariably those appearing before the committee are bureaucrats, usually of assistant deputy minister rank. Only very rarely do ministers appear (the Ombudsman Act prohibits him from investigating cabinet decisions).
35 The key to understanding this seemingly contradictory notion is that, under the act, the ombudsman makes a recommendation only if he concludes that a governmental decision was, inter alia, 'unreasonable, unjust, oppressive or improperly discriminatory.' To take a common illustration, if a person complained about being refused benefits by the Workers' Compensation Board, the ombudsman would have to satisfy himself (and later the committee) *not only* that in his judgment the complainant was entitled to benefits *but also* that the refusal was 'unreasonable.' In other words the Ombudsman could conclude that, had the decision been his, he would have granted benefits, but that the refusal to do so could not be characterized as unreasonable.
36 Select Committee on the Ombudsman, *Fifth Report* (November 1978), 98–9
37 The committee does not agree with this assessment; see its *Seventh Report* (September 1979), iv.
38 Though it was not concerned with this particular episode, a paper by a former senior adviser to the ombudsman warned of the committee's threat to the ombudsman's independence; see Brian Goodman, 'The Ontario Legislature's Select Committee on the Ombudsman,' International Ombudsman Institute Occasional Paper 19 (October 1982). A former committee chairman has argued that such fears are misplaced; see Robert W. Runciman, 'Ombudsmen and Legislatures: Allies or Adversaries?' *Canadian Parliamentary Review* VII (Autumn 1984), 15–17.
39 *Journals*, 22 November 1979, 211–14
40 For precise figures, see Table 5.1.
41 The distinction between 'taxes' and 'licence fees' is not always easily fathomed. For example, mandatory health insurance premiums, which generate close to $1 billion a year in revenue, are set by regulation. In 1978 Speaker Stokes reaffirmed rulings by earlier Speakers that challenges against legislation which permits the setting of health insurance premiums by regulation were in the nature of constitutional issues and thus beyond

the Speaker's competence; *Journals*, 13 March 1978, 32–3. An enthusiastic NDP member had argued that the practice offended against centuries of British parliamentary tradition, even unto Magna Carta.

42 Standing Committee on Regulations and Private Bills, *Second Report 1988* (June 1988)

43 Douglas Hartle, 'The Report of the Royal Commission on Financial Management and Accountability: A Review,' *Canadian Public Policy* v (Summer 1979), 382

CHAPTER 9 The process of reform

1 F.F. Schindeler, *Responsible Government in Ontario* (Toronto: University of Toronto Press, 1969)
2 Donald C. MacDonald, 'Modernizing the Legislature,' in MacDonald, ed., *The Government and Politics of Ontario*, 3d ed. (Toronto: Nelson, 1985), 50
3 Ontario, Select Committee on Rules and Procedures, *Report* (September 1969)
4 See Kenneth Bryden, 'Executive and Legislature in Ontario: A Case Study in Government Reform,' *Canadian Public Administration* XVII (Summer 1975), 235–52.
5 *Journals*, 9 June 1972, 117
6 For detailed accounts of the work of the Camp Commission and the processes behind the reforms of the 1973–78 period, see Graham White, 'Teaching the Mongrel Dog New Tricks: Sources and Directions of Reform in the Ontario Legislature,' *Journal of Canadian Studies* XIV (Summer 1979), 117–32, and 'The Life and Times of the Camp Commission,' *Canadian Journal of Political Science* XIII (June 1980), 357–75.
7 Ontario Commission on the Legislature, *First Report* (Toronto: Queen's Printer, 1973), 57
8 Ontario Commission on the Legislature, *Fourth Report* (Toronto: Queen's Printer, 1975), 4
9 Donald C. MacDonald, 'Modernizing the Legislature,' in MacDonald, ed., *Government and Politics of Ontario* (Toronto: Macmillan, 1975), 96–7
10 Ontario Commission on the Legislature, *Fifth Report* (Toronto: Queen's Printer, 1975), 43
11 Ibid., 56
12 *Journals*, 5 December 1975
13 Select Committee on the Fourth and Fifth Reports of the Ontario Commission on the Legislature, *Second Interim Report* (June 1976)

14 *Debates*, 16 December 1976, 6016–23
15 Select Committee on the Fourth and Fifth Reports of the Ontario Commission on the Legislature, *Final Report* (February 1977)
16 *Debates*, 1 December 1977, 2530; Lorne Maeck, the chief government whip, had been a member of the Morrow Committee.
17 Standing Procedural Affairs Committee, *Proposals for a New Committee System* (June 1980)
18 See Michael Breaugh, 'Proposals for a New Committee System in Ontario,' *Canadian Parliamentary Review* III (Winter 1980–81), 12–14.
19 Standing Procedural Affairs Committee, *Report on Witnesses before Committees* (October 1980)
20 Ontario Law Reform Commission, *Report on Witnesses before Legislative Committees* (September 1981). This report is an extraordinarily valuable source of information on a much wider range of topics than the title would suggest; for example, it contains an insightful treatment of the powers and privileges inherent in Canadian provincial assemblies (at 83–7).
21 Standing Committee on Procedural Affairs, *Report on Private Bill Procedures* (December 1981)
22 Standing Committee on Procedural Affairs, *Report on Standing Orders and Procedure (No. 1)* (December 1982)
23 On the Lefebvre Committee, see John A. Holtby, 'The Work of the Special Committee on the Standing Orders and Procedures,' paper prepared for the fall 1984 meeting of the Canadian Study of Parliament Group.
24 Transcript of the 10 February 1983 meeting of the Standing Committee on Procedural Affairs
25 *Journals*, 25 May 1982, 96
26 Standing Committee on Procedural Affairs, *Report on Standing Orders and Procedure (No. 3)* (June 1984)
27 *Debates*, 25 October 1984
28 *Debates*, 30 April 1982
29 The accord is reprinted in full in Rand Dyck, *Provincial Politics in Canada* (Toronto: Prentice-Hall, 1986), 325–7.
30 The preamble to the accord set out new ground rules for application of the confidence convention; these are discussed in Chapter 1.
31 Special Committee on Reform of the House of Commons, *Third Report* (June 1985)
32 Ministry of Treasury and Economics, *Reforming the Budget Process: A Discussion Paper* (October 1985)
33 Interview, 25 November 1986
34 *Debates*, 28 April 1986, 106

35 *Journals*, 10 July 1985, 53. According to the committee's interpretation, appointments of judges and deputy ministers were excluded from its purview, as were the eight hundred or more agency appointments made directly by ministers and a wide range of appointments to ad hoc bodies.
36 Standing Committee on the Legislative Assembly, *Report on Appointments in the Public Sector* (June 1986)
37 Ibid., 11
38 Cabinet Office, 'Government Response to the Report of the Standing Committee on the Legislative Assembly on Appointments in the Public Sector,' 27 October 1986, 5
39 The McGrath Committee recommended that parliamentary committees be able to veto appointments to a small number of regulatory agencies, but not appointments to Crown corporations; *Third Report*, ch. 5.
40 Ibid., 27
41 Cabinet Office, 'Response,' 7
42 The committee produced a document setting out the rationale for its recommendations and the requisite technical langauge; the untitled document was identified only by the phrase 'Revised 12 April 1988.'
43 In June 1988 – that is, after the ad hoc committee's recommendations had been circulating for some time – the Public Accounts Committee released its own report on the estimates process (*Special Report on the Estimates Process*). Although it was certainly informed by and generally supportive of the ad hoc committee's proposals, the Public Accounts Committee's conclusions were its own. Public Accounts dealt only with the estimates, not with opposition days or policy reviews in committee. Its report recommended the establishment of an estimates committee that would deal with six sets of estimates annually, though without time limits. Ministries not subject to full review would be subject to written questioning with the possibility of further questioning before the committee. In order to 'strengthen the accountability cycle,' one member from each party would sit on both the Estimates Committee and the Public Accounts Committee; the Estimates chairman would be one of these members. Finally, without specifying what it meant, the committee recommended that 'the Estimates Committee be given the power to recommend the reallocation of funding within each vote' (ibid., 12).
44 It was recommended that this process occur in six committees; but since the sixth committee would be the Government Agencies Committee, this would not represent anything new.
45 Untitled document, supra note 42, 5

46 Paul Thomas, 'Theories of Parliament and Parliamentary Reform,' *Journal of Canadian Studies* XIV (Summer 1979), 57
47 See, for example, David Arter, *The Nordic Parliaments: A Comparative Analysis* (New York: St Martins, 1984).

CHAPTER 10 The Ontario Legislature: An assessment

1 For a general discussion of legislative functions, see Gerhard Loewenberg and Samuel C. Patterson, *Comparing Legislatures* (Boston: Little, Brown, 1979), ch. 2; Michael Mezey, *Comparative Legislatures* (Durham, NC: Duke University Press, 1979), ch. 1; for discussions in the Canadian context, see John Stewart, *The Canadian House of Commons: Procedure and Reform* (Montreal: McGill-Queen's University Press, 1977), ch. 1, and Robert J. Jackson and Michael Atkinson, *The Canadian Legislative System*, 2d ed. (Toronto: Macmillan, 1980), 24–9.
2 David Smith, 'Approximating the Ideal: The Saskatchewan Legislative Assembly,' and Louis Massicotte, 'Quebec: The Successful Combination of French Culture and English Institutions,' in Graham White and Gary Levy, eds., *Canadian Provincial and Territorial Legislatures* (Toronto: University of Toronto Press, 1989)
3 Mezey, *Comparative Legislatures*, 272
4 Ronald Butt, *The Power of Parliament* (London: Constable, 1967), 31
5 *Comparing Legislatures*, 52
6 For an analysis of these factors at the federal level see C.E.S. Franks, *The Parliament of Canada* (Toronto: University of Toronto Press, 1987), ch. 3.
7 For an analysis of the representative function in a Canadian parliamentary context, see Allan Kornberg, Harold D. Clarke, and Arthur Goddard, 'Parliament and the Representational Process in Contemporary Canada,' in Harold D. Clarke et al., *Parliament, Policy and Representation* (Toronto: Methuen, 1980), 1–24.
8 Franks, *Parliament of Canada*, 174
9 Loewenberg and Patterson, *Comparing Legislatures*, 59
10 Joan Boase, 'Regulation and the Paramedical Professions: An Interest Group Study,' *Canadian Public Administration* XXV (Fall 1982), 332–53
11 David Rayside, 'Gay Rights and Family Values: The Passage of Bill 7 in Ontario,' *Studies in Political Economy* XXVI (Summer 1988), 109–47
12 Franks, *Parliament of Canada*, 215
13 Mezey, *Comparative Legislatures*, 8

14 Ibid., 6
15 Ibid., 218
16 Ibid.
17 Paul Pross, 'Parliamentary Influence and the Diffusion of Power,' *Canadian Journal of Political Science* XVIII (June 1985), 235–66
18 Ibid., 256
19 See Standing Committee on Procedural Affairs and on Agencies, Boards and Commissions, *Report on the Matter of Privilege Relating to the Action Taken by the Canadian Imperial Bank of Commerce against the Member for Riverdale* (January 1986).
20 For an elaboration of the theme of reasonable expectations for legislatures, see Graham White, 'Without a Doubt Our Legislatures Are Succeeding,' in Robert J. Fleming and Patrick Fafard, eds., *Canadian Legislatures: The 1986 Comparative Study* (Toronto: Office of the Assembly, 1986), 33–8.

Index

accord, Liberal-NDP: background, 11; committee reforms, 159; content, 11–12; effects, 12; legal status, 12, 264 n18; legislation arising from, 86; legislative reform, 236; and public accounts committee, 211, 236; and televising House proceedings, 196
accountability: of bureaucrats, 205–8, 212–14; effectiveness, 222–3; estimates, 152; and information, 222; meaning, 204–8, 222–3; members' interest in, 208; and ministerial responsibility, 205; press coverage and, 223; question period, 106; and regulations, 220–2; and responsible government, 204; and sanctions, 207; scrutiny versus control, 206
'ad hoc' reform committee. *See* parliamentary reform adjournment debate, 108–9
agencies, semi-independent. *See* semi-independent agencies
Alberta legislature, 50, 97, 284 n14, 290 n31
altruism, members', 35–6
amendments: to bills, 128–30; hoist, 124, 280 n11; money, 130; to private members' business, 134; reasoned, 123–4
appointments, legislative review of, 242–3, 294 n35
arena-transformative concept, 10, 18–20, 36, 67–8, 91, 152–3, 183, 203, 224, 248–9, 255–7
Assembly, Office of. *See* Office of the Assembly
Atkinson, Michael M., 35
attendance in House, 73, 81
audit act, 290 n. 22
auditor, provincial, 64, 151, 205, 209–12, 290 nn22–4
auditor-general, 212
Australia: state legislatures, 49

Bagehot, Walter, 252–3
Beauchesne, 76
Beer, Samuel, 77
bell-ringing, 85, 235, 238
bills, government: amendments, 128–30; budget, 144; carry-over to new session, 133; coming into force, 131–2; Committee of the Whole, 145, 129, 281 nn15, 19; committee

review, 122, 125–30; delay, 258; draft, 122; first reading, 121–2; government caucus, 121; 'legislation by exhaustion,' 120; omnibus, 120; origin, 279 n3; proclamation, 132; public hearings, 126–7; rate of passage, 118–19; recommittal to committee, 131; report stage, 130–1; reports on, 131; royal assent, 131; second reading, 123–4; third reading, 131; time required for passage, 119, 123, 125, 280 n8; time taken by, 117, 129
bills, private, 140–2
bills, private members': carry-over to new session, 135; committee stage, 135; frequency, 133–4; money bills, 133; passed, 139; procedure, 134; reasons behind, 136. See also private members' business
Board of Internal Economy, 41, 54, 60, 63–4, 74, 145, 162, 177, 188, 196, 199–203, 228, 238, 270 n48, 281 n17
Bradley, James, 196
Breaugh, Mike, 237, 244
British Columbia: legislative building, 186; legislature, 40–1, 83, 97
budget, 143–5
budgetary process: reform of, 159
budget bills, 144
budget debate, 89, 143
Butt, Ronald, 251

cabinet committee on regulations, 45–6
cabinet office, 41, 108
Camp, Dalton, 227
Camp Commission, 9, 55, 62, 83, 95, 96, 98, 112–13, 124, 158, 187, 193; on committees, 228; fifth report, 229; first report, 227; fourth report, 228; principles, 227; second report, 227–8
Canadian Radio-Television and Telecommunications Commission, 198
candidate recruitment, 15
Cassidy, Michael, 56
caucuses, 46–53, 67; chairman of, 47, 270 n59; committees of, 50–3; government, 47–9, 51, 121, 244; funding, 190; NDP, 50, 52, 71–2, 79; opposition, 123; Progressive Conservative, 50, 52
ceremonial activities, 89
chairman, committee: appointment, 165, 174–5; partisanship, 175; pay, 175; powers, 173–4; of Public Accounts Committee, 209; rulings, 130
chamber, legislative: description, 4–5
Charter of Rights and Freedoms, 74
chief government whip, 39, 44, 200, 231, 270 n48
civil servants, 42, 126, 146, 205–9, 212–14
Clarke, Charles, 55
Clarke, Harold D., 34
clerk assistant, first, 62
clerk of the House, 57, 61–4, 111, 198, 228, 272 n83
clerks, committee, 176, 178
clerk's office, 76, 108, 112, 178, 286 n31
clerk's table, 61–2
closure, 83–4
Commission on Election Finances, 188
Commission on the Legislature. See Camp Commission
Commissioners of Estates Bills, 142
Committee of Supply, 59, 146
Committee of the Whole, 59, 81, 125, 129–30, 144, 273 n6, 281 n15
Committee on Government Productivity (COGP), 45, 226

Index

committee reports: on bills, 131, 179; concurrence in, 181–2, 286 n37; debate on, 90, 181–2; dissenting opinions, 180; government response, 182; leaks, 180; minority reports, 180; procedure, 112, 286 n37; from Public Accounts Committee, 213; release, 286 n34; on special studies, 171, 179) 80

committees: activities, 166–8; atmosphere, 154–5; chairman, 165, 173–5; and civil servants, 126, 146; divisions in, 156; education function, 172; effectiveness, 171–3, 183; extent of activity, 87; fairness, 163; follow)up, 172, 213, 218, 290 n24; government reports, review of, 170; in camera meetings, 180; number of meetings, 160; partisanship in, 156; party discipline, 79; policy field, 158; and policy process, 169–70; procedure, 164; quorum, 155; reform, 158–60, 232; representation of parties, 161; review of bills, 123; schedule, 168–9, 275 n42; seating in, 155, 283 n2; select, 157, 164–5; size, 157–8, 161; special studies, 169–73; staff, 175–8; standing, 157, 165; standing orders, 160–1, 164; subcommittees, 164, 174, 230; substitution, 158, 161, 168; terms of reference, 161–2; time distribution, 166; transcripts, 178–9; travel, 71, 127, 156, 162, 284 n7; whips, 44; witnesses, 162–3, 232–4. *See also* names of committees

Commonwealth Parliamentary Association, 61

compendium of information, 95, 122

computer system, 191–2

concurrence: in committee reports, 181–2; in estimates, 149

confidence convention, 12, 148

consent: mobilization of, 257

constituencies, 7

constituency offices, 189, 230, 287 n11

constituency service, 35, 193–4, 229, 253

Constitution Act, 74, 138

constitutional amendment, 139

Conway, Sean, 42

critics, 49, 95, 123, 143, 147, 151

Crowe, Edward, 69

Davies, Cooke, 55

Davis, William, 9, 34, 199, 223, 233

debate, 80–3; on budget, 89, 143; in Committee of the Whole 130; concurrence, 149; of major issues, 253–4; relevance in, 80; second reading, 123

decline of parliament thesis, 5

decorum in House, 69

delaying tactics, 83–5, 121, 125, 235, 257–8, 283 n5. *See also* filibuster

deputy chairman of Committees of Whole House, 59–60

deputy ministers, 147

deputy Speaker, 59–60, 130

DesRosiers, Claude, 63

dining-room, legislative, 188

director of administration, 62

dissent by members, 78

divisions: in committees, 156; definition, 280 n12; at first reading, 122; on private members' business, 139; at second reading, 124; time expended on, 90. *See also* voting

Edighoffer, Hugh, 55, 58–9, 93

election finance, 16

electoral system, 15

'electronic Hansard,' 196 7

emergency debates, 57, 90, 113–15, 279 n46
Epp, Herb, 244
estimates: and accountability, 152; in Board of Internal Economy, 200–1; briefing books, 145; civil servants, 146; effectiveness, 147; opening statements, 147; press coverage, 148; reform, 151, 239, 244–5, 294 n43; schedule 145–6; supplementary 150; standing orders, 145; time expended on, 89–90
evening sittings, 72, 88
Eves, Ernie, 240
Executive Council Act, 39
executive-legislative relations, 5, 9, 19

Family Coalition Party, 265 n25
filibuster, 83–4, 86, 112, 275 n38, 276 n52. *See also* delaying tactics
Finance and Economic Affairs Committee, 160, 175
Fleming, Robert, 62
Fletcher, Frederick, 34, 65
Franks, C.E.S., 204–5, 253, 256–9
freedom of information, 110, 222
French, use of, 81–2, 180, 198, 274 n24
French Language Services Act, 274 n24
Froman, Lewis, 115
Frost, Leslie, 157

Goddard, Arthur, 34, 41
Government Agencies Committee, 160, 173, 214–16, 294 n44. *See also* Procedural Affairs Committee
government House leader, 39, 59, 87, 109, 113, 126, 181, 200
government House leader's office, 42–3, 181, 270 n54

government whip's office, 43, 93, 270 n53
grave disorder: adjournment for, 58
Grossman, Larry, 34, 104

Hansard, 191
Hansard interjectionist, 283 n1
hoist amendment. *See* amendment
Holtby, John, 272 n83
Horowitz, Gad, 16
House of Commons (Britain): candidate recruitment, 15; decorum, 70; expenditure committee, 152; hybrid bill, 282 n37; members' independence, 255; origin, 251; public accounts committee, 209; question time, 106; reform, 232; report stage on bills, 130–1; select committees, 161; Speaker, 54, 56–7; whips, 42; written questions, 108
House of Commons (Canada), 22; adjournment debate, 108; bell-ringing, 85, 235; bills, 129; budget rules, 144; committee reports, 179; committees, 129; comparison with Ontario legislature, 257; dining-room, 188; estimates, 146–7; interest groups, 259; Lefebvre committee, 234, 237; legitimacy, 251–2; members' statements, 93; membership turnover, 252; ministers' statements, 94–5; parliamentary secretaries, 46; press gallery, 198; public accounts committee, 209; question period, 97; reform, 232; regional caucuses, 50; report stage on bills, 130–1; review of regulations, 221; sergeant) at) arms, 63; Speaker, 54; Speaker's rulings, 57; standing order 43, 93; time limits on debates, 83;

written questions, 108. *See also* McGrath Committee

'householders,' 189–90

House leaders, 38–43, 77, 83, 113, 145, 169, 175, 200, 234, 239, 247; consultation among, 39–41, 125, 132, 229; staff, 40, 42, 233. *See also* government House leader

Hyson, Stewart, 136

ideology: members', 45–5; party, 33–4, 269 n33

incumbency, 192–3, 287 n17, 288 n25

India: parliament, 112

interim supply, 95, 149, 283 n46

Johnston, Richard, 171

Jones, Terry, 60

Krause, Richard 34

Lambert Commission. *See* Royal Comission on Financial Management and Accountability

'last-minute-rush' tactic, 88

'late show.' *See* adjournment debate

Laundy, Philip, 55

lawmaking function, 254–5

leaders, party, 37, 43, 96

leadership recruitment, 252

leaders' offices, funding, 190

Leduc, Lawrence, 33

legislation. *See* bills

'legislation by exhaustion,' 120

Legislative Assembly Act, 22, 38, 60, 62, 74, 186, 188–9, 199, 227–8, 234, 241, 245, 272 n8, 284 n14

Legislative Assembly Committee, 62–4, 160, 162–3, 186, 199, 244, 248. *See also* Procedural Affairs Committee

Legislative Building: description, 3–4; facilities, 185–7, 231; renovation, 186, 231

legislative chamber: description, 4–5

legislative counsel, office of, 122, 141, 178, 190

legislative-executive relations. *See* executive-legislative relations

Legislative Library: director, 63; research service, 176–7, 190

legislature: atmosphere, 70; budget, 201–2; as club, 72–3; duration of, 74; in nineteenth century, 6; legitimacy, 17; number of members, 7, 229; powers, 74

legitimacy, 17, 33, 127, 251–2

Lewis, Roderick, 62, 272 n82

Liberal party, 14

lieutenant-governor, 131, 264 n18

lobbyists, 255–6

Loewenberg, Gerhard, 252

Macdonald, John A., 5

MacDonald, Donald, 184

McGrath Committee, 56, 161, 205, 237, 242–3, 247, 294 n39

Maeck, Lorne, 293 n16

Management Board of Cabinet, 213

Management Board orders, 150–1

Manitoba legislature, 85, 89, 235

Mathews, Donald, 22

May, Erskine, 76

media studio, 191

Members' Conflict of Interest Act, 75

members of the legislature: addressed by riding name, 82; adoption by, 269 n41; age, 31–2, 268 n26; altruism, 35–6; attendance, 73; attitudes, 33–6; cable TV shows, 191; education, 30, 268 n25; experience, 22;

302 Index

ideology, 34–5; interpersonal relations, 70; municipal experience, 22–4, 67, 266 n5; occupation, 28–30, 268 n23; oratorical abilities, 80; origin, 26–8, 267 n16; pay and benefits, 38, 45, 175, 187–8; perceptions of roles, 35; policy goals, 35; policy influence, 129, 170; professionalization, 72; and reform, 247; religious affiliation, 25–6; representativeness, 32–3; sex, 24–5; staff, 72, 81, 189; and television, 197; turnover, 252
Members' Services Committee, 158
members' statements, 43, 92–4, 240, 248
Mezey, Michael, 256
Mill, J.S., 206, 253
Miller, Frank, 199
ministerial responsibility, 146, 205
minority government, 264 n11; effects of, 9, 12, 39, 229
Morley, J.T., 30
Morrow, Donald, 230
Morrow committee, 159, 195, 229–31, 293 n16
motions: non-confidence, 143; routine proceeding, 113
Mowat, Oliver, 6, 157

naming of members, 58, 63
New Brunswick legislature, 290 n31
New Democratic Party, 14
New Zealand: parliament, 112
Nixon, Robert, 110, 159, 184
non-confidence, 143
norms, legislative, 69
Nova Scotia House of Assembly, 35

Office of the Assembly, 54, 60, 63, 199, 201, 228, 288 n28

offices, members', 72, 185
Oliver, Farquhar, 226
ombudsman, 64–5, 216–220, 288 n19, 291 nn33–5
Ombudsman Act, 182, 220, 291 n34
Ombudsman Committee, 65, 172, 177, 216–20, 238, 290 n31
one-party dominance, 6, 33–4
Ontario Hydro, committee on, 236
Ontario Law Reform Commission, 233
Ontario Municipal board, 141
order, points of, 82, 94
orders of the day, 92

pairing, 270 n53, 272 n79
Parliament, Nelson, 55
parliamentary assistants, 45–6, 93, 97, 142, 270 n56
parliamentary calendar, 87, 239–40
parliamentary reform: 'ad hoc' committee, 244–5, 271 n73, 272 nn77–8, 276 n47; 277 n4, 278 n39, 279 nn42, 48, 280 n12, 282 nn31–2, 285 n18, 286 n33; committees, 232; explanations, 246–50; international influences, 248; and institutionalization, 249–50; and legislative bureaucracy, 249; nature, 225; 1986 rule changes, 239–42; 1978 rule changes, 232; 1976 rule changes, 226, 230–1
parties, definition, 284 n14; influence of, 75
partisanship, 70–2
party discipline, 43, 77–80, 91, 274 n20
party system, 7, 13–15
Paterson, Samuel, 252
Peterson, David, 82, 199, 264 n18, 274 n20
petitions, 110–12; as delaying tactic, 86, 112, 278 n40; frequency, 110–

11, 278 n38; government response, 111; and whips, 111
political culture, 16–18
Polsby, Nelson, 10, 20, 117, 183
prayer, opening, 92
precedents, 76
premier, 37, 46, 81, 87, 97
premier's office, 41, 95, 243
press gallery, 65–7; attitude towards legislature, 67; coverage of estimates, 148; and sitting times, 276 n46; views on television coverage of House, 196
'previous question.' *See* closure
Price, Richard, 34
Private Bills Committee, 158
private members' business: amendments, 134; 133–40; blocking of, 134–5; discussed in caucus, 50; effectiveness, 137, 140; in nineteenth century, 6; party influence on, 139–40; and policy process, 136; procedure, 134, 281 n29; scheduling, 281 n30; time expended on, 91; time limits, 134; votes, 134, 139. *See also* bills, private members'; resolutions, private members' privilege, 260–1
privilege, points of, 82, 94
Procedural Affairs Committee, 56, 83, 85, 87, 160–1, 196, 214, 233–9, 242, 248. *See also* Legislative Assembly Committee; Government Agencies Committee
procedure, parliamentary: pragmatism in, 77; unwritten practices, 77
professionalization: of legislature, 203; of members, 72
Progressive Conservative party, 14
'Proposals for a New Committee System,' 159, 232, 247

prorogation, 87, 275 n42
Pross, Paul, 258
province-building, 251
Public Accounts, 209, 290 n20
Public Accounts Committee, 64–5, 151, 173, 174–5, 176, 178, 205–6, 208–14, 236, 290 n20, 294 n43
public hearings, 126–7, 253

Quebec National Assembly: bills, 122; dining-room, 188; interpellation, 108; ministers' statements, 95; press gallery, 198; sitting days, 88; sergeant-at-arms, 63
question period, 46, 58, 81, 96–107, 225, 235; and accountability, 106; back-benchers, 99; effectiveness, 106–7; and government members, 105–6; in 1960s, 96; and media, 99, 106–7; members' participation, 104–5; opposition preparation, 99–101; opposition strategy, 98; party leaders, 96–9, 103; and premier, 104; Speaker, 59, 96; standing orders relating to, 96–7; time expended on, 90, 276 n53; time limits, 83
questions: asked by Conservatives, 103; asked by Liberals, 103, 277 n18; asked by New Democrats, 103; subjects of, 102–3; supplementary, 97; written, 108–10
quorum, 283 n5

Rae, Bob, 104
reasoned amendment. *See* amendments
reform. *See* parliamentary reform
Reforming the Budget Process, 144–5, 159, 238
'Reform of Parliament, The,' 206

regulations: under Ombudsman Act, 220; review by legislature, 220–2; setting licence fees, 291 n41; volume, 118
Regulations and Other Statutory Instruments Committee, 158, 176
Regulations and Private Bills Committee, 141, 220–1
Reid, Patrick, 209
Renwick, James, 279 n6
reports: reference to committee, 162; routine proceeding, 112. See also committee reports
representation function, 252–3
resolutions, private members', 133, 137–8
responsible government, 9–10, 204
Reycraft, Doug, 244
Robarts, John, 9, 38, 157, 225
routine proceedings, 92
royal assent. See bills
Royal Commission on Financial Management and Accountability, 206–7
rules: interpretation, 76–7; political context, 115. See also standing orders

safe seats, 15
Salsberg, Joe, 273 n10
Saskatchewan legislature, 83, 284 n14
Schindeler, F.F., 5, 9, 30, 75, 87, 89, 113, 120, 225
second reading. See bills
semi-independent agencies, 215–16, 242–3
seniority, 73
sergeant-at-arms, 63
session: length, 86–7, 225, 275 n38; timing, 86–7
sessional papers, 109

Shulman, Morton, 37
simultaneous translation, 198
sittings: days, 87, 276 n45; times of, 72, 88, 276 n46
Smith, Joan, 240
Speaker, 53–61; administrative responsibilities, 60–1, 200–1; authority, 54–6; and Board of Internal Economy, 200; casting vote, 58, 271 n75; censure of, 57; election of, 56, 60, 271 n72; and emergency debates, 113; independence, 54–5, 114, 227, 271 n75; jurisdiction over legislative building, 186, 228; length of tenure, 55; members' view of, 54; question period, 59, 96; powers, 58–9, 81, 85, 228; and reform, 247 role, 54; staff, 61; and warrants, 163
Speaker's rulings, 56, 62, 75–6, 114, 271 n73
Special Committee on the Reform of Parliament. See McGrath Committee
speeches: comments and questions on, 80; party rotation in, 81
Speech from the Throne, 60, 89
staff: of caucuses, 287 n10; of committees, 164–5, 175–8, 212; of Government House leader, 42–3; of House, 61–5, 201–3, 272 n91; of members, 72, 81, 189, 287 n11; of Speaker, 61
standing orders, 69, 75, 96–7, 108, 145, 160–1, 284 n14
statements: ministerial, 94, 95; personal, 95; policy, 95. See also members' statements
Stelling, Thomas, 63
Sterling, Norman, 237–8, 244
Stewart, William, 55
Stokes, Jack, 55, 57–9

subcommittees. *See* committees
sub judice convention, 274 n14
substitution. *See* committees
Sullivan, Barbara, 47
Supply Act, 149

task forces, party, 53
television in the House, 12, 72–3, 81, 195–99, 237; costs, 197; distribution system, 198; effects on members' behaviour, 197; introduction of, 230; quality of coverage, 195; and question period, 195; political effects, 196, 199, 288 n25; and press gallery, 196
third reading. *See* bills
Thomas, Paul, 36, 246
throne speech. *See* Speech from the Throne
Timbrell, Dennis, 34, 239
time: allocation, 83–4; distribution of, 89–91
time limits: on debates, 83; on private members' business, 134, 282 n31; on speeches, 83
tradition, parliamentary, 76–7
Treleaven, Richard, 59–60, 237–8

Truman, David, 69
Turner, John, 56–7, 59, 82, 150
turnout, 265 n31
TVOntario, 198
Twiss, James, 34

unparliamentary language, 82
unwritten practices, 77
upper chamber, 6

vice-chairman, 175
visitors, 276 n51
voting: party cohesion in, 78; on private members' business, 134. *See also* divisions

warrants: Speaker's, 63, 163, 285 n21; special, 150
Westminster model, 5, 10, 18–19, 73–4, 78, 257, 261
whips, 38–9, 42–5, 168–9, 239. *See also* chief government whip
White, Walter, 33
Whitney Block, 185–7
Winn, Conrad, 34
women in the legislature, 24–5, 72, 267 n10

Ministry of Education, Ontario
Information Services & Resources Unit,
13th Floor, Mowat Block, Queen's Park,
Toronto   M7A 1L2

Ministry of Education & Training
MET Library
13th Floor, Mowat Block, Queen's Park
Toronto   M7A 1L2